Exam overview

Paper 1 Reading (1 hour 15 minutes)

Part 1	multiple matching pp.6, 24, 60	a text preceded by 12–18 multiple matching questions
Part 2	gapped text pp.18, 30, 48, 66, 84	a text from which 6 or 7 paragraphs have been removed and must be replaced
Part 3	multiple choice pp.12, 36, 42, 72, 90	a text followed by 5–7 four-option multiple choice questions
Part 4	multiple matching pp.54, 78	a text preceded by 12–22 multiple matching questions

Paper 2 Writing (2 hours)

Part 1	compulsory task (approx 250 words) p.13 formal letter p.25 instructions and directions p.31 notices and announcements p.56 notes and messages p.92 brochure	a variety of task types (letters, articles, reports, reviews, leaflets, brochures, notices, etc.) based on up to 400 words of input material
Part 2	one task from a choice of four (approx 250 words) p.8 article p.20 leaflets p.25 instructions and directions p.38 competition entry p.44 report p.50 article p.62 informal letter p.67 formal letter p.74 report p.80 review p.86 letter of reference	a variety of task types (letters, articles, reports, reviews, leaflets, brochures, notices, etc.) specified in about five lines

Paper 3 English In Use (1 hour 30 minutes)

Part 1	multiple choice cloze pp.9, 51, 81	a text with 15 spaces followed by 15 four-option multiple choice questions
Part 2	open cloze pp.21, 63, 92	a text with 15 spaces: no possible options are given
Part 3	error correction pp.15, 39, 87	a text containing 16 specified errors to be identified and corrected
Part 4	word formation pp.27, 57, 81	two short texts to be completed with 15 words formed from given root words
Part 5	register transfer pp.33, 69, 87	two texts conveying similar information in different registers: the second (containing 13 gaps) must be completed in an appropriate way
Part 6	gapped text pp.45, 75, 93	a text with six spaces at phrase / sentence level: the text must be completed from a choice of 10 options

Paper 4 Listening (approximately 45 minutes)

Part 1	sentence completion note taking pp.10, 40, 46	a two-minute text with one speaker followed by 8–10 questions: you hear this twice
Part 2	sentence completion note taking pp.34, 58, 76, 88	a two-minute text with one speaker (possibly two) followed by 8–10 questions: you hear this once only
Part 3	sentence completion multiple choice pp.22, 64, 70, 94	a conversation between two or three speakers for about four minutes followed by 6–12 questions: you hear this twice
Part 4	multiple choice multiple matching pp.16, 28, 52, 82, 94	five short extracts of about 30 seconds each connected by theme: you hear these twice

Paper 5 Speaking (approximately 15 minutes)

Part 1	introductions pp.11, 35	three minutes: the candidates introduce themselves or each other and respond to the examiner's questions
Part 2	visual prompt pp.17, 41, 47, 77	3–4 minutes: the candidates comment on visual prompts and respond to their partner's comments
Part 3	problem solving pp.23, 53, 59, 83, 89	3–4 minutes: the candidates discuss and try to solve a task set by the examiner
Part 4	discussion pp.29, 65, 71, 95	3–4 minutes: a wider discussion of the topic raised in Part 3

Introduction

What is the CAE Study Pack?

The CAE Study Pack is a complete preparation for the Cambridge Certificate in Advanced English examination. It is particularly suitable if you are working on your own. However, it can also be used in class by your teacher. The Study Pack has been designed for use alongside the Landmark Advanced Student's Book, but you will find it equally effective if you are using a different advanced course. You will also find it extremely useful on its own if you want to improve your exam skills before taking CAE.

How is the book organized?

- **Exam overview** This gives you essential information about each Paper and the tasks you can expect to find.
- **Units** There are fifteen units, each based around a topic or theme that you will find useful as you prepare for the CAE exam.
- **Practice test** There is a complete practice test (together with answer sheets) which should form part of your final preparation before the exam.
- **Answer key** There is a detailed answer key which also gives information about why some answers are wrong. It includes learner tips and model answers for some of the writing tasks.

How are the units organized?

Each unit is divided into five sections covering the five papers in the CAE exam: Reading, Writing, English In Use, Listening, and Speaking. Each section provides practice in the different types of exam task and the skills that you need to deal with each task. Each section of a unit contains a number of key features.

- **Timing** At the start of each section a suggestion is given as to how long you should spend on the section. Timing is a very important factor in the exam. As far as possible you should try and follow the suggestions for timing.
- **Exam techniques** At the start of each section you will find an exam techniques box. In the first units of the book the exam techniques are described and an explanation is given for their use. As the course progresses and you become more familiar with the techniques, you will be asked to identify techniques. Finally, towards the end of the course, you will be asked to choose techniques appropriate to particular tasks.
- **Practice tasks** Each section contains a number of practice tasks. These tasks give you training in the exam techniques outlined at the start of the section and lead towards the exam task.
- **Exam task** Each section contains an exam task. This allows you to practise the techniques you have learnt.
- **Language development** The language development part of each unit extracts useful language from earlier material in the section and gives further practice. Whilst this is a useful part of the course, if you are short of time you may wish to leave this out.

- **Close up** The close up feature takes important examples of language from texts in the section and examines them in more detail.
- **Answer key** You will find the key to each section at the back of the book. It provides the correct answers and also gives information about why some answers are wrong.
- **How well are you doing?** Use this part to check on your progress and identify areas where you need more practice.

How should I work through the book?

There are many different ways to work through this book and you should choose one which suits you and your style of studying. Here are some suggestions, but you might think of a different way that suits you better. If so, do it.

- You could work through from beginning to end. This will give you a complete preparation for each exam task.
- If you want to brush up a particular skill, e.g. reading or listening, work through the appropriate sections of each unit.
- If you find particular tasks very difficult, e.g. multiple choice reading or error correction tasks in Paper 3, work through the areas that you find difficult.
- You could start working through the book from the beginning but later start concentrating on particular tasks that you find difficult.
- You could work carefully through the units in the first part of the book, working hard at developing the exam techniques. Then later in the book you could choose to leave out the practice tasks and concentrate on the exam tasks.
- Or you might choose a different way.

How can I do the Speaking exam tasks?

If you are working on your own, work through the practice tasks that come before the exam task. The practice tasks do not usually require you to speak. When you get to the exam task, take a few minutes to prepare what you are going to say. If you cannot record what you say, you could stop here. Or, you can get further practice by saying what you have prepared out loud. It may feel strange but it is actually useful practice!

If possible, record what you say. Then play back your recording. Listen for mistakes and think about ways to improve your performance. Record the task again if you think you can improve it.

If you have a partner, you can work through the practice tasks together, and then attempt the exam task together. If you are working with a partner, it will still be very useful to record your attempt at the exam task. You can then go back and spot mistakes and ways to improve what you said.

How is the exam marked?

The five CAE papers total 200 marks. The marks for each individual paper are scaled to a maximum of 40 marks. Each paper therefore carries equal importance.
It is not necessary to achieve a particular mark on all five papers in order to pass the examination. A candidate who gets an overall mark of 60% is likely to pass the exam.

Paper 1 (Reading)

In Parts 1 and 4 there is one mark for each correct answer. In Parts 2 and 3 there are two marks for each correct answer.

Paper 2 (Writing)

Each question has the same maximum number of marks. Each piece of writing is marked on its general impression and according to a mark scheme that is specific to each particular task.

The writing is assessed on how well the task has been completed, the accuracy of the language, the range of vocabulary and structures used, register and format, how the writing is organized, and its effect on the target reader. Marks are awarded on a five band scale, and it is worth remembering that Band 5 does not require a flawless, completely mistake-free performance.

Other factors which are taken into account are:

Length You should remember that a very short piece of writing will probably not complete the task satisfactorily, whereas a very long piece of writing may have a negative effect on the target reader. As a result, they will both probably lose marks.

Handwriting If your writing is difficult to read, it may be penalized one or even two bands on the scale depending on how illegible it is.

Spelling If poor spelling interferes with communication, it will be penalized.

Irrelevancy Material which is irrelevant or appears to have been learnt by heart will be penalized.

Layout Correct / acceptable layout forms part of the task achievement and is therefore important.

Paper 3 (English In Use)

Each correct answer gets one mark.

Paper 4 (Listening)

Each correct answer gets one mark.

Paper 5 (Speaking)

Candidates are assessed throughout the whole test in four areas:

Grammar and vocabulary Good marks are given for accurate and appropriate use of structure and vocabulary without continual pauses to search for the right words.

Discourse management Good marks are given for coherent, connected speech used to convey information, or to express or justify opinions.

Pronunciation This refers not only to the pronunciation of individual sounds but also to the appropriate linking of words and to stress and intonation. Having the accent of your native language will not lose you marks provided that it is not so strong that it interferes with communication.

Interactive communication This refers to general conversational skills: the ability to keep the conversation going, to take turns in the conversation, to develop it, and to help bring it towards a conclusion.

There will be two examiners for the Speaking Paper. The Assessor (who does not speak to the candidates) assesses the candidates in detail on the areas above. The Interlocutor (who speaks to the candidates) also assesses the candidates but on a more global scale.

Can I find my way round the book?

Now you have read the introduction and know what is in the book, find the answers to these ten questions. Do not take more than five minutes.

1 Can you lose marks for poor spelling in Paper 2?
2 How many people are usually in the room during Paper 5?
3 How many tasks can you choose from in Part 2 of Paper 2?
4 What is the difference between Parts 1 and 2 of Paper 3?
5 How long is Paper 4?
6 Which unit is about music?
7 Which pages practise the word formation tasks in Paper 3?
8 How long is Paper 5?
9 Which part of the listening do you hear once only?
10 Which is the longest paper?

➔ **Check your answers below.**

Key
1 Yes, if it interferes with communication. 2 Four: two examiners and two candidates. 3 Four. 4 In Part 1 you choose a word for each gap from four possible options; in Part 2 you do not have any options to choose from. 5 About 45 minutes. 6 Unit 9. 7 pp. 27, 57 & 81. 8 Approximately 15 minutes. 9 Part 2. 10 Paper 2: 2 hours.

Influences

Reading

🕐 (spend about 30 minutes on this section)

Paper 1 Part 1 and Part 4
Multiple matching

ℹ **Exam information** In Paper 1 Parts 1 and 4 you have to match the questions to the relevant information in the text or to a list of options.

▶ **Exam techniques**
- In the whole of Paper 1 there will be approximately 3,000 words of text to read. It is therefore important to be able to read quickly so that you can do the tasks in the time you are given. You will need to use a variety of different reading skills. You should know how to skim (to read a text through quickly to get a general idea of the meaning). This will prepare you for a more detailed reading of the text. Task 1 practises this.
- You also should know how to scan (to read a text quickly looking for the answer to a particular question and ignoring the parts that are not relevant). This will save you time because you will not need to read the whole text, just the relevant parts. When you scan a text for answers, look for key words and phrases. Task 2 practises this.

TASK 1 Read quickly through the reviews opposite (2 minutes maximum). Then answer 1–3 below.

1 Are the texts reviews of films, books, or plays?
2 Which is non-fiction?
3 Which are set in the first half of the twentieth century?

→ **Check your answers on p.111.**

TASK 2 There are some key words in *italics* under the first few questions. Finding these words in the reviews will help you find the answers to the questions.

Answer questions **1–14** by referring to the book reviews.

For questions **1–14**, answer by choosing from the list (**A–E**) below. Some of the choices may be required more than once.

Of which book can the following be said …

It is a novel.	**1** A **2** B **3** D
novel narrator	
It contains short stories.	**4** C
stories collection	
It tells the story of someone who almost goes mad.	**5** B
sanity	
It is the work of a writer who is still improving.	**6** C
development a significant advance	
It is part of a series of books.	**7** D
first volume	
It is about the relationship between some people who live close to each other.	**8** A
It is about someone who did not know who their parents were.	**9** B
It is about people who find life difficult to understand.	**10** A C
It is about someone who gets into trouble with the police.	**11** D
It tells the story of a man who led an adventurous life.	**12** E **13** D
It is a biography.	**14** E

A Undue Influence

B Island

C Midnight All Day

D A Star Called Henry

E Shackleton

→ **Check your answers on p.111.**

Note The key words in *italics* given for questions 1–7 would not appear in the exam.

A Undue Influence by Anita Brookner (Penguin)

This novel, like other Brookner novels, is about lonely people; here, they live quietly in central London, in flats and mansion blocks, and inflict their loneliness on each other. Claire Pitt is 29 and single. She works in the basement of a second-hand bookshop run by two old ladies, and worries about her dead parents.

Nearby, Martin Gibson is looking after his sick wife. Claire falls for him. Is Martin quiet and strange because of his situation? Would he be like this in better circumstances? Later, a horrifying possibility raises its head; that Martin is quiet and strange because he does not like Claire. As always, Brookner's net closes around you in the cleverest way.

B Island by Jane Rogers (Abacus)

Before she was adopted, returned, fostered, and returned, Nikki Black was Susan Lovage. But 'I'm nobody's Lovage. And with no father in the case – "unknown" neatly printed on my birth certificate – I fathered myself.' Jane Rogers's novel of the vengeful, bitter Nikki's search for her real mother ('when I was 28 I decided to kill her') is poetically, unendingly bleak. There is a cold understanding of the emptiness at the heart of some unfortunate people's lives, and an ability to tell stories within stories, to mix folklore with fiction.

Nikki finds her mother living on a remote Scottish island, and discovers that she has a brother, which sends her to the edges of sanity. The novel is both compelling and exasperating, Nikki's complaint justified, lyrical, and endless.

C Midnight All Day by Hanif Kureishi (Faber)

Kureishi is one of his generation's most perceptive writers, and his development has been fascinating to watch. The ten stories in this collection are acid, elegiac and spare. They deal with afterglows, fresh starts, regrets, the lovers left behind and lives not lived. Kureishi's eighties' survivors are not quite burnt out, but blunted, uncomfortable in middle age, confused by their life decisions.

The resonance of *Sucking Stones*, *Strangers When We Meet* and *That Was Then* is a significant advance on his collection *Love in a Blue Time* (1997). Even so, none of these pieces is as powerful as *Goodbye, Mother*. Kureishi is writing with growing conviction and is getting better and better.

D A Star Called Henry by Roddy Doyle (Vintage)

Set mainly in Dublin at the time of the First World War, this is the first volume of an epic undertaking, *The Last Roundup*, the author's account of the making of modern Ireland. The narrator is Henry Smart, born in the Dublin slums, whose father is a wooden-legged bouncer and professional killer.

Henry makes a name for himself in the Easter Rising of 1916, and later as one of Michael Collins's boys. He becomes a cop-bashing Republican hero (his father's wooden leg is useful), running from the RIC, the Black and Tans, and eventually falls out with the Republicans themselves. In agile, poetic language, the narrative rockets along. It is wonderfully readable; a love story, an act of political subversion, and a sentimental journey.

E Shackleton by Roland Huntford (Abacus)

Ernest Shackleton, who sailed with Scott on the Discovery expedition of 1900, went on to lead three Antarctic expeditions of his own. At the height of his fame, he was acclaimed as a national hero and knighted by Edward VII. But the world to which he returned in 1917 after his ill-fated voyage in the Endurance did not seem to welcome heroes who, unlike Scott, survived their hazardous journey. He finally obtained funds for another expedition, but died of a heart attack at the age of 47 as his ship reached the island of South Georgia. The adventures of this complex character make exciting reading.

Books Online. amazon.co.uk

Language development

Phrasal verbs *fall*

*Claire **falls for** him.*
*He eventually **falls out with** the Republicans themselves.*

1 Sometimes the same verb–particle combination can have two very different meanings. Look at the sentences and match the phrases in *italics* to a definition below.

1 They *fell for* each other the first time they met and they were married less than three months later.
2 I told him that I'd already booked a ticket on the first commercial flight to the Moon and he *fell for* it.
3 I put the vase on the window sill but it must have *fallen off* in the wind and broken.
4 Sales were very good in the first half of the year but they've *fallen off* recently.
5 I don't know why they *fell out* but they haven't spoken to each other all week.
6 He's terrified of going bald. He's tried everything to stop his hair *falling out*.

a to believe something that's not true
b to fall to the ground from where it was put
c to argue and stop being friends
d to fall in love with
e to come away from, e.g. the head
f to decrease

→ Check your answers on p.111.

2 Complete these sentences with appropriate forms of the verbs in exercise 1.

1 The meetings were popular to start with but attendance has .... over the last month.
2 She .... him as soon as she saw him. She just loved his blue eyes.
3 Where's my earring? It must have .... while I was drying my hair.
4 Have they .... again? I don't know why they got married in the first place.
5 He told you he was 45! You didn't .... that, did you? He's at least 60.
6 I wanted to put the vase on top of the bookcase but it was so large it kept ....

→ Check your answers on p.111.

Writing

(spend about 25 minutes on tasks 1 & 2; about one hour on task 3)

Paper 2 Part 2 Article

ⓘ Exam information There are two parts to Paper 2. The task in Part 1 is compulsory and there will be 400 words of text to read in order to complete the task. In Part 2 you have to choose one of four tasks. Many task types can appear in either Part 1 or Part 2. You may be asked to write an article for a magazine.

▶ **Exam techniques**
- Examiners have to read lots of answers so it is important to get their attention. Give your article an interesting heading to catch their eye. Task 1 practises this.
- If your writing is well organized, it is easier for people to read and understand. In English we usually organize our writing in paragraphs. Each paragraph contains ideas around a particular topic. Task 2 practises this.

TASK 1 Read the article by John Simpson opposite. Look at these alternative titles for the article and answer questions 1–4.

A Early influences   **C** My early life
B From Penge to publishing   **D** Simpson's start

1 Which title tells you who the article is about?
2 Which title tells you what this person did / does?
3 What do the titles in B and D have in common?
4 Which title do you prefer? Why?

→ Check your answers on p.111.

TASK 2 Look at the paragraph headings in the chart and the ideas below. Complete the chart by putting the ideas in the correct places as in the example.

1 Where I grew up	2 Nursery school	3 Primary school	4 Secondary school and my inspiration
	G		

A what Penge was like when I was young
B a teacher who impressed me
C why I was born in Lancashire
D what I wore at nursery school
E where we lived after the war
F how I stayed close to the person who inspired me
G *why I had an expensive education*
H where I was born
I what I learnt at nursery school
J the staff at primary school
K how this person helped me
L what I was good at
M what one teacher did at the same time as I left school
N where my primary school was

→ Check your answers on p.111.

My inspiration
By John Simpson
John Simpson is the BBC's world affairs editor.

My mother was bombed out three times in 1944, while she was pregnant, and my father was determined to send her as far away as possible for my birth, so I was born in Lancashire. However, we returned to Penge in south London soon after the war. These days Penge is quite posh, but in the late 40s it was a rougher area.

My father worked as a genealogist, among other things, so we didn't have a lot of money but he was determined to give me an expensive education. So I was sent to a horrible nursery school called the Crispin. I had to wear a bright purple jacket, and walking home in it was like wearing a badge that said, 'I have ambitions to be middle class, please punch me.' It did get me streetwise quickly, though, and I learnt to wear my jacket inside out.

I went on from there to a primary school in Dulwich which, with hindsight, was staffed by some very unpleasant people. Academically, I suppose I was good at the sort of things you might expect of a future journalist, writing, talking, and looking good with little effort.

At my secondary school, St Paul's, there was one English teacher, Mike Weaver, who made a profound impression. Mike went on to Cambridge University at the same time as me; he went to teach, I went to study. It was there that he had an even greater impact on my career. The outgoing editor of Granta magazine was looking for a replacement and Mike recommended me. It was my first break into journalism and I have much to thank him for.

The Guardian

TASK 3 You have been asked to write an article for an international magazine about a book which has had a great influence on your life. Describe your choice, say when and where you first read it, and explain the effect it has had on your life.

Use these ideas to help you plan and organize your writing.

Heading: think of something eye-catching
(you can do this after you have written the article)

⬇

Paragraph 1: say something general about the book
(this is introductory: talk about the book you have chosen, and when and where you first read it)

⬇

Paragraph 2: give a brief outline of the story
(this might take two paragraphs – but keep it short)

⬇

Paragraph 3: say something about the characters
(who they are, if they are sympathetic, how they develop)

⬇

Paragraph 4: say something about the style
(author and genre)

⬇

Paragraph 5: say something about its effect on you
(why you have chosen this book, what effect it has had on your life)

Write your article. Write approximately 250 words.

→ Compare your answer with the model on p.111.

English In Use

(spend about 25 minutes on this section)

Paper 3 Part 1 Multiple choice cloze

ℹ Exam information There are six parts in Paper 3. In Part 1 you are given a short text with 15 words missing. You have to choose from the four options given to fill in each missing word.

▶ **Exam techniques**
- Always read the text through and get a general idea of the meaning before you start to fill the spaces. If you understand what the text is about it will help you choose the correct words. Task 1 practises this.
- The questions in Part 1 generally test vocabulary rather than grammar. However, the word you choose must also fit grammatically so you will need to look carefully at the other words in the sentence. This part tests words which have a similar meaning but are different grammatically, words which often go together, idioms, phrasal verbs, and linking words. Task 2 practises this.

TASK 1 Read the article in task 3 and mark these sentences T (true) or F (false).

1 Stevenson's wife burned the first draft of *The Strange Case of Dr Jekyll and Mr Hyde*.
2 Stevenson was paid £1,500 for *The Strange Case of Dr Jekyll and Mr Hyde*.

→ Check your answers on p.111.

TASK 2 Look at this example sentence from the article.
Robert Louis Stevenson is one of Britain's most respected and enduring authors but his wife was less than (**0**) *impressed* with his literary talents.

0 A impressed   **B** attracted   **C** excited   **D** influenced

Impressed is the right answer. *Attracted* and *excited* would be followed by the word *by* not *with*. *Influenced* does not make sense in this context.

Now look at four possible versions of the second sentence. Complete each version with the correct word given from (1) and (2).

After reading the first draft of his most famous book, *The Strange Case of Dr Jekyll and Mr Hyde*,

1 A judged   **B** decided   **C** examined   **D** described
2 A put   **B** lit   **C** threw   **D** set

a) Fanny Stevenson ....*judge*............ (1) it 'utter nonsense'
   and .... (2) it into the fire.
b) Fanny Stevenson ....*described*............ (1) it as 'utter
   nonsense' and ....*lit*............ (2) the fire with it.
c) Fanny Stevenson ....*decided*............ (1) it was such 'utter
   nonsense' that she ....*set*............ (2) fire to it. *at fire to burning*
d) Fanny Stevenson ....*evaluated*............ (1) it, thought it was
   'utter nonsense', and ....*put*............ (2) it on the fire.

→ Check your answers on p.111.

TASK 3 Now finish the exam task.

For questions **3–15** read the text below and then decide which word best fits each space.

The Strange Case of Dr Jekyll and Mr Hyde

Robert Louis Stevenson is one of Britain's most respected and enduring authors but his wife was less than (**0**) *impressed* with his literary talents.

After reading the first draft of his most famous book, *The Strange Case of Dr Jekyll and Mr Hyde*, Fanny Stevenson (**1**) ..... it was such 'utter nonsense' that she (**2**) ..... fire to it.

This shameful ending to the first draft of the novel has been (**3**) ..... in a letter to the poet WE Hanley. It lay (**4**) ..... in the attic of Mr Hanley's (**5**) ..... for 115 years.

Mrs Stevenson, who was (**6**) ..... of her sick husband but also his fiercest (**7**) ....., wrote in 1885: 'He wrote pages and pages of complete nonsense. (**8**) ....., he has forgotten all about it now, and I shall burn it after I show it to you. He said it was his greatest (**9**) .....'

The letter is (**10**) ..... to fetch up to £1,500 when it is (**11**) ..... at Phillips, in London, on 17 November. Liz Merry, the head of the book (**12**) ....., said: 'This should end (**13**) ..... about what happened to the first draft of *Dr Jekyll* – it seems clear she burned it.'

But the discovery of the letter (**14**) ..... another mystery. Was Stevenson's first attempt at his most successful novel (**15**) ..... 'nonsense'?

	A	B	C	D
0	impressed	attracted	excited	influenced
1	judged	decided	examined	described
2	put	lit	threw	set
3	informed	revealed	expressed	shown
4	forgotten	unaware	ignorant	absent
5	survivors	generations	descendants	ancestors
6	sympathetic	protective	defensive	preserving
7	referee	judge	observer	critic
8	Fortunately	Properly	Favourably	Occasionally
9	job	composition	labour	work
10	intended	expected	hoped	guessed
11	traded	exchanged	auctioned	bid
12	department	part	class	zone
13	opinion	assumption	imagination	speculation
14	creates	makes	produces	causes
15	exactly	quite	indeed	rightly

→ Check your answers on p.111.

Listening

⏱ (spend about 25 minutes on this section)

Paper 4 Part 1 Note taking

ⓘ Exam information There are four parts in Paper 4. In Part 1 you listen to one person speaking for about two minutes. Sometimes the speaker is introduced by another person. You will hear the piece twice and you will have to complete some notes or sentences.

▶ **Exam techniques**
- Read the questions carefully and think about the type of information you need to write down for each question. Think about how that information might be given to you. Could it be a number, a price or sum of money, or a particular part of speech (a noun or an adjective, for example); could it be a name or a place, or a length of time or a percentage? It will be much easier if you know what type of information you are listening for. Task 1 practises this.
- Make sure you are familiar with the chart. Task 2 practises this.
- Don't expect to get all the information the first time you listen. Make a mental note where to listen for it the second time. Tasks 2 and 3 practise this.

TASK 1 Look at the chart below. In which columns will you expect to put

a numbers?
b adjectives?
c sums of money?

→ **Check your answers on p.111.**

TASK 2 🎧1.1 You will hear a woman talking about different mobile phones. As you listen, complete the notes for questions 1–8.

Phone	Price	Comment
Motorola [___1]	[___2]	least cool
Nokia 8850	[___3]	coolest and [___4]
Nokia 8210	[___5]	[___6]
Ericsson T28	–	[___7]
Nokia 5110	–	[___8]

TASK 3 Listen to the recording again and check your answers.

→ **Check your answers on p.112.**

Speaking

🕐 (spend about 25 minutes on this section)

Paper 5 Part 1 Introductions

ℹ **Exam information** There are four parts to Paper 5. In Part 1 the examiner will ask you questions and/or prompt you to ask your partner questions. These will ask you for personal information about you and your partner.

▶ **Exam techniques**

• This part of the exam is fairly predictable. In task 1 you will find a selection of the type of questions most commonly asked. Practise asking and answering them so that you are prepared for this part of the exam.

• Don't just say one or two words. Try to give full and interesting answers. This will show that you can contribute to the conversation and demonstrate good communication skills. It will also impress the examiner. Tasks 2 and 3 practise this.

TASK 1 🎧 1.2 Look at 1–8 and listen to the recording. Match the answers you hear to the questions. Some questions are answered more than once.

1 Where do you live?
2 What do you like about living there?
3 How long have you been studying English?
4 What do you enjoy about studying English?
5 What do you dislike about studying English?
6 Have you done anything interesting recently? What?
7 What do you think is the most memorable event in your life?
8 What are your future plans?

➔ Check your answers on p.112.

TASK 2 Listen to the answers on the recording again. Tick the appropriate boxes for each answer.

This answer…	A	B	C	D	E	F	G	H	I	J
is longer	☐	☐	☐	☐	☐	☐	☐	☐	☐	☐
gives an opinion	☐	☐	☐	☐	☐	☐	☐	☐	☐	☐
gives a reason	☐	☑	☐	☐	☐	☑	☐	☐	☐	☐
is personal	☐	☐	☐	☐	☐	☐	☐	☐	☐	☐
gives extra information	☐	☐	☐	☐	☐	☐	☐	☐	☐	☐
opens up other topics for discussion	☐	☐	☐	☐	☐	☐	☑	☐	☐	☐
tells how the speaker feels / felt	☐	☐	☐	☐	☐	☐	☐	☐	☐	☐

Which answers are not so good? Think about how the speaker could improve them.

➔ Check your answers on p.112.

TASK 3 Work in pairs. (If you are working alone, look at p.4.) Ask and answer the questions in task 1. If possible, record your answers. Then play them back and think about how you might improve them.

How well are you doing?

Look back at the different sections in this unit and assess your performance for each one. Choose from A–C below.

Reading (multiple matching) ...

Writing (article) ...

English In Use (multiple choice cloze) ...

Listening (note taking) ...

Speaking (introductions) ...

A No problem; I feel quite confident about this type of question.

B OK, but I need some more practice.

C I definitely need more practice. I find this type of question difficult.

Reading

🕐 (spend about 35 minutes on this section)

Paper 1 Part 3 Multiple choice questions

ℹ️ **Exam information** In this part of Paper 1 you have to answer between five and seven multiple choice questions. The questions are in the same order as the information in the text. For each question there are four possible options.

▶ **Exam techniques**
- Paper 1 Part 3 tests your detailed understanding of a text. You will need to read the text carefully before choosing the correct options. First, however, it is a good idea to read it through quickly to get a general idea what it is about. This will prepare you and make a second, more detailed reading of the text much easier. Task 1 practises this.
- When you have a general idea what the text is about, read it through again slowly and carefully, this time getting a detailed understanding. Then look at the questions, making sure you read all the options carefully. Then go back to the text to answer the questions. Task 2 practises this.

TASK 1 Read the article through quickly (take only 2–3 minutes). Choose the option which best describes it.

The article is about

A a family who are living in a hi-tech home.

B how people will be chosen to live in a hi-tech home.

C an experiment in living in a hi-tech home.

D how technology has advanced over the last ten months.

➡ **Check your answer on p.112.**

Orange announces Europe's first intelligent home

FAMILIES are queueing up to take part in trials of the first house in Britain to be operated entirely by a mobile telephone.

Orange, the second largest mobile phone company in Europe, has spent £2 million transforming an old farmhouse in Hertfordshire into a 'superhome' where making the coffee, mowing the lawn, buying the groceries and turning on the washing machine can all be done by remote control from a phone.

From April 1 a family will spend six weeks learning to live with the control phones and a host of gadgets dreamt up by some of the world's best-known manufacturers. Their progress, and that of other families who will follow them, will be monitored by teams at the universities of Surrey and Portsmouth.

The designers had an imaginary family in mind when they drew up the plans for the house. David, the father, is a travel writer and broadcaster who works a lot from home, and Clare, his wife, is a reflexologist. The children – James, Melissa and Christopher – are aged 14, 7 and 10 months respectively. The baby's cot is, naturally, fitted with noise and body temperature monitors and a camera in the room can send images of the child to screens around the home.

Now the search is on for parents and children who fit the designers' profile as closely as possible. Orange hopes to find them from among its staff or customers and an initial request for volunteers has had an overwhelming response. The company says it has been inundated by would-be guinea pigs willing to help the scientists discover just how much automation real people enjoy in their lives.

The house is powered partly by solar cells on the glass roof of the newly-built conservatory. Heating is supplied by a different sort of solar cell on the garage roof and the water used by the household for washing is recycled and used for flushing the lavatories. All this is established technology. What makes the Orange house different is that the phone can not only run the bath, it can set the temperature and depth – and it never overflows. After a day's work, the inhabitants can turn on the central heating or cooker. On their way home, they can open up the house remotely and turn on the lights.

The household gadgets and systems can also be controlled by handheld computers. Giving verbal commands to 'Wildfire', Orange's voice recognition system, can turn up the temperature, switch on the television, and turn off the lights. All these, according to Orange, could be routine fixtures in millions of homes in a few years.

As the house is developed, its central computer will note the groceries ordered on the internet and once the purchases have been delivered and put away, scanners in fridges, bins or cupboards will note the items as they are used up and add them to the household's list of things to re-order. The house is evolutionary, says Orange. Ultimately, the computer could offer recipes based on the fridge or cupboard contents and use data from health-monitoring equipment, which the house boasts in its small gym, to come up with tailored and nutritious eating plans.

Sue Lambert, who is in control of the project, said the organizers were unsure of the outcome: 'We do not know how far people will want to control heating, lighting, security, cooking or whatever, if at all. It is about how people use the technology and whether it makes things easier or not. Does it bring people together or will they just disperse into their own rooms? Do people want that one remote control for life? This experiment is sociological as well as technological.'

Sunday Telegraph

TASK 2 Read the article again and then answer questions 1–5.

For questions **1–5**, choose the correct option A, B, C, or D. Give only one answer to each question.

1 The house
  A has been specially built by Orange.
  B is full of gadgets designed by Orange.
  C belongs to two universities.
  D has been converted at a cost of £2 million.

2 Who will live in the house?
  A David, Clare, and their three children.
  B Volunteers, probably Orange staff or customers.
  C No one. It's an imaginary situation.
  D Scientists from the universities.

3 The house is special because
  A all the technology is new.
  B appliances and systems are controlled by phone.
  C the water is recycled.
  D it only uses established technology.

4 Eventually the house will be able to
  A decide what you should eat.
  B do the shopping for you.
  C prepare and cook your food for you.
  D plan an exercise programme.

5 Why has the experiment been set up?
  A To test the technology and see how people react to it.
  B To see how people in the house interact with each other.
  C To show how life will be easier in the future.
  D To see if the new technology works.

➜ **Check your answers on p.112.**

Writing

🕐 (spend about 30 minutes on tasks 1–3; about an hour on task 4)

Paper 2 Part 1 Formal letter

ℹ **Exam information** In Paper 2 Part 1 the task will be based on a text (or texts) of about 400 words. You will need to read, understand, and use the information from the text(s) in order to complete the task.

▶ **Exam techniques**
  • When you read the question and the text(s), underline the important information. If the question has more than one part, underline each part. This will help you to remember to answer the whole question. When you read the text(s), underline all the information that will need to be included in your answer. Task 1 practises this.
  • Think about who you are writing to and what the situation is. This will help you decide how formal or informal your letter should be. The examiner will expect you to use appropriate language – formal or informal – depending on the circumstances. Tasks 2 and 3 practise this.

TASK 1 Read the question and the texts below and underline the information that will be important in answering the question.

The college where you study is consulting students and staff about the number of computers available for use in the college and the rules for their use. The policy document is given below.

You have made some notes about points that you wish to bring to the attention of the Principal. Write a letter to the Principal giving your opinion on the document.

PETERSHAM COLLEGE

**Information technology and computing
Policy document**

The college-wide information technology and computing policy committee has made a number of recommendations to the college administration regarding the provision and use of computers within the college.

1 The ten computers currently in use in the college IT room should be replaced with 20 new and considerably more powerful PCs.

2 Students should be charged a standard termly fee for Internet use. A figure of £15 per term has been suggested.

3 The college reserves the right to check students' e-mail at any time to check for unsuitable or illegal content.

4 Students may not download any material from any source without the permission of a member of the college IT staff.

We would appreciate hearing the opinions of students and members of staff on these proposed changes. All views will be taken into consideration before a decision is reached.

Amanda Williams

Amanda Williams
Principal

Notes on policy document:
  • *keep old computers? what's wrong with them?*
  • *or 12–15 new ones OK (max. class size 15)*
  • *censor Internet (unsuitable material)*
  • *check websites and programs (not just e-mail)*
  • *no downloading: 1) cheating (using other people's work)*
    2) unsuitable material

➜ **Check your answers on pp.112–113.**

TASK 2 In fact, the notes on p.13 were written by Barry Trench, an art history teacher in the college. Read his answer to the question and look at the pairs of sentences below. Choose the more formal sentence from each pair to fill the appropriate space (A)–(D) in the letter.

1 a Finally, I hope that the college will not allow any downloading of material at all.
  b And then, of course, you shouldn't let students download anything from the Internet at all.

2 a I am not opposed to a charge for Internet use.
  b I'm not against people paying to use the Internet.

3 a These points are important and you should think about them before you decide what to do.
  b I feel these points are important and should be given consideration before any decisions are made.

4 a Why do we need any new computers in the first place?
  b Firstly, I fail to see the need for any new computers at all.

Dear Ms Williams

I would like to draw your attention to a number of points concerning the IT and computing policy document. … (A)

… (B) The ones we have are only three years old and are perfectly adequate for student use. If, however, you do decide to invest in new hardware, I suggest that a purchase of 12 to 15 computers would be sufficient, given that the maximum class size in the college is 15.

… (C) However, I feel it is essential that Internet use is censored in some way so that students are not able to access unsuitable or illegal material. For similar reasons, I feel that the college should not just check student e-mail but should also monitor the websites and the programs that students use.

… (D) From an academic point of view, this could well encourage students to pretend that material from the Internet is actually their own work.

I hope you will consider these points when arriving at a decision.

Yours sincerely,

Barry Trench

Barry Trench
Art History Department

→ **Check your answers on p.113.**

🔍 **Close up**

How would you write the opening and closing sentences from the letter in less formal English?

1 *I would like to draw your attention to a number of points concerning the IT and computing policy document.*

2 *I hope you will consider these points when arriving at a decision.*

→ **Check your answers on p.113.**

TASK 3 Match the phrases with similar meanings. Mark the more formal phrase F and the more informal phrase I.

1 Many thanks for …
2 I was wondering if you could …
3 I would like to apologize for …
4 Could you send me …
5 Write soon.
6 I would like to complain about …
7 I'm dead against …
8 It will be totally inadequate.

a I'm really sorry about …
b I look forward to hearing from you.
c Thank you very much indeed for …
d I am completely opposed to …
e I would be grateful if you could send me …
f It won't be nearly enough.
g Please could you …
h What were you thinking of?

→ **Check your answers on p.113.**

TASK 4 The notes that you made about the policy document on p.13 were very different from Barry Trench's notes. Read your notes below and write a letter to the Principal. Write about 250 words.

Notes on policy document
- *new computers – yes! v. necessary: old ones v. slow*
- *20 not enough (600 students at college)*
- *Internet – free (£15 a term too much)*
- *checking e-mail? – NO. Privacy?*
- *download materials – YES. Responsibility?*

Use these ideas to help you with your writing.

Underline the information in the notes above that you should include in your letter.

⌄

Note down any other ideas and any useful language that you might need.

⌄

Think of reasons for your ideas and opinions.

⌄

Organize your information, ideas, and useful language into paragraphs.

⌄

Remember you are writing to the Principal of the college. Think about how formal or informal your letter should be.

English In Use

(spend about 35 minutes on this section)

Paper 3 Part 3 Error correction

ℹ Exam information In Paper 3 Part 3 you are given an error correction exercise. There are two types of this exercise. In one type you have to correct errors of spelling and punctuation; in the other you have to identify extra, unnecessary words which have been added to the text.

▶ **Exam techniques**
- Be aware of words which are commonly misspelt in English. Make a list of any English words that you have problems spelling. Learn them! Task 1 practises this.
- Be aware of common punctuation problems. Make sure you know when to use capital letters and full stops, when to put inverted commas and question marks, and where you should use commas and apostrophes. Task 2 practises this.
- Read the text through to get a general idea of the meaning before you start looking for any errors. Understanding the meaning of the text will often help you spot errors of spelling and punctuation. Task 3 practises this.

TASK 1 Read the text below. Correct the spelling of the four words that are underlined. Then find five more words which are misspelt and correct them.

Our company has decided to buy some important hardware components from a new sauce. Up until last year we had always prefered British-made components. Unfortunatly, however, market conditions have changed dramatically on acount of the rise in value of the pound and so we have had to look for cheaper items. Initially we looked at the market that was developping in the Far East. Their were a number of advantages, particularly cost, but we found that we were unable to find components of the right wait to go into our laptops. The peices we were given as samples were far too heavy. However, a South American company was able to provide what we wanted at a reasonable price and we recieve our first shipment next week.

➡ Check your answers on p.113.

TASK 2 There is one punctuation mistake in each sentence below. Correct it.

1 'Let's ask them! They've got a dictionary so they must know the answer, said Kelly.
2 The new iMac computer, which is already a design classic has helped considerably to restore the fortunes of Apple.
3 We've decided to make it a rule that english should be the language used throughout our company.
4 Its not uncommon to see eagles in parts of the far north of Scotland.
5 The title of the conference is: 'How should governments approach the problem of global warming.'
6 'Let's stop It's the end of the exercise.'

➡ Check your answers on p.113.

TASK 3 Read through the article in task 4 and answer these questions.

1 Why are the families being filmed?
2 Why are the cameras hidden?
3 What will the scientists do with the information?

➡ Check your answers on p.113 after doing exam task 4.

TASK 4 Now do the exam task.

In most lines of the following article, there is either a spelling or a punctuation error. For each numbered line **1–16**, write the correctly-spelled word or show the correct punctuation. Some numbered lines are correct. Indicate these lines with a tick (✔). The exercise begins with three examples.

BIG TEDDY IS WATCHING YOU

Miniature cameras hiden in cocoa tins and teddy bears around	**0** hidden
the home are to be used to investigate peoples true reaction to	**00** people's
new technology.	**000** ✔
They will silently tape the behaviour of children towards home	**1** ....
computers, recording how often they are used and why they are	**2** ....
used.	
The cameras will also record the influense of the Internet on	**3** ....
everyday life as well as the usefullness of such technologies as	**4** ....
e-mail or home banking.	
Sixteen famillies around the country who are already using the	**5** ....
new technology at home will be monnitored over the next two	**6** ....
years in the £180,000 programme which will be aided by an	**7** ....
award from the Economic Funding Council.	
Dr David Morrison of Leeds University, the reserch scientist	**8** ....
who is heading the project said using cocoa tins and teddy	**9** ....
bears, as well as other household objects, to hide the cameras	**10** ....
was something they had developped to ensure more natural	**11** ....
reactions.	
We all expect technology to open up a new world for us but	**12** ....
maybe it wont. The social history of the telephone, for example,	**13** ....
shows that it consolidated our relationships rather than	**14** ....
expanded our circle of friends,' he said.	
The information they acquire, Doctor Morrison added would	**15** ....
contrabute to the new technology debate and could also be of	**16** ....
benefit to industry and commerce.	

Independent on Sunday

➡ Check your answers on p.113.

Listening

(spend about 25 minutes on this section)

Paper 4 Part 4 Multiple matching

ⓘ Exam information In Paper 4 Part 4 you will be given either multiple choice questions or a multiple matching task. You will hear five extracts which are thematically related. The multiple matching task will be in two parts. In each part there will be five questions where you are asked to match the extract you hear to a list of eight options.

▶ **Exam techniques**
- Key words will often help you answer questions in Paper 4. Before you listen to the recording, think about what words you might hear. Task 1 practises this.
- Try and read both tasks before you listen to the recording. You will hear the recording twice. It is a good idea to try and complete the first task after the first listening and the second task after the second listening. Task 2 practises this.

TASK 1 In exam task one you are asked to identify five people's occupations. Put the words below into an appropriate column in the chart. Some words may go in more than one column.

| vote sculpture treatment oils rough draft orphan symptoms |
| watercolours govern software election manuscript classes disk |
| problem kids collage subject |

writer	teacher	artist	doctor	social worker	politician	student	computer programmer

➜ **Check your answers on p.113.**

TASK 2 🎧2.1 You will hear five short extracts in which people are talking about the influence of technology on their lives and their attitude towards it. Listen to the recording twice.

TASK ONE

For questions **1–5**, match the extracts with the people, listed **A–H**.

A a writer	Speaker 1 [1]
B a teacher	
C an artist	Speaker 2 [2]
D a doctor	Speaker 3 [3]
E a social worker	
F a politician	Speaker 4 [4]
G a student	
H a computer programmer	Speaker 5 [5]

TASK TWO

For questions **6–10**, match the extracts with each speaker's attitude towards technology, listed **A–H**.

A It makes my job easier.	
B It provides me with lots of information.	Speaker 1 [6]
C It helps me shop.	Speaker 2 [7]
D It provides a new challenge.	Speaker 3 [8]
E It gives me news and sports updates.	Speaker 4 [9]
F It helps me keep in touch with people.	Speaker 5 [10]
G It keeps me entertained.	
H It makes me angry.	

➜ **Check your answers on p.113.**

Language development

Nouns with *-ion*

1 Look at these phrases from the recording:

*… avenues and methods of **expression** …*

*… there's vital **information** …*

Now complete the chart.

VERB	NOUN
express	expression
create	
inform	
revise	
revolt	
donate	
admit	
examine	
act	
operate	

➜ **Check your answers on p.113.**

2 Answer these questions as in the example. Use words from exercise 1.

What happened in France in 1789?
A revolution.

1 What do surgeons perform in hospitals?
2 What does 'The Big Bang' theory explain?
3 What do you give to charity?
4 What do film directors say when they start to shoot a scene?
5 What sign will you see on the door of an art gallery that you do not have to pay to go into?
6 What do you take at the end of the school year? And what should you do before you take them?
7 What do you get from an encyclopedia?

➜ **Check your answers on p.113.**

Speaking

🕐 (spend about 25 minutes on this section)

Paper 5 Part 2 Speaking

ℹ Exam information In Paper 5 Part 2 you are asked to speak for about a minute without interruption about some photographs or pictures. You will also have to comment on what your partner says.

▶ **Exam techniques**
- Listen carefully to the instructions you are given. Make a mental note of what you have to do; it is important to do what you are asked and not to talk generally about the pictures. Then take a few seconds to think about how you are going to answer the question before you start speaking. Task 1 practises this.
- When you are describing a picture, you cannot always be sure what is happening. Use appropriate language to show that you are not sure. You will then show the examiner that you are able to express uncertainty in English. Task 2 practises this.
- If you don't know the exact word for something, don't panic. Use the words you do know to explain what you mean. This will show the examiner that you have good communication skills. Task 4 practises this.

TASK 1 Look at the pictures below. The examiner says: 'I would like you to describe the two pictures, say what you think is happening in each one, and discuss any possible connection between the two pictures.' Think about what you would say.

TASK 2 🎧2.2 Listen to someone describing the pictures and answer the questions below.

1 These are all ways of speculating. Tick (✔) the phrases you hear.
   - ☐ … looks as if …
   - ☐ … something like that …
   - ☐ It looks like …
   - ☐ … this might be some kind of …
   - ☐ … it could be …
   - ☐ … maybe …
   - ☐ I guess they might be …
   - ☐ Perhaps …
   - ☐ I suspect it's …

2 What tense is often used when describing pictures or photos?

3 Does the speaker know the correct English word for what the people are doing in picture 2? How does he deal with this?

→ **Check your answers on p.113.**

TASK 3 Work in pairs. (If you are working alone, look at p.4.) Look at the pictures. Describe one each and discuss what connection you think there might be between them. If possible, record your discussion. Then play it back and think how you might improve it.

TASK 4 🎧2.3 Now listen to two native speakers discussing the pictures in task 3.

1 Listen to the first part of the recording. Look at the phrases and sentences below from the recording. Underline the words and phrases that show the speaker is speculating and not absolutely sure about what he or she is saying.
   a my picture seems to be in a busy office type thing
   b there's stuff – computers in front of them or something
   c he's obviously had some happy news
   d it seems to be like an industrial area kind of like offices
   e he's just come out of the office maybe
   f maybe telesales or something
   g could be telesales or a switchboard or something
   h I get the idea this guy's in a more superior position
   In which phrase or sentence does the speaker seem certain about what he or she is saying?

2 Listen to the second part of the recording. Complete the phrases and sentences below with the words you hear on the recording.
   a It .... this one's business …
   b He .... talking to a loved one.
   c He .... just got a job there.
   d He .... their boss and he's out to lunch and they're working hard.
   e Maybe it's some stockbroker. Money market ....

→ **Check your answers on p.114.**

How well are you doing?

Look back at the different sections in this unit and assess your performance for each one. Choose from A–C below.

Reading (multiple choice questions)	…
Writing (formal letter)	…
English In Use (error correction)	…
Listening (multiple matching)	…
Speaking (speculating)	…

A No problem; I feel quite confident about this type of question.
B OK, but I need some more practice.
C I definitely need more practice. I find this type of question difficult.

Reading

(spend about 30 minutes on this section)

Paper 1 Part 2 Gapped text

ⓘ Exam information In Paper 1 Part 2 you are given a text with six or seven paragraphs missing. You are given the missing paragraphs in a jumbled order and there is one extra paragraph. You have to choose the correct paragraph for each gap in the text. Only one paragraph will fit correctly into each gap.

▶ **Exam techniques**
- Look at the title to get an idea of what the text is about. This will help you to understand the text more easily when you read it through. Task 1 practises this.
- Read the gapped text through carefully. Get an overall idea of the meaning of the text and think about how it is organized. Think about the order in which the information or the argument is presented. Having a clear idea of how the text is organized will help you when you decide how to replace the missing paragraphs. Tasks 2 and 3 practise this.

TASK 1 Read the title of the text in task 3 and choose the best option below.

The text is probably about:
1 how to make good sandwiches
2 how to run a sandwich bar
3 why sandwiches are bad for you

TASK 2 Read the text through. Change your answer to task 1, if necessary.

TASK 3 Match the descriptions (a–i) to the paragraphs in the gapped text. The first two have been done for you.

a *The initial idea*
b Making progress
c What we offer
d The start of the day
e Why we are successful
f *Early research*
g How we got the money
h Early decisions
i The end of the day

Roll-play? No – the working reality of a sandwich bar

a Sonya and I wanted to start a business of our own, rather than work in a big company environment. We considered a number of different businesses but felt there was a gap on many High Streets for a quality sandwich shop – an alternative to the standard fast food choice of McDonald's or Burger King.

f We did quite a lot of research, such as questionnaires and pedestrian counts, building up as much information as we could. We weren't fixed in terms of where we wanted to set up, as the ideal location was all-important, so we visited Leeds, Bristol, and Portsmouth as well as Southampton.

1

We had just a few thousand pounds between us so it was a matter of approaching the banks. The Midland Bank agreed to lend us £30,000 under the Small Firms Loan Guarantee Scheme, where part of the loan is guaranteed by the government. We also secured £5,000 from a business trust.

2

We had fixed ideas about what we wanted to sell. The baguettes had to be just right: not too thin and not too big. We decided right from the start that our French bread would indeed be French and we'd get it from a distributor and part-bake it. We were ready to open in December 1995, well into the Christmas season and typically a very good month for business. We opened right from the start with four staff.

3

Gradually the business pulled round and we got into a routine with our systems, which are vital for any fast-food operation. There tend to be some very busy periods during the day. You certainly don't want queues. And you need staff who work well together.

4

We offer a variety of breads from sun-dried tomato to white farmhouse and if you take into account our salad toppings as well as fillings we offer 44 million combinations of sandwich.

5

The daily routine involves staff coming in at 7.30a.m. to start doing the preparation. The more work that can be done in advance, the more time you can save when the shop gets full of people. And then by 8a.m. we are open for the breakfast trade.

6

We close at 6p.m. (7p.m. on Thursday) but some nights we have to work late. Sonya and I are now working on opening a new shop in Southampton, and also further expansion.

I think where we've succeeded is that we've never compromised on what we offer. We are a sandwich bar and have never ventured into selling jacket potatoes or chips. It's our intention to open other outlets and possibly franchise the concept and become a national operation. We have the energy, and time, on our side.

Daily Express

➔ Check your answers on p.114.

TASK 4 Now do the exam task.

You must choose which of the paragraphs **A–G** below fit into the numbered gaps in the article opposite. There is one extra paragraph which does not fit in any of the gaps.

A Once we had the money organized we had to find a place. The site we chose was a former clothes shop which made it ideal because it already had the right kind of floor and lighting. The lease was typical of properties in the area at between £30,000 and £35,000 and we had to put in an oven, counter, upstairs preparation area, tills, fridges and freezers, making our start-up costs around £50,000.

B The first day, however, was a real trial. We took £200, less than even half of what we need to break even, and we had the prospect of the less busy January and February season approaching.

C The busy time is obviously lunchtime but that can extend to 3.30p.m. Our business continues longer than many sandwich bars where that lunch-hour trade is the be-all and end-all.

D Our families were incredibly supportive and helpful. My father, a carpenter by trade, helped out with the shop fitting, while Sonya's aunt was a fund of useful ideas for sandwich fillings and types of bread. She was so enthusiastic she wanted to help out in the shop but we felt that at 86 she was better off at home.

E Other preparations that we felt were important included trying to gain some practical experience. Sonya had worked in a small Gloucestershire café and I had spent two months in McDonald's.

F Getting the right people was very important and we rejected about nine out of ten people. It is important to build an efficient team who can work together in a friendly way, and deal politely and efficiently with the public.

G However, people are generally still conservative in this market. Our biggest sellers are chicken, cheese, ham and tuna. More exotic fillings such as marinaded red pepper and goat cheese have fewer takers. Four or five types of bread are very popular.

→ Check your answers on p.114.

Verb–noun collocations

1 Match the verbs on the left with an appropriate phrase on the right.

to start   a lot of research
to do   a new shop
to gain   an efficient team
to get into   a business
to build   a routine
to open   some practical experience

→ **Check your answers in the article on pp.18–19.**

2 Complete the text below with the correct form of phrases from exercise 1.

'When I left school, I got a job in a newsagent's shop. It was quite a big shop – there were two or three staff – and I really enjoyed working there. After a year or two, when I had .... ¹, I thought to myself 'I could do this' so I decided to .... ² for myself. To begin with I .... ³ to find out where would be a good area to set up. Then I bought a shop, recruited three staff, and started. After a while we .... ⁴, and things went well. When I realized that I had .... ⁵ in this shop and that they could run the business on their own, I became more ambitious and started to think about .... ⁶. That was five years ago. I've now got ten.'

→ **Check your answers on p.114.**

Writing

🕐 (spend about 20 minutes on tasks 1–4; about an hour on task 5)

Paper 2 Part 2 Leaflets

ⓘ **Exam information** In Part 2 of the Writing Paper you have to choose one of four tasks. See p.3 for the complete list of tasks that you might be asked to do. You may be asked to write the text for a leaflet.

▶ **Exam techniques**
- With leaflets and brochures, the layout is often very important. Think about it carefully before you start planning your writing. Think about how the leaflet would look in your language. NB Do not draw pictures in the exam; you don't get any extra marks. Columns are not necessary either, but clear layout is. You will get better marks if you lay your leaflet out so that the information is easy to grasp. Task 1 practises this.
- The language and style of leaflets and brochures is important. Think about what you are trying to do: give advice, inform, order, etc. Think also about who will be reading the leaflet. The language you use may be different depending on the purpose of the leaflet and who will read it. Tasks 2, 3, and 4 practise this.
- Before you start the leaflet, write down as many ideas as you can. Having a lot of ideas will make writing easier. You will be able to concentrate more on how to express yourself rather than what to say. Remember: you don't have to use all the ideas you think of, just the best ones. Task 5 practises this.

TASK 1 Look at the layout of leaflets A and B and answer these questions.

1 The points in leaflet A are all short. Why do you think this is?
2 In leaflet B, some of the points are even shorter. Do you think this is an improvement on leaflet A?
3 Leaflet A starts with a question. What is the effect of that?
4 What is this • called? Why do the leaflets have one at the start of each point?
5 Leaflet A has a number of different sub-headings (*Starting out, Making progress,* etc.). Why has the writer done this?
6 Leaflet B is written in two parts. Why?
7 Which leaflet do you prefer? Why?

→ **Check your answers on p.114.**

Ⓐ

Skateboard SAFETY ⓝⓢⓤ

Have you just bought a skateboard?
Then remember these simple ideas!
SKATEBOARDING IS FUN BUT IT CAN BE DANGEROUS
These simple ideas can help you avoid accidents and be a better skateboarder.

STARTING OUT
- If you're a beginner, practise with a friend first. Most bad accidents happen during the first month.
- Learn everything slowly, including new tricks. If you lose your balance, don't wait to fall off. Step off and start again.

MAKING PROGRESS
- Learn how to fall (by rolling if possible) without the skateboard. Most serious skateboard injuries are broken bones.
- Go down gentle slopes at first. Never go down a slope where you can't run off the board.
- Running or jumping onto skateboards can be dangerous.

WHAT TO WEAR
- Wear protective equipment: knee pads, elbow pads, helmet and gloves. Wear long sleeves and trousers too – and flat-soled shoes.

CHOOSING WHERE TO SKATE
- Practise in places where you can improve your skills. Don't go on busy pavements and streets. Don't go in places where other skateboarders have had accidents.
- Don't skateboard on wet or uneven surfaces.
- …

Published by the National Skateboard Union

Ⓑ

SKATEBOARD SAFETY

SKATEBOARDING IS FUN BUT IT CAN BE DANGEROUS

DO'S
- Practise where you can improve your skills.
- Practise with a friend first – if you are a beginner.
- Learn everything slowly – including new tricks.
- Go down gentle slopes at first.
- Learn how to fall (by rolling) without the skateboard.
- Wear protective equipment: knee pads, elbow pads, helmet and gloves.
- Wear long sleeves and trousers – and flat-soled shoes.
- …

DON'TS
- Don't go on busy pavements and streets.
- Don't go where other skateboarders have had accidents.
- Don't wait to fall off if you lose your balance. Step off and start again.
- Don't go down a slope that is so steep you can't run off the board.
- Don't run or jump onto skateboards.
- Don't skateboard on wet or uneven surfaces.
- …

UNIT 3

TASK 2 Look again at leaflets A and B and answer these questions.

1 What is the purpose of the leaflets? Choose the best answer.
   a to inform   **b** to advise   **c** to explain   **d** to order
2 Which leaflet achieves its purpose a little more strongly? How?
3 Many of the verbs in the leaflets are in the imperative (*practise, learn, go, wear*). Why do you think this is?
4 What age group do you think the leaflets are aimed at? Do you think this has influenced the language in any way?
5 In what way would the language used be different for
   a a leaflet persuading teenagers to come to a new youth club?
   b a leaflet explaining to pensioners plans for a new free bus pass for the over-60s?

TASK 3 The last point has been left out of both leaflets. For leaflet A, choose the wording below which you think is the most direct, concise, and effective.

A It's a good idea to think about where your skateboard might go if you are thinking of jumping off it. The problem is that it could run into someone else who didn't see it coming and it might injure them quite badly.
B Before you jump off your skateboard, make sure you know where the board is likely to go. If someone is standing nearby, be very careful. Don't let your board run on and injure someone else.
C Be careful when you are jumping off the skateboard. Have a look and see where it is likely to go. Make sure it doesn't hit someone and hurt them.

→ **Check your answers to tasks 2 and 3 on p.114.**

TASK 4 For leaflet B, write one or two extra sentences to add to the leaflet, based on the ideas in task 3 above.

→ **Check your answers on p.114.**

TASK 5 You work in a factory which makes and sells fireworks. Your customers are ordinary people who are buying fireworks to give displays to groups of up to about 25 or 30 of their friends or family. Your boss has asked you to produce a safety leaflet to go in every box of fireworks.

Write the leaflet in approximately 250 words.

Use these ideas to help you plan and organize your writing.

> Use your common sense and make a list of as many different things as possible that people need to think about when handling fireworks.
>
> Group your ideas into different categories.
>
> Decide which of your ideas to keep and which (if any) to leave out.
>
> Decide on a suitable layout for your leaflet.
>
> Decide how to fit your ideas into the layout you have chosen.
>
> Write your leaflet.

English In Use

🕑 (spend about 30 minutes on this section)

Paper 3 Part 2 Open cloze

ℹ **Exam information** In Paper 3 Part 2 you are given a short text with 15 words missing. You have to fill in the missing words. Unlike Part 1, you are not given any words to choose from. Remember to put *only one word* in each space.

You are unlikely to need the same word more than once. You are also unlikely to need a contraction (*don't, isn't,* etc.).

▶ **Exam techniques**
  • As with Part 1, read the whole text through carefully and get a good idea of the meaning before you start to fill in any spaces. Understanding the whole text will be a great help when trying to fill the spaces. You may also find clues later in the text that help you to fill some of the earlier spaces. Task 1 practises this.
  • Don't worry if there are some words in the text that you don't understand. In this part the spaces usually test *grammar* words rather than vocabulary. Task 2 practises this.
  • Remember to use only one word for each space and never leave a space empty. You don't lose marks for a wrong answer and there is always a chance you will guess correctly.

TASK 1 Read through the article on p.22 and answer these questions.

1 How is passport control going to be changed?
2 By how much is it expected that air traffic will increase over the next ten years?
3 What two reasons have made the changes to passport control necessary?
4 How do the Immigration Service feel about this idea?

→ **Check your answers on p.114.**

TASK 2 Look at the words below. Tick (✔) the words which are *grammar* words.

- [ ] their
- [ ] has
- [ ] with
- [ ] can
- [ ] prevent
- [ ] immigration
- [ ] bypass
- [ ] to
- [ ] by
- [ ] hi-tech
- [ ] will
- [ ] occupy
- [ ] long
- [ ] this
- [ ] queue

→ Check your answers on p.115.

TASK 3 Now do the exam task. You will find the first five answers among the words in task 2 above.

> For questions **1–15** complete the following article by writing each missing word in the correct space. Use only one word for each space. The exercise begins with an example (**0**).
>
> **PALM PRINT I.D. TO REPLACE PASSPORTS**
>
> Immigration officers are to (**0**) *be* replaced by machines at a major UK airport – probably Heathrow – in a trial of a computerised passport control system (**1**) .... identifies travellers by their palm prints.
>
> By pressing (**2**) .... hands on a monitor, and then slotting a card into a machine, passengers holding an air ticket will be able to bypass queues (**3**) .... walk into the customs hall in 15 seconds.
>
> The Fastgate system has been developed by computer giant IBM and is the latest technological initiative designed (**4**) .... prevent border officials being overwhelmed (**5**) .... passenger numbers.
>
> In the next ten years, 50 per cent more air journeys (**6**) .... expected to be made to and from the UK, leaving the Government (**7**) .... a logistical nightmare concerning frontier checks.
>
> There is a limit to the number of immigration officers (**8**) .... can be employed and the space that they occupy at airports. Faced with (**9**) .... prospect of long snaking queues congesting British airports, technological innovation has been in order.
>
> The need for reform has been compounded by the increasing sophistication (**10**) .... forgers, who are able to produce passports which can fool experienced passport control officers.
>
> The project has been attacked though by Britain's Immigration Service Union, which (**11**) .... warned against putting (**12**) .... much faith in machines over the tried and tested system of human hunch and intuition.
>
> General Secretary Martin Slade said: "(**13**) .... you can design it, you can beat it. I (**14**) .... not trust it. There isn't a computer system in the world that does (**15**) .... have a bug in it."
>
> **Independent on Sunday**

→ Check your answers on p.115.

Listening

🕐 (spend about 30 minutes on this section)

Paper 4 Part 3 Sentence completion

ℹ️ **Exam information** In Part 3 you will hear a conversation between two or three speakers. You will either have to complete some sentences or answer some multiple choice questions. If you are completing sentences, you will not need to write more than three words for each answer. Part 3 tests your understanding of people's attitudes and opinions as well as your grasp of specific information.

▶ **Exam techniques**
- Read the questions and note what information you can get from them. You can find out quite a lot from the questions to prepare you for what you are about to hear. Task 1 practises this.
- Once you have read the questions, don't just sit and wait for the recording to start. If you have time, think about what sort of vocabulary might come up in the conversation. This will also help to prepare you for the listening. Task 2 practises this.
- Look at the questions as you listen to the recording. This will focus your mind on what you are listening for. Task 3 practises this.

TASK 1 Read the exam question and sentences in task 3 below. Answer these questions.

1 Do you think the press are interested in Katie?
2 Are there any advantages to being famous?
3 What might the answer to (6) be?

TASK 2 Tick (✔) the words and phrases you think you might hear in the recording.

- [ ] tabloid newspapers
- [ ] a bookcase
- [ ] a huge star
- [ ] an agent
- [ ] interviews
- [ ] restaurant
- [ ] to intrude into one's life
- [ ] a flower shop
- [ ] business affairs
- [ ] superstitious
- [ ] garage
- [ ] glamorous

→ Check your answers to tasks 1 and 2 on p.115.

TASK 3 🎧 **3.1** You will hear a radio interview with an actress about the problems of being famous. For questions 1–8 complete the sentences. Listen to the recording twice.

> Katie thinks many people are [1] than her.
> Katie feels she shouldn't [2] about press intrusion.
> Katie's dealings with the press are handled by her [3].
> Katie is [4] by photographers.
> Katie doesn't mind journalists if they get the [5].
> The advantage of being famous is that it's not necessary for her to [6].
> Katie has a [7] in the film she is making at the moment.
> Katie doesn't want to talk about her other project, the [8] she has started working on.

→ Check your answers on p.115.

Speaking

⏱ (spend about 25 minutes on this section)

Paper 5 Part 3 Agreeing and disagreeing

ℹ **Exam information** In Paper 5 Part 3, you have to discuss a problem-solving task with your partner. At the end of the task you will have to report the outcome of your discussion to the examiner.

▶ **Exam technique**
- There will not necessarily be a right or a wrong answer to the problem-solving task. What is important is that you communicate with and listen to each other, and that you use good communication skills to make sure that you each have a roughly equal share of the conversation. You may agree or disagree with your partner, but if you disagree, you should disagree politely. Tasks 1 and 2 practise this.

TASK 1 🎧 **3.2** Two people are discussing how important various different factors are in influencing the way people vote for a political party. First look at the following list of factors. Then listen to the conversation and mark sentences 1–3 T (true) or F (false).

- the party promises to lower taxes
- the leader of the party is good-looking
- the party maintains good international relations
- the party wants to raise educational standards
- the party wants to provide good quality healthcare
- the leader of the party has a charismatic personality
- the members of the party are generally seen to be honest
- the party has a record of good economic management

1 The man thinks health and education are particularly important.
2 The woman thinks people do not care whether politicians are honest.
3 They agree that good economic management is the most important factor.

➔ **Check your answers on p.115.**

TASK 2 Listen again to the conversation.

1 Note the words and phrases that the speakers use to agree and disagree with each other.
2 Note the words and phrases the speakers use to ask each other for their opinions.

➔ **Check your answers in the transcript on p.115.**

TASK 3 Work in pairs. (If you are working alone, look at p.4.) Discuss the question below. If possible, record your discussion. Then play it back and think about how you might improve it.

Put the factors below in order according to how important you think they are in influencing the way people decide which car to buy.

- how fast it will go
- how big / small it is
- how much it costs
- how much it costs to maintain
- how comfortable it is
- how prestigious the make is
- what safety features it has
- what appeal it has to the opposite sex

How well are you doing?

Look back at the different sections in this unit and assess your performance for each one. Choose from A–C below.

Reading (gapped text)	...
Writing (leaflets)	...
English In Use (open cloze)	...
Listening (sentence completion)	...
Speaking (agreeing and disagreeing)	...

A No problem; I feel quite confident about this type of question.
B OK, but I need some more practice.
C I definitely need more practice. I find this type of question difficult.

Reading

🕐 (spend about 35 minutes on this section)

Paper 1 Part 1
Multiple matching

ℹ️ **Exam information** Paper 1 Part 1 will contain between 12 and 18 multiple matching questions. These questions test your ability to find particular information, opinions, or attitudes within a text.

▶ **Exam techniques**
- The questions for Parts 1 and 4 of the Reading Paper come before the text. This is to encourage you to read the questions first and then scan the text to find the answers. However, it is still a good idea to look through the text quickly first to get a general idea of the meaning. Task 1 practises this.
- Once you have a general idea about the text, read the questions carefully so you know what information you are looking for. Then find the answers in the text. Try not to waste time reading the whole text slowly from beginning to end. Task 2 practises this.

TASK 1 Read through texts A–G quickly (2–3 minutes maximum). Then mark these sentences T (true) or F (false).

1 All the animals listed are extinct. F
2 Some of the animals listed are birds. T
3 None of the animals listed lives in the sea. F
4 Many of the animals listed are endangered. T

TASK 2 Now do the exam task.

→ Check your answers on pp.115–116.

For questions **1–16**, answer by choosing from the list (**A–G**) below. Some of the choices may be required more than once. When more than one answer is required, these may be given in any order.

According to the text, which of the animals listed

used to be able to fly?	**1**	
can still fly today?	**2**	
seem to live well in zoos?	**3**	**4** . . . . .
do not mind contact with humans?	**5**	**6** . . . . .
is hunted by farmers because it kills their animals?	**7**	
no longer lives in the wild?	**8**	
is hunted by farmers because they think it kills their animals?	**9**	
are small compared to other examples of their species?	**10**	**11** . . . . .
runs away from people?	**12**	
used to be in danger of extinction but is not now?	**13**	
are protected by law?	**14** . . . . . **15** **16**	

A Galapagos Flightless Cormorant

B Snow Leopard

C Pygmy Hippopotamus

D Trumpeter Swan

E Przewalski's Horse

F Giant Anteater

G Humpback Whale

Ⓐ Galapagos Flightless Cormorant

The Galapagos flightless cormorant evolved in an isolated island environment that was free of predators. The birds had no need to fly and eventually became flightless. However, the Galapagos Islands have not remained free of predators, and, consequently, this cormorant is now one of the world's rarest birds.

Through the years, dogs, cats, and pigs were introduced to the Islands and have had a drastic effect on the cormorant population. As well, these birds have no fear of man and can be easily approached and picked up. There are now only about 1,000 flightless cormorants left and the species is listed as rare.

Ⓑ Snow Leopard

Found above the tree line and near permanent snow in central Asia's dry mountainous country, the snow leopard has been prized as a hunter's trophy, destroyed as a predator of domestic animals, and sought as a source of valuable fur. Complete information as to its numbers is not available, but almost everywhere it is considered to be rare or in decline. Currently, the most serious threat to its survival is loss of habitat due to human expansion. More than 150 snow leopards live in zoos where they have been bred successfully. The snow leopard is now listed as an endangered species and is legally protected. In some places, however, enforcement of regulations is difficult.

C Pygmy Hippopotamus

The name hippopotamus comes from Greek and means 'river horse'. Hippos, however, are not related to horses, but to pigs.

Although hippos once ranged through Europe and Asia, they are now found only in the African interior and on game reserves. The pygmy hippo, which is the smallest species, occurs in West Africa, especially in or near rivers, lakes, and swamps.

Common hippos live in herds and are well adapted to life in the water. By contrast, the pygmy hippo is a shy, solitary, forest dweller that is still hunted by the natives for its meat. When encountering people, it flees at once into the nearest river or swamp. Their life span is about 35 years, and they have adapted well to life in zoological gardens, a hopeful sign, as they are threatened with extinction in their natural habitat. The major threats to this species are deforestation and hunting.

D Trumpeter Swan

The trumpeter swan, largest and rarest of the world's eight swan species, was once a common nesting bird in north, west, and central North America. It was hunted extensively by natives for food and feathers, and its numbers began to decline when a market developed in European settlements for its skin, feathers, down, and quills. The decline continued with the gradual loss of nesting, feeding, and wintering habitats, especially in the United States, to expanded land use. By the early 1900s, the bird's extinction was thought near. Now legally protected in Canada and the United States and provided with sanctuaries, its numbers have slowly increased through emergency winter feeding, habitat restoration, and controlled relocation of populations. More than 5,000 trumpeter swans presently take to the air, of which about 500 pairs can be found in Canada. Although still carefully monitored, they have been removed from the list of endangered species.

E Przewalski's Horse

This stocky, pony-like animal, named after the Russian naturalist who discovered it in 1879, is the only surviving species of wild horse. Only 1.2m high (its domestic counterpart averages 1.6m) it once inhabited the vast grasslands of central Asia, but beginning in the early 1900s, hunting pressure, competition for grazing land and water, and interbreeding with domestic Mongol ponies contributed to its increasing scarcity in its natural state.

Strict legal protection since 1926 in Mongolia appears to have failed to save the last wild population. The most recent reliable sighting of this horse occurred in 1968. It now survives only in zoos. If it adapts well to this environment, there is hope that captive breeding stock can be used in the future to re-establish the species in the wild.

F Giant Anteater

The giant anteater of South America is about the size of a German Shepherd dog. It is covered with stiff, straw-like hair which grows up to 40cm long on the tail.

As the name suggests, anteaters eat ants and termites in vast quantities, sometimes up to 30,000 insects in a single day. The anteater will rip open a termite hill with its clawed hand and work its tubular snout into the opening, sticking its long, worm-shaped tongue down into the heart of the colony and trapping the insects on its tongue's sticky coating.

Docile and inoffensive by nature, the anteater's principal enemies are the puma and the jaguar. These large predators must be careful in their attacks, however, as an embrace by the anteater's powerful forelimbs can prove fatal. Giant anteaters are hunted in South America for their meat and for trophies. They are also killed because they are mistakenly believed by farmers to kill dogs and cattle.

G Humpback Whale

Distinguished by its short, stout body and long, curved flippers which are often a third of the total body length, this slow-moving animal is usually easily approached, even by humans. The average length of the Pacific adult males is 12.5m and of females 14.6m. The average weight is 30 tons.

The humpback is often observed throwing itself out of the water in gigantic somersaults and crashing back into the sea again. It rolls on the surface, sometimes leaping out of the water, flippers beating the air as if it were attempting to fly.

Humpbacks are preyed upon by humans and killer whales. These whales have been hunted to near extinction, and only about 2,500 exist today.

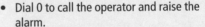

http://www.nature.ca/notebooks/english

 (spend about 40 minutes on task 1; about an hour on task 2)

Paper 2 Parts 1 and 2
Instructions and directions

> **ⓘ Exam information** In Paper 2 you might be asked to write some instructions and/or some directions. In Part 1 these might be part of the question – you would have to complete another task as well. In Part 2 they would be the whole question.

▶ **Exam techniques**
- As with leaflets, in the previous unit, layout and style are important when you are writing instructions or directions. Clarity is vital: in appropriate circumstances the layout can be used to help make your writing clearer. Tasks 1–4 practise this.
- It is also important that your instructions or directions are expressed in an appropriate, logical order and in clear, simple language. They will then be easy to understand and to follow. Tasks 1–4 practise this.

TASK 1 Look at questions and answers 1–3. Answer a–e/f below each one.

1 You work at a hotel. You have been asked to write a notice to go in each room telling guests what to do in case of fire. You should tell them how to raise the alarm, where to go, and how to get there.

> **EMERGENCY PROCEDURE**
> **In case of fire**
> - Dial 0 to call the operator and raise the alarm.
> - If there is no reply, dial 9-999 to call the fire brigade. Then break the glass in the fire alarm in the corridor outside. This will sound the alarm bell.
> - Leave your room quickly. Do not stop to pick up personal possessions.
> - Go quickly to the nearest assembly point indicated on the map below. Use the stairs. Do not use the lifts.

a How many parts are there to the question? Underline the different parts.

b Does the notice answer the question fully?

c Is the notice clear?

d Does the notice need a heading? Does it have one?

e What verb form is mainly used? Why?

f Is it clearly presented? What punctuation feature is used to help the clarity?

2 A friend is coming to stay in your house while you are away on holiday. Tell them how to get in touch with your doctor and give directions to the Health Centre.

> *And of course you'll need to know where the doctor's is just in case any of you get ill. I'm afraid Dr Hudson lives in the next village – Kingley. It's about five kilometres away so you'll have to drive. Turn left out of the front gate and go along the road to the end. Turn right there and go straight on until you start to come into Kingley. Take the first turning right (Ashburton Avenue) and you'll see the Health Centre on the left. The phone number is 9468743 and it's best to ring and make an appointment. In an emergency you can also ring that number out of hours.*

a Who will read these directions? How will this affect the layout and style compared with question 1 on p.25?

b Does the paragraph above answer the task fully?

c Are the directions clear?

d Do the directions need a heading? Do they have one?

e What verb form is used? Why?

f Would it have been appropriate to present these directions in the same way as the instructions in question 1, i.e. with short paragraphs and bullet points?

3 You work for a company which makes fire extinguishers. You have been asked to write some instructions to go on the side of the extinguishers so that people know how to use them.

1
First of all you need to hold the extinguisher in an upright position. There's a thing like a plug near the top. Make sure that's pointing away from you and pull the plug out.

2
Then press the trigger. You'll have to break the seal as you do this but don't worry – it's supposed to happen like that. You'll find that it will work best if you move the extinguisher from side to side as you use it so that you cover a wider area of flames.

3
The best place to stand (if you can) is about a metre back from the fire. You should then point the extinguisher at the base of the fire.

4
Make sure you don't breathe in any of the fumes that come from the extinguisher.

a Who will read these instructions and in what situation? What, therefore, will be the most important features of the instructions?

b Do the instructions above answer the task fully?

c Are the instructions clear?

d Do the instructions contain all the important features you mentioned in question a?

e Do the instructions need a heading? Do they have one?

TASK 2 Which of the answers (1–3) above are satisfactory and which are not?

→ **Check your answers on p.116.**

TASK 3 Think about the reasons for your answers to **tasks 1 and 2**. Mark the sentences I if they are true for instructions, D if they are true for directions, and X if they are not true.

Instructions and directions
- [ ] should always be in short paragraphs with bullet points.
- [ ] should be appropriately presented.
- [ ] often use the imperative (*Go …*, *tell …*, etc.).
- [ ] should be in a logical order.
- [ ] will never be in the form of a letter.
- [ ] should be in clear and simple language.
- [ ] must have a heading.
- [ ] should contain all the necessary information.
- [ ] can sometimes be written in ordinary paragraphs.

→ **Check your answers on p.116.**

TASK 4 Rewrite and improve the instructions in **task 1 question 3**.

→ **Check your answers on p.116.**

TASK 5 You have to go away suddenly on business. You write a note to your neighbour, who is not at home, asking him / her to sort out a number of things for you because you don't have time. Explain where necessary how to do them.

For example:
- turn the heating up if the weather gets very cold
- take / get rid of the food in the fridge
- stop the papers being delivered
- switch off / on the burglar alarm
- feed your cat
- other ideas

Write your note containing the instructions in about 250 words.

> Think about what you will ask your neighbour to do. Make notes.
>
> Think about what layout to use (just one paragraph? just bullet points? a combination of the two?)
>
> Think about what language to use (formal? informal? chatty? polite?)
>
> Organize your notes and ideas into a plan.
>
> Write your note.

Note In the exam you would not be given example ideas, as in task 5 above.

English In Use

🕐 (spend about 35 minutes on this section)

Paper 3 Part 4 Word formation

ℹ **Exam information** In Paper 3 Part 4 there are two texts of up to 130 words each. You have to complete 15 spaces with a correct word formed from the prompt words you are given.

▶ **Exam techniques**
- Read the text all the way through first to get the general meaning. Do not worry about the spaces at this stage. You will need to understand the text in order to decide what form of each word to choose. Task 1 practises this.
- Think about what possible different forms there are of the words you have been given. Then think about what part of speech these different forms are. Task 2 practises this.
- Think about what part of speech is needed to fill each space. Task 3 practises this.
- Deal with each text separately. This will avoid any confusion. Task 4 practises this.

TASK 1 Read the article in task 3. Mark these sentences T (true) or F (false).

1 There are fewer vultures in India than there were.
2 Scientists know what is causing the problem.

TASK 2 Match the words on the left with their appropriate grammatical function on the right, as in the example.

0	die	noun
	death	verb
	dead	adjective
1	catastrophe	adverb
	catastrophic	adjective
	catastrophically	noun
2	extinct	noun
	extinction	adjective
3	nature	adjective
	natural	noun
	naturally	noun (person)
	unnatural	adverb
	unnaturally	prefix + adjective
	naturist	prefix + adverb
4	alarm	adverb
	alarming	verb or noun
	alarmingly	adjective
5	expect	adverb
	expected	adjective
	unexpected	verb
	unexpectedly	noun
	expectedly	prefix+adjective
	expectation	prefix+adverb

➡ Check your answers on p.116.

TASK 3 For questions 1–5 in the exam task below, choose your answer from the words in task 2.

For questions **1–8**, read the text below. Use the words to the right of the text to form one word that fits in the same numbered space in the text. Write the new word in the correct gap. The exercise begins with an example (**0**).

VULTURES DISAPPEARING

Vultures, often seen as symbols of (**0**) *death*, are themselves dying out. Their numbers are falling (**1**) .... in India, their main stronghold, and experts fear they face (**2**) ....

British and Indian animal welfare bodies have mounted an urgent investigation to find out what is happening to the birds, which are fast disappearing from their (**3**) .... habitats, where they often congregate in large numbers. They are trying to find the cause of the decline which has become all the more (**4**) .... because it is so totally (**5**) ....

At the moment the cause remains a mystery. (**6**) .... carcasses lying around the country testify that there is no (**7**) .... of food. One theory is that increased monsoon rainfall may be responsible, as vultures have a notorious (**8**) .... of the wet.

Independent on Sunday

0	DIE
1	CATASTROPHE
2	EXTINCT
3	NATURE
4	ALARM
5	EXPECT
6	EAT
7	SHORT
8	HATE

➡ Check your answers on p.116.

Note In the exam, there is no previous task with words to choose from, as there is for task 3. There is only one set of instructions for both texts. The second text contains seven spaces, and is numbered 9–15.

For questions **1–8**, read the text below. Use the words to the right of the text to form one word that fits in the same numbered space in the text. Write the new word in the correct gap.

DANGER – WELSH!	
The language which includes some of the world's longest words is (**1**) .... to cause problems because (**2**) .... might take too long to absorb new electronic warning signs. The (**3**) .... of danger on motorways in Wales has prompted the Welsh assembly to commission (**4**) .... tests on the likely effect of planned bilingual text. The fears follow government (**5**) .... of new Variable Message Signs on British motorways, with up to four lines of illuminated text. The screens are the direct result of the need to convey complex and changing (**6**) .... on motorways with which (**7**) .... painted signs cannot cope. The worst case scenario could involve (**8**) .... taking the first exit off the A5 – to Llanfairpwllgwyngyllgogerychwyrndrobwllllantysiliogogogoch.	**1** THREAT **2** DRIVE **3** POSSIBLE **4** SCIENCE **5** APPROVE **6** INFORM **7** CONVENTION **8** MOTOR
The Guardian	

➜ Check your answers on p.116.

Language development

Noun – verb – adjective – adverb

1 Complete the chart below.

NOUN	VERB	ADJECTIVE	ADVERB
threat			
	–	possible	
science	–		
	approve		
	inform		
convention	–		

2 List the opposites of all the words in the adjective and adverb columns.

3 Which words in the noun and verb columns have opposites? What are they?

➜ Check your answers on p.116.

Listening

(spend about 30 minutes on this section)

Paper 4 Part 4 Multiple choice questions

ℹ️ **Exam information** In Part 4 of the Listening Paper you hear five short extracts of about 30 seconds each, all on a related topic. You will be told the topic in the instructions for this part of the paper. There will either be multiple choice questions or a multiple matching task. If there are multiple choice questions, there will be two questions about each speaker, and each question will have three possible options.

▶ **Exam techniques**
- You will have time to read the questions before the recording starts. Use this time and read the questions carefully. You may be able to guess what the topic is. This will help you when you hear the recording. Task 1 practises this.
- It may seem obvious but … look at the questions while you listen. You need to see the exact words as you listen to be sure of answering accurately. Task 2 practises this.

TASK 1 Read the multiple choice questions in task 2 opposite. Answer this question.

What do you think each speaker is talking about? Work out topics for four out of the five speakers.

Speaker 1 (questions 1 & 2)   Speaker 4 (questions 7 & 8)
Speaker 2 (questions 3 & 4)   Speaker 5 (questions 9 & 10)
Speaker 3 (questions 5 & 6)

➜ **Check your answers on p.116.**

4.1 You will hear five short extracts in which different people are talking about dangerous sports. For questions 1–10, choose the correct option A, B, or C. Listen to the recording twice.

1 The speaker
  A   decided not to jump.
  B   was paid to jump.
  C   jumped even though she was nervous.

2 The speaker was worried about
  A   her eyes.
  B   falling into the water.
  C   wasting her money.

3 The speaker
  A   has fallen a few times.
  B   had to rescue an injured friend.
  C   was once badly injured.

4 The speaker prefers
  A   planning a climb to climbing.
  B   climbing on his own.
  C   difficult climbs.

5 The speaker takes precautions against
  A   sunburn.
  B   the cold.
  C   breaking her leg.

6 The speaker thinks that skiing today is
  A   far too expensive for most people.
  B   cheap enough for everyone to afford.
  C   affordable to many people.

7 The speaker is intending to
  A   continue to race as a hobby.
  B   retire at the end of next season.
  C   turn professional.

8 The speaker thinks the most important thing to have is
  A   a lot of money.
  B   a good car.
  C   a good team.

9 The training lasted a couple of
  A   days.
  B   hours.
  C   weeks.

10 When she jumped, the speaker felt
  A   frightened.
  B   excited.
  C   emotional.

→ **Check your answers on p.116.**

Speaking

🕐 (spend 25–35 minutes on this section)

Paper 5 Part 4 Discussion

ℹ **Exam information** In Paper 5 Part 4 you will be expected to take part in a wider discussion of the issues raised in Part 3.

▶ **Exam technique**
Remember that you are being examined on your ability both to speak and to develop a discussion. You should try and give full answers with reasons, give your opinion, and develop the discussion. You should also involve your partner in the conversation. This will show your skills at conversation and communication. Tasks 1 and 2 practise this.

TASK 1 **4.2** Look at the discussion question below. Listen to the different pairs of people discussing it. Tick (✔) the sentences you agree with for each discussion. You may agree with more than one sentence.

Add to the list below of *Dangers of the Modern World* and discuss which items on your list are the most dangerous:
mobile phones, mad cows, the hole in the ozone layer, …

Discussion 1
☐ The man develops the discussion well.
☐ The man speaks too much.
☐ The woman is rude when she interrupts.

Discussion 2
☐ The man speaks too little.
☐ Both speakers share the conversation equally.
☐ The conversation develops fairly naturally.

Discussion 3
☐ The woman does not encourage the man to speak.
☐ The man does not really participate in the conversation.
☐ The man does not say enough to get a good mark in the exam.

→ **Check your answers on p.117.**

TASK 2 Work in pairs. (If you are working alone, look at p.4.) Read and discuss the question below. If possible, record your discussion. Then play it back and think about how you might improve it.

How dangerous do you think the following activities are?
Put them in order of danger.

flying in a commercial plane
climbing in the Himalayas
crossing the road
motorcycling

being in the army
paragliding
swimming in the Amazon
having your appendix removed

How well are you doing?

Look back at the different sections in this unit and assess your performance for each one. Choose from A–C below.

Reading (multiple matching)   …
Writing (instructions and directions)   …
English In Use (word formation)   …
Listening (multiple choice questions)   …
Speaking (discussion)   …

  A   No problem; I feel quite confident about this type of question.
  B   OK, but I need some more practice.
  C   I definitely need more practice. I find this type of question difficult.

5 Dilemmas

Reading

🕐 (spend about 35 minutes on this section)

Paper 1 Part 2 Gapped text

ℹ **Exam information** Paper 1 Part 2 tests your understanding of how texts are organized and how they develop.

► **Exam techniques**
- Read through the gapped text quickly to get an idea of what it is about. Task 1 practises this.
- There will be words in the text which will help you to put the missing paragraphs back in the right place. Look especially for cohesive words: pronouns (*he*, *she*, etc.), demonstratives (*this*, *that*, etc.), possessive adjectives (*his*, *her*, etc.), link words and phrases (*however*, *although*, *the next day*, etc.). Task 2 practises this.

TASK 1 Read quickly through the gapped text and answer these questions.

1 How many people went on the trip?
2 What problems did they face?

→ **Check your answers on p.117.**

One length forward, two lengths back.

It was meant to be a relaxing break following a science conference – a three-day kayaking trip off the west coast of Vancouver Island, before returning to Toronto. Instead it turned into a succession of near-disasters, albeit along some of Canada's most beautiful shore.

All had gone well the first day. Slipping out early from our hotel beside Vancouver's Stanley Park we skipped the last session of the conference and drove to Horseshoe Bay ferry terminal with a couple of two-person kayaks firmly attached to the van roof, and wet-bags filled with provisions. Brenda was the senior member of this gang of four. Besides being a leading surgeon, she was an experienced ocean kayaker. David and I were reassured that we would have no problems. Michael, a family friend of Brenda's, completed the group.

| 1 | |

Waking to heavy rain, we discovered a sea of mud around the tent. Aware that the weather could worsen considerably, we decided to head back to Tofino. It was soon apparent that rough seas and a strong wind were against us. The next few exhausting hours were spent battling against the tide: progress made with great effort would be quickly lost in a strong gust. During one stretch, we kayaked beside the same tall pine tree for about 30 minutes, holding our own against the tide, but unable to go forward.

| 2 | |

Both Native Indians, they ran a Family Recovery Centre for alcoholics and their families, with an emphasis on traditional concepts and practices. They told us about their work and how it was helping the local community.

| 3 | |

The following morning the water looked calm; the sky, although certainly not blue, was not black either. Determined not to waste the opportunity, we headed back onto the water. Our destination was Meares Island, a breathtaking, ancient rainforest with trees many hundreds of years old and of vast diameters, damp and dense undergrowth, and eagle nests high above. Emerging again at the shoreline after hiking a trail through this wonderland we were met with heavy rain and choppy seas.

| 4 | |

We were soon buffeted by wind and rain. Halfway across, the kayaks were caught in the rough swell where two currents merged: waves smacked into us and we were knocked and blown about. Michael and I were battling along when suddenly we heard a shout behind. Brenda and David had gone over into the freezing water, their kayak was upside down and they were struggling to hold on in the high waves.

| 5 | |

Michael called the coastguard from the nearest house: they arrived within minutes asking for directions, and then we waited. Many, many tense minutes passed before the coastguard again came into view and we both had tears in our eyes when we counted two extra figures in the boat.

| 6 | |

That tragedy had been averted made the travails of the subsequent tale seem trivial, but they are worth relating. As soon as we were able, we left Tofino and drove across Vancouver Island at high speed and in gale force winds, only to miss the ferry by minutes. The later sailing meant we reached the airport check-in desk one minute before the last flight of the day left for Toronto.

| 7 | |

So much for relaxation – but at least we all survived.

The Independent

TASK 2 Read through the gapped text again carefully. Look at the paragraphs below which have been taken out. Use the underlined words and phrases to help you fit the paragraphs into the numbered gaps. Remember there is one paragraph which does not fit.

A Later, they arranged for the seaboat that serves the native communities along the coast to return us to Tofino. That night, we rented a log cabin on Long Beach and were lulled to sleep by the sound of waves pounding on the shore.

B Brenda had managed to right the kayak and clamber back in, and had been attempting, without a rudder, to paddle closer to land while David clung to the side.

C Once on Vancouver Island we drove across the mountainous interior to the Pacific Rim National Park with its endless log-strewn beaches, and north to Tofino, starting point for any kayaking trip among the small islands of Clayoquot Sound. Despite much controversy in recent years over logging in the region, it remained a largely unspoilt wilderness. We paddled out to the islands until late afternoon, enjoying calm seas and a blue sky and admiring the mountains before eventually setting up our campsite facing the Pacific Ocean.

D Twenty-twenty hindsight reveals our subsequent decision to have been most unwise. Rather than retracing our meandering outward journey between the islands, which would have provided shelter from the wind, we chose the shorter and more direct route, crossing an open stretch of water.

E Vancouver Island is the largest island off the west coast of North America. It boasts everything for the discerning tourist, from rugged wilderness to grand colonial architecture. The climate is mild, particularly at the southern end where it is protected from the ocean by a northerly promontory of Washington State.

F We turned to go back but Brenda furiously shouted us away, waving us to the shore for help. Realizing that it was the only possible hope, we left them, and desperately fighting the heaving swell, headed for land. Looking back before we turned in towards Tofino, all we could see were waves.

G The airline was persuaded to hold the flight as Brenda was due to operate on a very sick child the next morning. Our luggage was to follow on a subsequent flight: but when we received our bags, all the outdoor and camping equipment had been meticulously stolen.

H Eventually a lull in the storm allowed us to slowly but doggedly cross to an adjacent island where we pulled into a dock. As the wind rose again we were about to attempt the difficult task of rounding the headland when two men came out of the forest. Scanning the bay with binoculars for eagles, they had spotted the kayaks from their home on the hill. After driving us all back there, they calmly made hot tea while describing the whale population in the area and the behaviour of eagle families in the bay.

→ **Check your answers on p.117.**

Note In the exam, there would be no underlined words and phrases to help you fit the paragraphs into the gaps in the base text.

Writing

(spend about 20 minutes on tasks 1 & 2; about 20 minutes on task 3)

Paper 2 Part 1 Notices and announcements

ℹ **Exam information** In Paper 2 Part 1 you may be asked to write a notice or an announcement. You will first have to read and process some information.

▶ **Exam techniques**
- Notices and announcements are usually intended to inform, to persuade, to warn, or to advise. Think about the purpose of your writing. Then try and make sure that this purpose is clearly expressed in your writing. This will impress the examiner. Task 1 practises this.
- Think about the layout and organization of your writing. As with leaflets and brochures, you should use the layout and organization to catch the reader's eye and convey information clearly and concisely. Task 2 practises this.

TASK 1 Look at the note below. Tick (✓) the purpose of the notice you have to write.

☐ to inform   ☐ to give advice
☐ to persuade   ☐ to warn

Chris

As the last stress management day was so successful I thought we should hold another one at the end of next month. Like last time we'll aim it at local business people – especially those in small businesses in the area. Could you work out an announcement that we can circulate via the usual channels? It'll be on Saturday 12th December. I've booked the small library at Peckover School again and we'll start at 10 and hopefully finish at about 5 o'clock. As usual we'll provide tea and coffee, but they should bring their own lunch. They'll also need pen and paper and a cushion – for the relaxation exercises. It's probably a good idea to make sure they park in the school car park, not in the street outside – the traffic wardens are very vigilant, especially on a Saturday. £50 for the day. Payment in advance to me at the usual address. If you could e-mail me a copy before you send it out, that would be great.

Cheers

Jan

TASK 2 Read the note on p.31 again. Then look at notices A–C below. Complete the chart by giving each notice marks out of three in each category. (1 = very good, 2 = OK, 3 = poor)

	A	B	C
Does the notice catch the eye?			
Are different sizes of writing, layout, etc. used to good effect?			
Is the information clearly expressed?			
Does the notice contain all the information?			
Is the information arranged logically?			
Is the style of language appropriate?			
Is the notice easy to read?			
Has the writer added some of their own ideas?			

→ **Check your answers to tasks 1 and 2 on p.117.**

STRESS MANAGEMENT DAY

Saturday 12th December
10 am to 5 pm
in
the small library Peckover School
Please bring pen, paper, lunch
Park in school car park
Cost: £50 payable in advance to:
Jan Evetts, 121 Pepper Rd, Evesham WR6 1QT

Because of its recent success and popularity, Evetts business services is once again planning to hold one of its popular Stress Management Days at Peckover School. It will be on Saturday 12th December at 10 am and will cost £50. Please pay in advance the fee of £50 to Jan Evetts. You should bring a pen and paper with you because you may wish to take notes, also a cushion in case we do some relaxation exercises. That will make it more comfortable for you. It would be a good idea to park in the school car park as the traffic wardens are pretty strict on Saturday mornings. The session will finish at 5 p.m.

Tired?

Stressed?

Overworked?

Need a break?

Or even a holiday?

We can help...

Evetts Business Services
STRESS MANAGEMENT DAY
Saturday 12th December
10 a.m. to 5 p.m. the small library Peckover School

(please park in the school car park)
Come along to our popular and successful Stress Management Day.

- Learn how to prioritize your work.
- Deal decisively with daily dilemmas.
- Discover the secrets of relaxation.
- Find out how to keep your cool under pressure.
- Get rid of unwanted worries.
- Build confidence in your own abilities.

Please bring: – pen and paper
                – a cushion
                – some lunch (tea & coffee will be provided)

Cost: £50 payable in advance.

Please send cheques to:
Jan Evetts, 121 Pepper Rd, Evesham WR6 1QT

TASK 3 You have received the note below. Write a notice of approximately 100 words.

> Pat
>
> Heavens! What a mess! I've lost my bag and everything in it and I think it happened when I was round at your offices yesterday. You know the bag I mean. It's a blue canvas thing like a briefcase but it's got a soft cover. And when I say I've lost everything I mean everything. My laptop was in it – fortunately owned by the company so not my financial loss, but the data doesn't bear thinking about; my phone was in it – and a lot of the phone numbers stored in it I don't have anywhere else; my diary – Heaven knows what I'm supposed to be doing; my notes of all last week's meetings in a large blue folder; and so on and so on. Could you put a notice up somewhere in the building so that people keep a look out for it. You know what it looks like. It's also got my initials on and a sticker from Paris with a picture of the Eiffel Tower on it. You can give my phone number as a contact. It'll have to be the landline number of course as my mobile's in the bag! And I'll come over and pick it up if someone finds it. I'd also be quite happy to give a reward to whoever finds it. Let's say £35 – it'll be worth it.
>
> Thanks a lot.
>
> Martyn (Gray)

Decide what information from Martyn's note needs to go into the notice. (Note that quite a lot of the information is not helpful to anyone looking for the bag.)

Think about the purpose of the notice.

Think about how to lay out your notice so that it catches people's eye. What part of the information might be the most interesting?

Think about how people will know they have found the right bag.

Think about what people should do if they find the bag.

Add your own ideas where possible / appropriate.

Plan your notice and write it out.

English In Use

🕐 (spend about 35 minutes on this section)

Paper 3 Part 5 Register transfer

ℹ️ **Exam information** In Paper 3 Part 5 there are two short texts containing the same information but in different registers. You have to complete the 13 spaces in the second text by putting one or two words in each space. You may not use any of the words from the first text when filling the spaces, except articles, common prepositions, etc.

▶ **Exam techniques**
- Read both texts and identify the difference in style between the two. You need to be clear about the style of both of the texts before you start to complete the spaces. Task 1 practises this.
- Remember that in English there are often several different ways of saying the same thing. This part of Paper 3 tests your knowledge of how to say the same thing in a different register. Task 2 practises this.

TASK 1 Read both texts in task 3 and decide which description below fits each text.

☐ very formal: between two people who only meet in formal situations

☐ formal / businesslike but friendly

☐ informal / friendly: between people who get on well but are not close friends

☐ very informal: between two close friends

TASK 2 Complete the blanks in the right-hand column with words from the box.

achieve	express	agree	attend	redecorate	reduce
aware					

1 to be at a meeting – to .... a meeting
2 to say what I think – to .... my views
3 to be in favour of – to .... with something
4 to do something – to .... something
5 to do up – to ....
6 to cut something – to .... something
7 to know something – to be .... of something

Where you think there is a difference in register between an item in the left-hand column and its equivalent in the right-hand column, mark the more informal expression I and the more formal expression F.

➔ **Check your answers on p.117.**

TASK 3 Now complete this exam task. Use some of the expressions in task 2.

For questions **1–13**, read the following note, written by a club member. Use the information in the note to complete the numbered gaps in the letter to the club secretary. *Use no more than two words* for each gap. The exercise begins with an example (**0**).

A INFORMAL NOTE

Maggie,

I'm afraid I can't make the youth club meeting on Thursday after all. The boss wants me to go to Spain – she only let me know last night.

Anyway, I've written to Mrs Burgess to let her know I can't come and also I wanted a chance to tell her what I think about a couple of the things that will come up for discussion. One is what should we do with the extra money? I know some people think we should keep the fees the same or even cut them a little but I really think the club house needs doing up. It's in a terrible state – some paint and some new wallpaper would be a start. To my mind, this really is the best thing to do.

She also thought it would be a good idea if we met more often. Well, for once I agree with her. (It doesn't happen very often, does it?) We might get more done.

Have a nice meeting! I'll think of you as I tuck into my paella.

George

B FORMAL LETTER

Dear Mrs Burgess,

I (**0**) *regret* to inform you that I will be unable to (**1**) .... the meeting on Thursday 14th April as I have been asked to travel to Spain on (**2**) .... at very (**3**) ....

I would like to take this (**4**) ...., therefore, to (**5**) .... my views on two important items on the agenda. The first is the (**6**) .... of what to do with our financial surplus. I am (**7**) .... that there are some members who feel that this would be best used to keep our membership fees as they are or even to (**8**) .... them. My feeling, however, is that this would not be the best (**9**) .... action and that the money should be used to (**10**) .... the club house.

The second item concerns your (**11**) .... that the committee should meet every month rather than every two months as it does at the moment. I am very much in (**12**) .... this idea and I feel that we would (**13**) .... much more if we were to meet more frequently.

Yours faithfully,

G J Florey

G J Florey

➔ **Check your answers on p.117.**

Listening

(spend about 25 minutes on this section)

Paper 4 Part 2 Sentence completion

ⓘ **Exam information** In Paper 4 Part 2 you will hear the recording once only. You will either have a note taking task or a sentence completion activity, which will test your understanding of specific information. You should not have to write more than three words in answer to a question.

▶ **Exam techniques**
- As you only hear the recording once, it is very important to be familiar with the questions before you listen. This will help you find the answers quickly and easily. Task 1 practises this.
- Your answers must be grammatically correct. Think about the grammar when you write down your answers. Tasks 2 and 3 practise this.

TASK 1 Read exam task 2 and answer these questions.

1 Who is speaking?
2 What are they speaking about?
3 Can you refuse alcohol?
4 Do you think it's a good idea to drink beer? Why / why not?
5 Do you think it's a good idea to drink Coke?
6 How important do you think it is to make conversation?

➜ **Check your answers on p.117.**

TASK 2 🎧5.1 You will hear an image consultant talking about how business people should present themselves in restaurants. As you listen, complete sentences 1–8.

In a restaurant you should first	**1**	.
Say	**2**	if you want to refuse alcohol.
You may appear	**3**	if you order a pint of beer.
You will appear	**4**	if you ask for Coke.
You want to appear	**5**	while you are at the table.
Have some interesting ideas for	**6**	.
Don't talk to people about	**7**	.
After lunch it's a good idea to	**8**	.

TASK 3 Look back at your answers above. Are any of them more than three words long? If so, make them shorter. Are they grammatically correct? If not, change them.

➜ **Check your answers on p.117.**

Language development

Compound nouns

1 Find the two underlined expressions in the transcript on p.118. You will notice they are fixed expressions made up of two nouns. These are called compound nouns.

2 Make more combinations by matching words from each column as in the example.

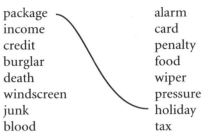

package	alarm
income	card
credit	penalty
burglar	food
death	wiper
windscreen	pressure
junk	holiday
blood	tax

3 What does *it* refer to in each sentence below? Choose from the compounds in exercise 2.

1 'I think I've left it at home. I'll have to pay cash.'
2 'It went off at about two o'clock in the morning and woke the whole street.'
3 'It was very high so she's given me some pills.'
4 'If they raise it again, I'm certainly not going to vote for them in the election.'
5 'They still have it in some states in the US but I think they should abolish it.'
6 'It was wonderful. We had great weather and a wonderful hotel.'
7 'I know I shouldn't really eat it but it's so cheap and convenient.'

➜ **Check your answers on p.118.**

Speaking

(spend about 25 minutes on this section)

Paper 5 Part 1 Introductions

ⓘ Exam information Paper 5 Part 1 lasts about three minutes and gives you the opportunity to use general social language with your partner and the examiner.

▶ **Exam techniques**

- Listen to what your partner says. You should make the conversation seem as natural as possible so you will need to pay attention to what he or she says. Task 1 practises this.
- It is important that both you and your partner have a roughly equal share of the conversation. Do not take over the conversation. Make sure you encourage your partner to speak. Task 2 practises this.

TASK 1 🎧 **5.2** **Listen to the recording. Only one of the sentences below is correct. Correct the others.**

1 The woman is halfway through her university course.
2 She is studying Tai Chi at university.
3 She spent ten weeks in China this year.
4 Her university course takes three years to complete.

→ **Check your answers on p.118.**

TASK 2 Listen to the recording again. Notice how the man encourages the woman to keep talking. Write down the words he uses in the chart below.

TECHNIQUE	EXAMPLE (S)
repeating a key word / phrase	
asking a short question	
making a comment	*How interesting!*
asking for more information	
asking for clarification	
changing the topic	

How does the woman indicate that she thinks she has spoken enough and now it is the man's turn to say something about himself?

→ **Check your answers on p.118.**

TASK 3 Work in pairs. (If you are working alone, look at p.4.) Ask and answer the questions below. Take it in turns to use some of the techniques above to encourage your partner to keep talking. If possible, record your answers. Then play them back and think about how you might improve them.

- What have been the most interesting events in your life over the last year?
- What has been the most enjoyable holiday you can remember? Why was it so enjoyable?
- What are your plans for the next few months?
- What do you imagine your life will be like in five years' time?

How well are you doing?

Look back at the different sections in this unit and assess your performance for each one. Choose from A–C below.

Reading (gapped text)	...
Writing (notices / announcements)	...
English In Use (register transfer)	...
Listening (sentence completion)	...
Speaking (introductions)	...

A No problem; I feel quite confident about this type of question.
B OK, but I need some more practice.
C I definitely need more practice. I find this type of question difficult.

Reading

🕐 (spend about 40 minutes on this section)

Paper 1 Part 3 Multiple choice questions

ⓘ Exam information You have 75 minutes for Paper 1 and there are four parts. It is sensible to spend an equal amount of time on each of the four parts. You will therefore have about 15–20 minutes for each part in the exam.

▶ **Exam techniques**
- Remember to read the headline and skim the article quickly. Ignore any words you don't know at the moment. Task 1 practises this.
- With the multiple choice questions, you will have to read the text and the options carefully. The options may have similar wording to each other and each option may at first appear to be correct. If you have time, it is worth checking that the options you haven't chosen are wrong. Task 2 practises this.

TASK 1 Read the headline of the article. Skim through the text quickly. Tick (✔) the correct option below.

This article is about

1 ☐ Bill Gates.
2 ☐ someone who knows Bill Gates.
3 ☐ someone who looks like Bill Gates.
4 ☐ someone who works for Bill Gates.

➜ **Check your answer on p.118.**

Just call me Bill

He is the defining face of our time: an icon and role model for the age of the global cyber-mogul. And, on this occasion at least, he isn't even the real deal. Journalist Adam Sternbergh meets the alternative William Gates III.

Though he is, in many ways, unremarkable, and we have never met before, and he hasn't given me any particular clues to help me pick him out, it's not hard to spot Steve Sires in the lobby of his downtown Toronto hotel, simply because he's the only man here who looks exactly like Bill Gates, the computer millionaire and head of Microsoft. 'I figured you'd recognize me,' he says, rising from his chair to shake my hand, in his Bill Gates glasses, with his Bill Gates hair, smiling his Bill Gates smile. 'If you didn't, then I guess I'd be in trouble.'

Steve Sires is a 42-year-old civil engineering consultant who married his high-school sweetheart on the day they graduated, runs his own business from his home just outside Seattle and, twice a month or so, gets paid to jet across the continent and look like Bill Gates. He's hired for business functions mostly – product launches, industry seminars and conferences. He isn't the only professional Bill Gates lookalike in the world – he knows of three others – but he is, by most accounts, the best.

Leaving his hotel, we walk over to a busy business-district restaurant. I'd made a reservation for two, under 'Gates'. I'm worried this might annoy Sires, but he just laughs and admits that it's something he's never tried himself. The hostess doesn't even blink when I drop the name. As she leads us to our table I imagine a few furtive glances sent our way, but they're likely just that, my imagination. Sires assures me that he causes much more hubbub back in Seattle, where the real Gates is occasionally known to walk among the masses.

'People have reported spotting Bill at Burger King or eating popcorn at a movie,' Sires says. 'Of course, who knows if they saw him or me? I wonder how many times people see me and think "Why in the world would Bill Gates be shopping in a cheap supermarket like Costco?"'

After spending almost ten years working in Alaska, Sires moved to the Seattle area in the early 1990s; he had no idea why people kept stopping him on the street or asking him for stockmarket tips in the checkout line. 'I didn't know who this Gates guy was,' he says. 'Turns out I lived 20 minutes from his house.'

TASK 2 Read question 1 below and the four options. Then read the first three paragraphs of the article carefully to find the correct answer. Work out why the other options are wrong.

1 Steve Sires
   A is paid by Bill Gates to attend parties and conventions.
   B runs a business organizing parties and conventions.
   C is easy to recognize.
   D only needs to work twice a month.

→ **Check your answer on p.118.**

Sires initially shrugged off the much-remarked-on resemblance. Then, two years ago, his wife cut out a newspaper ad placed by a local agent who handles lookalikes – 150 or so, from Bill Clinton to famous comedian, George Burns. 'My wife said, "What do you think of this?" And I said "So?" and put the ad away.'

He didn't know she'd already called the agent. 'He got me a job at the grand opening of a performing arts centre. I did it for free. But my picture was picked up by Associated Press.'

Soon, Sires was travelling to events in Holland and Singapore as 'Bogus Bill', his appearance fee running to several thousand dollars. ('Don't quote the actual price,' he says. 'By the time this gets printed, it may have gone up.') At events he's introduced as the 'special guest from Redmond' or the 'world's richest man', but never as Gates.

'I'll do some comedy, and by the mid-point of the speech, when everyone's cracking up, I'll put something in the script like, "I'll take care of the Justice Department. I'll just buy Washington."'

Afterwards people will line up for an hour to get his autograph. 'When I sign books, I write "Bill Gates" in quotes,' he says. 'I've had people ask "What's with this quote-unquote?" And I say, "Well, I'm not the real Bill Gates." If they still don't believe me, I'll pull out my driver's licence to prove it. I did that with one and she goes, "That's just a fake you had made so you can trick people."'

Our dinner proceeds without interruption, without a single autograph hunter rushing to the table. (After all this is Bogus Bill we're talking about, not Bogus Ricky Martin.) I imagine an incognito evening like this is probably a relief for Sires, and I ask him if he ever purposely throws on a baseball cap and a pair of contact lenses to spend a day as, unarguably, Steve Sires.

'No – but sometimes I do try to look *more* like Bill,' he says. 'It's a kick. I get to stay in nice places, try new foods, see new cultures. I count it as a blessing from God. How else to explain it?'

And so, by the grace of God, Steve Sires is famous. Actually, what he has is better than fame – it's celebrity, without any of the complications of actually being Bill Gates. 'I've got a great deal,' he admits. 'I get a little attention. It's fun to get a *little* attention. But at the end of the day, I can always go home to my real life.'

As we're finishing dinner, I ask him what he would say to Gates if they ever met. 'I don't know', he replies. 'But I had a dream once. We met on the street. I had the feeling he knew everything about me, my wife, my kids, where I lived, my job, everything. All he said was, "Hi, Steve." That was it. But I could tell he knew everything. I'll tell you, that was uncomfortable.'

Independent On Sunday

TASK 3 Now complete the exam task by answering these questions in the same way as in task 2. Give only one answer to each question.

2 In the restaurant
   A Bill Gates is a regular customer.
   B the writer thinks that people are looking at them.
   C Steve Sires booked the table in his real name.
   D a lot of people talk to Steve.

3 When Steve first realized he looked like Bill Gates,
   A he started selling stockmarket tips.
   B he contacted a local agent.
   C he immediately started making public appearances for money.
   D he didn't think it was particularly important.

4 When Steve makes public appearances,
   A he introduces himself by his real name.
   B people often ask to see his driving licence.
   C some people really believe he is Bill Gates.
   D he pretends he really is Bill Gates.

5 How does Steve Sires feel about looking like Bill Gates?
   A He enjoys it but he also likes having his own life.
   B He finds it a bit confusing at times.
   C He would prefer to be famous as himself.
   D He really wishes he was Bill Gates.

→ **Check your answers on p.118.**

🔍 **Close up**

Find the sentences below in the text. They are all in colloquial American English. How would you say them in British English?

He isn't even the real deal.

Then I guess I'd be in trouble.

I didn't know who this Gates guy was.

I did it for free.

What's with this quote-unquote?

This is Bogus Bill were talking about.

It's a kick.

→ **Check your answers on pp.118–119.**

Writing

⏱ (spend about 25 minutes on tasks 1–3; about 1 hour on task 4)

Paper 2 Part 2 Competition entry

ⓘ **Exam information** In Paper 2 Part 2 you may be asked to write a competition entry. This is not the same as a letter. There may be a 'prize' on offer or the best entry may be 'published' in a magazine or newspaper.

▶ **Exam techniques**
- Think about what sort of writing might win a competition. The first sentences will be very important. The judges of the competition (like the examiners who mark your exam papers) will have a lot of entries to read. If you can grab their attention in the first few sentences you will make a good impression. Task 1 practises this.
- The final paragraph or conclusion of your entry is also important. This is the last thing that will remain in the reader's mind. For examiners it may be the last thing they read before they give your work a mark. Task 2 practises this.
- Read the question carefully and underline the different things you have to do. Task 3 practises this.

TASK 1 Read this exam task. Then look at the introductions of the three entries A, B, and C. Which do you think is best? Why? What is wrong with the others?

You see this advertisement in an English language magazine.

Win A Round-The-World Trip

Traveller's Choice, the award-winning travel company, is offering free round-the-world air tickets stopping off in five different places, one in each continent: Europe, Asia, Australasia, America, and Africa (sorry, not Antarctica!). To win this once-in-a-lifetime journey, make a list of the five places you would like to go to (one in each continent), explain why you would like to visit them, and tell us why you are the person we should choose to send on this journey.

Write your entry in 250 words.

A In Europe I'd like to go to Athens. I'd spend a couple of weeks there. I'd like to see the Acropolis and the Parthenon. I'd also do one or two trips outside the city. I fancy going to Olympia to see where the Olympic Games started and I'd like to see the theatre at Epidaurus. I've heard that it's quite amazing.

B An opportunity to win a 'round-the-world' trip. I couldn't believe it. My hand was shaking a little as I put down the advertisement. My mind was racing as I reached for the atlas. Where should I go? What could I see? The choice was almost limitless and yet I could only stop once in each continent. I fumbled slightly as I took the large book off the shelf. It fell from my grasp, tumbling to the floor, falling open. I looked down. India. Its familiar shape lay at my feet. I looked again. Mumbai. That would be my first destination.

C Every journey needs a purpose. Every journey, expedition, excursion, trek, safari, quest, and pilgrimage. A pilgrimage? A pilgrimage to each continent to visit a place of particular religious significance. First, Europe: …

→ Check your answers on p.119.

TASK 2 Read the conclusions of the three entries. Which do you think is best? Why? What is wrong with the others?

A This journey, therefore, would complement my studies perfectly. My account of it and any photos I take will form part of my thesis, a valuable step towards my ambition to become a teacher.

B And I feel sure that the experience of making this journey will stay with me forever. It will give me the opportunity to broaden my horizons, to witness vastly different cultures and customs, and to meet people with a wide range of perspectives on life. I would greatly welcome that opportunity.

C And finally, of course, I could never afford a trip like this on my own so it would be absolutely fantastic if I won.

→ Check your answers on p.119.

TASK 3 Read the advertisement in task 1 again. Underline the important parts. There are three parts to the question. What are they?

→ Check your answers on p.119.

TASK 4 Now write your own answer to the exam task.

Decide which five places you would like to go to.

Make a list of reasons for wanting to visit each place.

Decide why you think you should be the person chosen.

Decide how to organize your writing: how many paragraphs will you have? What will each paragraph be about?

Decide how to start your entry. Make it an attention-grabbing opening.

Decide how to end your entry. Make it a memorable ending.

Write your entry.

Make sure you have answered each part of the question, and check your writing through for mistakes.

English In Use

⏱ (spend about 25 minutes on this section)

Paper 3 Part 3 Error correction

ℹ **Exam information** In the error correction exercise there will be 16 lines of text for you to examine carefully. Remember that up to five lines might be correct.

▶ **Exam techniques**
- Read through the text quickly to get a general idea of the meaning. Task 1 practises this.
- Read the instructions carefully so that you know which type of error correction question you are dealing with (extra words or spelling and punctuation mistakes). Task 2 practises this.
- Read the text carefully. Although there is an extra word in most *lines*, it is important to read the text *sentence by sentence*. You will find it easier to spot the extra words if you do this. Task 3 practises this.

TASK 1 One of sentences 1–3 below is false. Read through the article in task 3 quickly and decide which one.

1 Left-handed people get injured more often than right-handed people.
2 Injuries to left-handed people happen because most equipment is designed by right-handers.
3 Left-handed people are naturally awkward.

➜ **Check your answer on p.119.**

TASK 2 Read the instructions in task 3 and answer this question.
What mistake are you looking for in each line?

➜ **Check your answer on p.119.**

TASK 3 Now do the exam task.

In most lines of the following text, there is one unnecessary word. It is either grammatically incorrect or does not fit in with the sense of the text. Find the word and write it in the space at the end of each numbered line. Some lines are correct. Indicate these with a tick (✔). The exercise begins with two examples (**0**).

SHORTER, TOUGHER LIFE FOR LEFT-HANDERS	
Left-handed people are suffering by injuries and premature death because equipment at workplaces is designed solely for the use of right-handers, a trade union said it yesterday.	**0** by .... **00** ✔ .... **1** ....
The GMB union, which all represents an estimated 225,000 left-handed workers, said that this design prejudice is being responsible for a real number of types of injury, including RSI (repetitive strain injury), among left-handed employees.	**2** .... **3** .... **4** .... **5** ....
In support of its other argument the GMB quoted a 1991 study which found that significantly more than left-handers were killed in accidents and, on the average, died nine years before their right-handed counterparts. Equipment was designed by right-handed people forces very left-handed workers to make damaging, unnatural and awkward movements.	**6** .... **7** .... **8** .... **9** .... **10** ....
To quite mark today's International Left-Handers Day, Kim Sunley, a GMB health and safety researcher, called on to designers and employers to make it easier for left-handers, who can make up 13 to 30 per cent of the British population.	**11** .... **12** .... **13** ....
A spokesperson for GMB dismissed claims so that the union had been overreacted: 'We are trying to celebrate left-handedness. But left-handers do live in a world that's the wrong way round.'	**14** .... **15** .... **16** ....
Independent on Sunday	

➜ **Check your answers on p.119.**

Language development

Prepositional phrases

Look at these phrases from the text:
*... is designed solely **for the use of** right-handers, ...*
***In support of** its argument the GMB ...*

Complete the sentences below with an appropriate phrase from the box.

as a consequence of	for the purpose of
in relation to	on the basis of
in a variety of	in the absence of
in contrast to	by way of

1 .... updating our records, could you please fill in this form?
2 We chose him for the job .... his experience in Asia.
3 Unfortunately, ... the bankruptcy, we were forced to sell off the business.
4 I'll take responsibility for the decision .... the managing director.
5 Your monthly salary will vary .... the amount of goods you sell.
6 I'm afraid I can't offer you much .... refreshment.
7 They sell rugs and carpets .... shapes and sizes.
8 This year's exam results were excellent – very much .... the poor grades people got last year.

➜ **Check your answers on p.119.**

Listening

Paper 4 Part 1
Sentence completion

ℹ Exam information The recordings may contain a variety of accents: British, American, Australian, etc. You can prepare for this by listening to a variety of speakers, as in this book. Remember that in the exam all the speakers will be speaking standard English at natural speed so you should not have any problem understanding them. Remember that Part 1 will be a monologue and that you will be listening for specific information.

▶ **Exam techniques**
- Read the sentences carefully to prepare for the listening. Task 1 practises this.
- The sentences will be in the same order as the information on the recording. Look at the sentences while you listen and be ready to move on to the next sentence if you are not sure of an answer or if you miss one. Task 2 practises this.

TASK 1 Look at the sentences in task 2. Then read this paragraph. One sentence in the paragraph contains false information. Which one?

Scientists have been discussing the possibility of making the planet Mars more like Earth by introducing gases into the Martian atmosphere. This would have the effect of raising the temperature and creating an atmosphere rich in carbon dioxide. The process could be speeded up to such an extent that scientists are in no doubt that considerable progress would be made within 60 years.

→ **Check your answer on p.119.**

TASK 2 🎧 **6.1** Listen to the recording once.

You will hear part of a radio programme about Mars. For questions **1–8** fill in the missing information.

Scientists are interested in changing the [____1____] of Mars to make it more like Earth.

The surface of Mars is [____2____] , and very cold.

One idea is to introduce gases which would cause a [____3____] resulting in a rise in temperature.

The introduction of man-made gases would raise the temperature to [____4____] .

An atmosphere rich in carbon dioxide would support [____ and ____5____] .

To speed up the process they could use a large [____6____] .

People who think that we could raise the temperature on Mars to 15° Celsius within 60 years are [____7____] .

Other scientists say this will take [____8____] .

TASK 3 Listen to the recording again and check or complete your answers.

→ **Check your answers on p.119.**

Note In the exam, you will always hear Part 1 recordings twice.

Speaking

🕐 (spend about 30 minutes on this section)

Paper 5 Part 2 Commenting

ℹ️ **Exam information** As well as having to describe and compare a set of photographs or pictures, you will also be asked to comment on what your partner says. You will only have about 20 seconds in which to respond. However, it is important to show the examiners that you have been listening to your partner and can make a contribution to the discussion.

▶ **Exam techniques**
- Listen carefully to what your partner says so that you know what to react to. While you are listening, think of things to say when it is your turn to speak. Task 1 practises this.
- Try and build on or respond to what your partner has already said. Add your own ideas. Remember it is not necessary to agree with your partner. Task 2 practises this.

TASK 1 🎧 6.2 Listen to the recording. Answer the questions below.

1 What sort of mine does the speaker think it is?

2 What does he say about the men?

3 What does he say about the connection between the pictures?

4 What contrast does the second speaker make?

5 What other connection does she make?

→ Check your answers on p.119.

TASK 2 Listen to the recording again. Tick (✔) the phrases below that you hear the woman use to comment on what the man says.

☐ I see you mentioned …

☐ Another thing I noticed was …

☐ I was surprised at your comments about …

☐ I was interested that you …

☐ I notice that …

☐ Have you noticed that …

☐ It's interesting / surprising that …

→ Check your answers on p.119.

TASK 3 Work in pairs. (If you are working alone, look at p.4.) Discuss the questions below. If possible, record your discussion. Then play it back and think about how you might improve it.

Describe the photos above. Compare and contrast them and say what the advantages and disadvantages of the lifestyle of each person might be. Decide which lifestyle you would prefer given the choice.

Describe the photos above. Compare and contrast them and say what the advantages and disadvantages of living in each place might be. Decide where you would prefer to live given the choice.

How well are you doing?

Look back at the different sections in this unit and assess your performance for each one. Choose from A–C below.

Reading (multiple choice questions)	…
Writing (competition entry)	…
English In Use (error correction)	…
Listening (sentence completion)	…
Speaking (commenting)	…

A No problem; I feel quite confident about this type of question.
B OK, but I need some more practice.
C I definitely need more practice. I find this type of question difficult.

Reading

🕐 (spend about 35 minutes on this section)

Paper 1 Part 3
Multiple choice questions

ℹ **Exam information** The multiple choice questions are given in the same order as the information in the text. The final question may be a question about the text as a whole: for example, the writer's purpose, attitude, or opinion.

▶ **Exam techniques**
- It is helpful to predict what the text will be about before you start reading. How can you do this? Check your answer on p.120. Task 1 practises this.
- Identify which paragraph or paragraphs contain the answer to each question. You can then read those paragraphs again very carefully in order to decide which answer is correct. Task 2 practises this.

TASK 1 Look at the headline of the article. Tick the ideas below that you think might be discussed in the article.

> **Are you reading me?**
> Being deaf makes it all the harder to study. Stephen Hoare looks at the problems and the successes

- ☐ different kinds of deafness
- ☐ housing for the deaf
- ☐ job prospects for the deaf
- ☐ dyslexia
- ☐ provision in schools for deaf people
- ☐ grants for deaf people
- ☐ numbers of deaf in the community
- ☐ sign language
- ☐ university life for the deaf
- ☐ blindness

TASK 2 Read the article opposite carefully. Then read the multiple choice questions in task 3. Identify the paragraph(s) which contains the answer to each question and complete the chart below.

question	paragraph(s)		question	paragraph(s)
1	c		4	
2			5	
3			6	

→ Check your answers to tasks 1 and 2 on p.120.

TASK 3 Read the article opposite and then do the exam task.

> Answer questions **1–6** by choosing the correct option, **A, B, C,** or **D**. Give only one answer to each question.
>
> **1** Catherine believes that deaf students who want to get to university must
>   **A** have a good role model.
>   **B** have a lot of support from their family.
>   **C** be able to lip-read.
>   **D** work harder than other students.
>
> **2** The main problem for deaf students at university is that
>   **A** it is difficult to get phonic earpieces.
>   **B** most learning takes place through the spoken word.
>   **C** very little extra provision can be made for them.
>   **D** fellow students won't talk to them.
>
> **3** According to the writer, The Joint Universities Deaf Education centre
>   **A** sends teachers out to schools to teach deaf people.
>   **B** collects comprehensive facts and figures about disabled people.
>   **C** finances deaf people through higher education.
>   **D** encourages businesses to employ deaf people.
>
> **4** At university Catherine found it depressing that
>   **A** her difficulties often went unnoticed.
>   **B** it was difficult for her to be independent.
>   **C** her deafness gave her a lot of pain.
>   **D** the staff found it difficult to talk to her.
>
> **5** Catherine believes that
>   **A** it should be easier for deaf people to get to university.
>   **B** disabled students should help with the cost of any special support.
>   **C** everyone who is intelligent enough has the right to be at university.
>   **D** universities already provide excellent support for the disabled.
>
> **6** The main purpose of this article is to
>   **A** describe Catherine Cassidy's life as a deaf student.
>   **B** inform readers about current provisions for deaf people at university.
>   **C** persuade deaf people to go to university.
>   **D** praise Queen's University, Belfast for its policies on deaf students.

→ Check your answers on p.120.

Are you reading me?

Being deaf makes it all the harder to study. Stephen Hoare looks at the problems and the successes

(a) Catherine Cassidy has every reason to be proud. This summer she graduated with a 2:1 honours degree in zoology and biological sciences from Queen's University, Belfast, where she won awards for water-polo and swimming. She is going on to study for an MSc and has ambitions to be a scientific journalist. She is also profoundly deaf.

(b) Catherine is oral-deaf, which means she can lip-read. Deaf students who cannot lip-read need interpreters to translate speech into sign language, while partially deaf students can benefit from various different types of hearing aid.

(c) I interviewed Catherine via e-mail. Given the patchy nature of special needs provision in British schools, she told me getting to university was an achievement in itself. Disabled students need an enormous amount of determination to succeed, and there are few role models. She says: 'You have to work considerably harder than your peers and have to be prepared to commit yourself. Luckily, I have had a phenomenal level of support from my family.' Catherine is one of 22 deaf students at Queen's.

(d) The Disability Discrimination Act insists that universities increase their intake of special needs students to reflect the numbers of disabled in the community, and all now set targets for admissions. But there are difficulties. First, there are no reliable figures on the numbers of disabled in the community, hence universities are unsure of the percentages they should be aiming to recruit.

(e) Second, definitions of disability are hard to pin down. Some students on the edges of disability with conditions such as dyslexia might require very little extra provision, while others might have a severe physical handicap requiring specially adapted computers, or online learning support.

(f) Of all the disabilities, deafness is probably the one that is hardest to cope with at university. Dr Roddie Cowie, a senior lecturer in psychology at Queen's, explains: 'Universities run on talk. Knowledge is communicated in lectures, seminars, talking to fellow students – reading is only secondary. For deaf students, casual spontaneous discussions are out.'

(g) Fortunately for Catherine, Queen's is a centre of excellence for the teaching of deaf students on account of a special project, Succeed, set up in 1995 with a grant of £95,000. The Joint Universities Deaf Education centre (Jude) organized a special phonic earpiece that enabled Catherine to listen to lectures.

(h) Now self-financing, Jude has been extended to the other further and higher education institutions of Northern Ireland. Jude is setting an example in what can be achieved. Sharon Easton, deaf student support officer, says: 'One of our officers visits schools to make deaf people aware that higher education is a possibility. Another part of our role is to talk with employers. We're offering them deaf awareness training – how to adapt to the needs of deaf employees, and where to apply for grants. There is no reason why a deaf person shouldn't manage any job within reason.'

(i) Jude's funding may be secure but there are no universally agreed standards of provision and no handy funding formulae. The Higher Education Funding Council for England, Hefce, is currently working with the UK Department for Education and Employment and local authorities to draw up funding proposals. A spokesman for Hefce says: 'Robust data on numbers and types of disability is unbelievably difficult to come by. The cost of provision for an individual student could be anything from £50 to £3,000. We are committed to removing cost barriers.'

(j) Support and encouragement was an essential part of Jude's offering. Catherine says: 'Having a tailor-made service gave me independence that was a key element to my enjoying university life.' But Catherine presented a major challenge for the staff at Jude: her skill in lip-reading made communicating with her seem so effortless that many people did not believe she had a problem. At times this experience has been painful. Catherine says: 'People have labelled me "not really deaf". It is like telling me I don't count. And this can be very disheartening, very demoralising.'

(k) At the end of the day, Catherine believes that excellent and well-focused special needs support should be available to all disabled students at university whatever the cost. She says: 'You are accepted by a university on the basis of your ability to learn and carry out mental tasks. You have a right to be there – people should not judge the mental capability of a person by any physical disability.'

The Guardian

🔍 Close up

Find and underline these phrases in the article. Check that you understand what they mean.

profoundly deaf	severe physical handicap
sign language	specially adapted computers
partially deaf students	online learning support
special needs provision	student support officer
special needs students	physical disability

Translate them into your own language.

🕐 (spend about 20 minutes on tasks 1–3; about an hour on task 4)

Paper 2 Part 2 Report

ℹ️ **Exam information** In Paper 2 Part 2 you may have to write a report.

▶ **Exam techniques**
- You should organize your report into clear paragraphs. Each paragraph should have a clear aim or subject. It is often a good idea to give your paragraphs separate headings. Task 1 practises this.
- Reports are usually written in an appropriate impersonal style. You should therefore avoid expressing your personal feelings or opinions except perhaps in a conclusion. Tasks 2 and 3 practise this.

TASK 1 Add these headings to the boxes above the appropriate paragraphs in the report.

> Guided tours
> Introduction
> Nightlife
> Museums
> Shopping
> Outside Oxford
> Conclusion
> Other attractions

➜ Check your answers on p.120.

TASK 2 Read the report again. One paragraph is written in an inappropriate style. Which one and how is it inappropriate? Look at the other paragraphs and read sentences 1–9 below. Mark them T (true) or F (false).

1 The language is clear.
2 The writer expresses a lot of opinions.
3 There are a lot of facts.
4 Some of the language is rather vague.
5 It is easy to find specific information in the report.
6 The paragraph headings make the report difficult to read.
7 There is a lot of unnecessary information.
8 The report is well organized.
9 Only one paragraph expresses a personal recommendation.

➜ Check your answers on p.120.

TASK 3 Rewrite the paragraph on museums in a more appropriate style.

➜ Check your answer on p.120.

OXFORD

This report has two aims: first, to describe the tourist and leisure facilities available in Oxford; second, to make a recommendation as to whether Oxford should be included in our *Grand Tour of Britain* itinerary and, if so, to decide how long groups should stay.

A number of guided tours are available. Particularly good is the two-hour Oxford Walking Tour, taking groups round the centre of Oxford and into a number of the University colleges. A bus tour of the city on an open-top bus is also available.

There are a few museums in Oxford. We loved the Ashmolean. It's got lots of exhibits from all over the place: coins, paintings, drawings, and so on. The University Museum, the Museum of Oxford, and the Museum of Modern Art aren't too bad either.

Oxford has a wide variety of shops. The Covered Market is especially worth visiting, with its array of gift and clothes shops and numerous cafés.

The Botanic Gardens is fascinating. It is 370 years old and houses 8,000 species of plants. The Oxford Story is an imaginative exhibition outlining the history of the University. The River Thames and the River Cherwell both flow through Oxford and provide an opportunity to go boating.

Blenheim Palace, a few miles north of Oxford and birthplace of Sir Winston Churchill, is the country's largest private house and is surrounded by beautiful landscaped gardens.

Oxford boasts two theatres: the Playhouse and the Apollo. Both offer regular performances. There are four cinemas in the town and a number of nightclubs. Oxford's many restaurants offer a wide variety of different cuisines.

We thoroughly recommend the inclusion of Oxford in the *Grand Tour of Britain*. We feel that a two-day stay with appropriate optional excursions and tours would be suitable. This would give visitors time to appreciate the variety of attractions that the city has to offer.

TASK 4 You have been asked by the national tourist organization in your country to report on the town where you live with a view to it being included in a Grand Tour of the country. You should write a report:
- describing the tourist and leisure facilities in the town
- recommending whether the town should be included in the Grand Tour
- giving reasons for your recommendation

Write your report in about 250 words.

> Write down all the important features of the town that you need to mention.
>
> Organize the features into different groups. (Use the report on Oxford as a model, but add further groupings of your own if necessary.)
>
> Think of headings for each group.
>
> Decide on your recommendation.
>
> Decide on reasons for your recommendation.
>
> Write your report. Remember:
> lay out your report clearly
> use clear, factual language
> end with your recommendation

English In Use

🕐 (spend about 30 minutes on this section)

Paper 3 Part 6 Gapped text

ℹ️ **Exam information** In Paper 3 Part 6 you are given a text from which six phrases or short sentences have been removed. You have to complete the text by choosing the correct option for each gap from a list of ten.

▶ **Exam techniques**
- It is helpful to have a good understanding of the text before you look at the options. What should you do first? Check your answer on p.120. Task 1 practises this.
- This task particularly tests how phrases and sentences fit together to form a text. Think about how the different options might fit in with the phrases and sentences around each gap. Think about grammar and about meaning. Task 2 practises this.

TASK 1 Read the article carefully without worrying about the gaps. Tick (✔) the points below that are mentioned in the article.

The article talks about

☐ what many people think of airline food.

☐ what pilots eat.

☐ the problems of preparing airline food.

☐ how to complain about airline food.

☐ some recent developments regarding airline food.

☐ what professional chefs recommend regarding airline food.

→ **Check your answers on p.120.**

TASK 2 Look at the article again and read options A–J below the text. Think about these questions with regard to gaps 0–5.

gap 0: Which option can stand alone between two commas and link to the phrase *it's not unreasonable*?

gap 1: What kind of menus do top chefs usually produce?

gap 2: What further information is offered about what the professor will do? Which preposition follows *research*?

gap 3: What do we find out about what *the problem* is connected to?

gap 4: What do we find out about the effect of ovens?

gap 5: What do we find out about strong flavours?

→ **Check your answers on p.120.**

TASK 3 Now do the exam task.

For questions **1–6**, read the following text and then choose from the list **A–J** the best phrase given below it to fill each of the spaces. Each correct phrase may only be used once. Some of the suggested answers do not fit at all. The exercise begins with an example (**0**).

TASTE IN AIRLINES

Mankind has mastered flight, but has not yet conquered the skill of serving up decent food in the skies. Surely, (**0**) *J*, it's not unreasonable to expect a small miracle to be presented on the plastic plate. Yet, for the vast majority of travellers, airline food remains lukewarm and unappetising.

Now, at last, there are signs that the problem is being addressed. British Airways recently spent millions of pounds to improve catering, and called on top chefs to recreate the kind of menus (**1**) ...... Surrey University plans to appoint a professor of airline food, who will lead research (**2**) ......

But the airlines have a lot of ground to make up. A recent survey of transatlantic meals by the renowned food critic, Egon Ronay, found most to be 'very poor indeed – an insult to the palate as well as to the intelligence.'

But the problem is (**3**) ....., according to Christopher Smith, a lecturer in food and beverage management at Surrey University. 'The quality of the food used is high in terms of products, hygiene and safety.' Part of it is simple logistics.

In-flight meals have to be prepared hours in advance, chilled to 5°C, then reheated on board. Delays on the runway or turbulence preventing meals being served immediately mean that food sits too long in ovens, (**4**) ......

And, for reasons experts do not yet understand, altitude and cabin pressure numb the palate. Food and drink lose much of their taste at around 35,000 feet, which leaves airline caterers struggling to find strong flavours (**5**) .....: garlic, for instance, is generally taboo.

The consensus for the experts is: (**6**) ...... Several professional chefs said they would be much happier with a fresh, well-prepared sandwich or cold bean salad rather than a more ambitious but poorly executed meal.

Independent On Sunday

A which dries it out
B that won't offend
C keep it simple
D not necessarily the food itself
E whenever you wish
F usually found in high-class restaurants
G like smoked salmon
H into such areas as preparation and supply
I as we began to taxi for take-off
J *given the cost of air travel*

→ **Check your answers on p.120.**

🔍 **Close up**

Look at the article again. Find and underline any words and phrases to do with flight or flying. Check you understand what they mean.

→ **Check your answers on p.120.**

Listening

🕐 (spend about 25 minutes on this section)

Paper 4 Part 1 Sentence completion

ℹ️ **Exam information** There will be eight to ten questions in Paper 4 Part 1.

▶ **Exam techniques**
- It is helpful to know what kind of information you need to find out before you start listening. Will it be particular types of words – nouns, adjectives, etc.? Will it be particular types of information – percentages, prices, etc.? How can you find this out before you start listening? Task 1 practises this.
- What should you do while you listen? Task 2 practises this.
➜ **Check your answers on p.120.**

TASK 1 Look at the sentences for completion in task 2. Answer these questions.

Which question(s) could be answered by:
1 a percentage
2 a reference to time
3 a number
4 an adjective

➜ **Check your answers on p.120.**

TASK 2 🎧7.1 You will hear part of a radio report about a new medical treatment. For questions 1–8, fill in the missing information. Listen to the recording twice.

Richard Branson, Courteney Cox and Spice Girl, Mel G, have all had [1] surgery.

The treatment has been available in the US for a [2] than in Britain.

The report states that Courteney Cox was [3] before her operation.

Last year almost [4] people signed up for the operation in the US.

The operation is expensive, but it is very [and   5].

The success rate for the operation is [6].

A [7] has started in the US to help people whose eyesight is worse as a result of the operation.

If the operation goes wrong, there is [8] the surgeons can do.

➜ **Check your answers on p.120.**

Language development

Idioms *eye*

1 When the presenter asks *Might there be more to all this than meets the eye?* what does she mean? Look at the transcript on p.120 if you need help.

➜ **Check your answer on p.120.**

2 Match the idioms to the meanings.

1 to pull the wool over someone's eyes
2 to have eyes in the back of one's head
3 to be in the public eye
4 to keep an eye on something
5 to catch someone's eye
6 to be more to something / someone than meets the eye

a to watch something and make sure it is safe
b to deceive or lie to someone
c to get someone's attention
d to be able to see in all directions at once; to be aware of what's happening all around you
e to be more interesting / complex than one might at first think
f to be known about by everyone

➜ **Check your answers on p.120.**

3 Complete sentences 1–6 with the correct form of an idiom from exercise 2.

1 I'd hate to be a pop star. You're .... all the time. You never get any privacy.

2 Could you .... my bags while I make a phone call? I'll only be a few minutes.

3 He said he was ill but I don't believe him. I think he's ....

4 It's always the same with this waiter. It's impossible to ....

5 How was I supposed to know what was happening outside! I don't ....

6 You know the man who works in the Post Office and seems really boring? There's .... – he's an award-winning novelist.

➜ **Check your answers on p.121.**

Speaking

🕐 (spend about 25 minutes on this section)

Paper 5 Part 2 Comparing and contrasting

ℹ **Exam information** Paper 5 Part 2 is your best opportunity to speak without interruption. It is a good chance to show the examiners how much you know.

▶ **Exam techniques**

- Make the most of this part of the Speaking Paper. Use the pictures to show the language you know. Tasks 1, 2, and 3 practise this.
- You are often asked to compare and contrast the pictures. You should know how to compare and contrast in English. Task 2 practises this.
- Remember: if you find there are some words you don't know, talk about the pictures using words you do know. If you communicate your meaning, you will not lose marks for not knowing a word. (Look back at Unit 2 for ways of talking about things when you don't know the right words.) Task 3 practises this.
- Practise speaking for one minute so that you get used to the time limit. You don't want the examiner to stop you before you have answered the question. Task 3 practises this.

TASK 1 Look at the pictures below: both are to do with the idea of *sight*. Think about how you might compare and contrast them. Think also about how strong the connection is between the two pictures.

TASK 2 🎧 **7.2** Listen to someone describing and comparing the pictures in task 1. All the expressions below can be used to compare and contrast the pictures. Tick (✔) the ones you hear.

- ☐ to compare them
- ☐ there was no comparison
- ☐ they are completely different
- ☐ more uncomfortable
- ☐ whereas
- ☐ much quieter
- ☐ not so loud
- ☐ busier than
- ☐ not as easy as
- ☐ while
- ☐ but
- ☐ compared to

→ **Check your answers on p.121.**

TASK 3 Work in pairs. (If you are working alone, look at p.4.) One person look at the pictures marked A; the other person look at the pictures marked B. Listen to the examiner's instructions. If possible, record your answers. Then play them back and think about how you might improve them.

A 🎧 **7.3**

B 🎧 **7.4**

How well are you doing?

Look back at the different sections in this unit and assess your performance for each one. Choose from A–C below.

Reading (multiple choice questions)   …

Writing (report)   …

English In Use (gapped text)   …

Listening (sentence completion)   …

Speaking (comparing and contrasting)…

A No problem; I feel quite confident about this type of question.
B OK, but I need some more practice.
C I definitely need more practice. I find this type of question difficult.

8 Control

Reading

🕐 (spend about 40 minutes on this section)

Paper 1 Part 2 Gapped text

ℹ **Exam information** In Paper 1 you will find texts from a variety of sources: newspapers, magazines, journals, non-literary books, brochures, etc.

▶ **Exam techniques**
- Before you start reading, you should try and get an idea what information you might find in the text. How can you do this? Task 1 practises this.
- You should get a good idea what the text is about and how it is organized before you look at the missing paragraphs. How can you do this? Task 2 practises this.
- It is important to notice how paragraphs might relate to each other. How can you do this? Task 3 practises this.

➜ **Check your answers on p.121.**

TASK 1 Read the title of the article opposite. Tick (✔) questions 1–5 below which you think might be answered by the text.

1 ☐ What is this new idea?
2 ☐ Why has it been introduced?
3 ☐ Is anyone against it? Why?
4 ☐ Who introduced it?
5 ☐ Where is the scheme in operation?

TASK 2 Read the article opposite and find the answers to the questions in task 1 above. (Take no more than three minutes.)

➜ **Check your answers on p.121.**

TASK 3 Read the missing paragraphs A–H below the article and think about the answers to the questions below which refer to each paragraph.

A What is *it*? Who is *she*? Where is she first introduced in the article? Is she in favour of the scheme or against it?

B Do you think this paragraph introduces the view of the police? Why / Why not? Are there any other quotes from the police in the article? If so, where will this paragraph come in relation to it / them?

C Who are *they*? Why do they object? Will an explanation of the system come near the beginning or the end of the article?

D Are Liberty for or against the scheme? What will *However* contrast their view with? Does Deborah Clark have anything else to say? Where?

E Who is Ms Clark? What else has she said? Will she be referred to first in the article as Deborah Clark or Ms Clark?

F *Fraudulent* reflects a word in the previous paragraph – what might it be? *The print* refers back to the previous paragraph too – how?

G Both cheques and credit cards are mentioned in the text but are they contrasted anywhere? If so, where? Is there any mention elsewhere in the text about the comparative safety of credit cards? Is the opinion of the banking world mentioned anywhere else in the text?

H What does *this security system* refer to? How does *Bluewater* refer back?

TASK 4 Use the questions above to help you complete the exam task opposite.

➜ **Check your answers on p.121.**

For questions **1–7**, you must choose which of the paragraphs **A–H** fit into the numbered gaps in the text. There is one extra paragraph which does not fit in any of the gaps.

Shoppers made to put thumbprints on credit card slips in war on fraud

By Robert Mendick

Shoppers paying by cheque or credit card are having to leave their thumbprints behind in the latest scheme to combat high-street fraud. The simplicity of the new security system, which is cheap and so far proving to be an effective deterrent, has delighted police and traders alike. It is operating in over 1,000 stores across the country including 45 at the Bluewater complex in Kent, Europe's largest shopping centre.

1

However, the thumbprint scheme perturbs human-rights campaigners, who say it is an infringement of civil liberties and will undoubtedly lead to an increase in state control over the individual with a consequent loss of freedom and liberty.

2

In fact, shops within the scheme are now refusing to accept credit cards or cheques from customers who will not use the pad to give a thumbprint. They argue that genuine customers will have no reason to refuse; it is only potential fraudsters who will not want to oblige.

3

The pioneering system was first introduced from the US in the summer by Margaret Reid, a Scottish businesswoman based in Dunfermline, and is spreading rapidly up and down the country. Ms Reid, managing director of Thumbs Up Security Ltd, spotted its potential while on a holiday in Dallas when she was asked to leave her thumbprint behind when cashing a cheque.

4

In the US, thumbprinting has been so successful that criminals have tried cutting their skin to evade detection. 'Some fraudsters have been found to slice off the skin of their thumb, but we are not worried about it because it would be obvious on the print,' Ms Reid said. Last week, shoppers at the Princes Quay shopping centre in Hull became the latest consumers to have to give a thumbprint as well as a cheque guarantee card. The scheme is already operating in large parts of Kent and in some areas of London.

5

'There will be a knock-on effect; for example, an impact on burglary and theft as credit cards and cheques become virtually useless to the thief because of a high chance of detection of fraud.'

6

She feared that the scheme could lead to fingerprint scans replacing signatures as the means of security identification which in turn could lead to a national identity scheme via the back door.

7

Whether or not Liberty's protestations have an effect, one thing is certain: shopkeepers and police are determined to win the war against thieves and fraudsters.

The Independent

A 'It's a massive deterrent and an effective deterrent,' she explained. 'It has been 100 per cent successful so far in the UK. In five months in British shops where the scheme is running, to date nobody has made a fraudulent transaction.'

B Local police were quick to point out that the thumbprints would not form a national database. PC Dave Watson, the Humberside force's crime-prevention officer, said: 'Law-abiding customers need not fear this scheme. The process is simple and they are only verifying that they are the genuine holders of the credit card or cheque.

C The system that they object to so strongly merely requires shoppers paying by cheque or credit card to press their thumbs on an inkless disc pad and leave a thumbprint on either the back of the cheque or the credit card slip. The pad costs £5 and lasts for 500 imprints.

D However, Liberty, the civil-rights organization, expressed concern. 'What it means is that it leaves a lot of personal information sitting around on cheques and there is a huge potential for abuse,' said Deborah Clark, Liberty's director of public affairs.

E 'It is the tip of the iceberg,' said Ms Clark. 'If the police have access to these records and there is a crime that has been committed, then that is one thing. But if banks were holding databases of fingerprints that is a completely different matter.'

F In the case of fraudulent transactions, police can use the print and check it on the national fingerprint database, which contains five million prints. Research has found that 78 per cent of people who commit fraud already have a criminal record.

G 'Cheques have become problematic for the consumer in this day and age,' said Barry Middleton of Barclays Bank. 'People no longer carry cheque books around with them. Credit cards are smaller, more convenient, and despite some instances of fraud, they are actually much safer.'

H The reason for the introduction of this security system, especially at Bluewater, is simply the fact that credit-card fraud has been a key growth area for criminals. In the 12 months to April, according to estimates, it rose to £226m – an increase from £189m the previous year.

🔍 **Close up**

Find the words or phrases in the gapped text above that mean the following:

1 worries
2 saw how something might develop
3 to avoid being found out
4 almost
5 by means of / by way of

➜ **Check your answers on p.121.**

Writing

(spend about 20 minutes on tasks 1–4; about an hour on task 5)

Paper 2 Part 2 Article

ⓘ Exam information Parts 1 and 2 in Paper 2 carry an equal number of marks. You will lose marks for handwriting that is difficult to read and for poor spelling.

▶ **Exam techniques**
- What should you do as you read the question? Task 1 practises this.
- What should you do before you start to plan and write your answer? Task 2 practises this.
- When you have listed all your ideas what should you do? Task 3 practises this.
- How can you immediately catch the reader's attention and make them want to continue reading? Task 4 practises this.

→ **Check your answers on p.121.**

TASK 1 Read the question below and underline the key points that you need to include in your answer. How many points are there? What are they?

English Now!, the international magazine for learners of English, has invited its readers to write an article about their experiences learning English as a foreign language. You should say where you learnt your English, what you liked and didn't like about the classes, and give some tips as to how readers can become better learners.

Write your **article** in about 250 words.

→ **Check your answers on p.121.**

TASK 2 Look at the question again. Write down as many ideas as you can to include in your answer.

TASK 3 Look at the notes for an answer to the question in task 1. Check them against the main points that you underlined. Cross out any ideas that you think are irrelevant. Add any of your own ideas that you think are better.

learnt at school
- *teacher wore terrible clothes*
- *school food was awful*
- *English lessons poor*
- *four lessons a week (Mon, Wed x2, Fri)*
- *teacher was very strict*
- *we never spoke English in class*
- *exercises were boring*

likes
- *speaking English*
- *going out (in UK)*
- *being in UK*
- *meeting people from other countries*
- *comfortable desks & chairs in UK school!!*
- *good class in UK*
- *friendly teacher*
- *English jokes*

tips
- *eat breakfast*
- *exercise every day*
- *write new words on little pieces of paper and keep them in your pocket until you know them*
- *speak English sometime every day*
- *read a lot of English*
- *don't do your homework if you can think of a better way of spending your time*
- *eat chocolate (chocolate and breakfast both give you energy!)*

learnt in UK
- *stayed 10 weeks (Jan–Mar)*
- *great teacher (funny)*
- *never been so cold in my life*
- *stayed with UK family*
- *10 yr. old daughter; 8 yr old son*
- *son supported Liverpool football club*
- *wonderful food (surprise!)*
- *learnt a lot and had a good time*

dislikes
- *homework*
- *grammar*
- *short words in English (especially prepositions!)*
- *classmates who ask the teacher boring questions*

→ **Check your answers on p.121.**

Now organize your ideas into a plan.

TASK 4 Look at these three techniques for starting an article and at three openings to the question. Match each opening to a technique. Which do you like best and why?

a   a controversial or unexpected statement

b   something factual but enthusiastic

c   a joke or story

1   'Why do cows study English?' 'Because it a-moo-ses them.' That was one of my first teacher's 'English jokes'! He was called Monsieur Lamaison, he was very tall and he thought he was very funny. I didn't like him or his jokes, and he didn't like me. As a result, I didn't like English. But that changed when I went to Britain for three months on a course.

2   You wouldn't believe how much I hated English! I hated the teacher. I hated the classes. I hated the language. But not now. Let me tell you why.

3   I've always loved English. From the very first time I heard the words 'Coca-Cola' right up to watching the film *Gladiator* last night on television. For a time, when I was in my early twenties, I lived and breathed English too – studying for a bachelor's degree at university in Melbourne, Australia.

→ **Check your answers on p.122.**

TASK 5 Think of a good opening for your answer to task 1.

Now write your article in about 250 words.

→ **Compare your answer with the model article on p.122.**

English In Use

⏱ (spend about 30 minutes on this section)

Paper 3 Part 1 Multiple choice cloze

ℹ **Exam information** The areas that are usually tested in Paper 3 Part 1 include: phrases and collocations, idioms, phrasal verbs, and linkers.

▶ **Exam techniques**
- It will help your understanding if you know what the text is about before you start reading. How can you work this out? Check your answer on p.122. Task 1 practises this.
- If you are not sure which option is correct, work out which options are incorrect. This is also a useful way of checking answers you feel sure about.

TASK 1 Read the title of the article and choose the best option from 1–3 below.

The article is probably about

1 children who learn to drive motor racing cars to help them recover.

2 getting children to hospital faster when they are sick.

3 moving children around the hospital after an operation.

→ **Check your answer on p.122.**

TASK 2 Read the article through carefully, ignoring the spaces. Then look at these answers and explanations about questions 1–5.

Decide which word best fits each space.

1 A put   **B** sent   **C** called   **D** set

This question tests your knowledge of phrasal verbs. Which phrasal verb means to ask someone to come and help? The answer is *to call in*. *To send in* means to ask someone to go and help. *Put in* and *set in* do not fit in this context.

2 A habit   **B** discipline   **C** arrangement   **D** order

This question tests the meaning of an individual word in the context of the whole scenario. All the words fit grammatically, but what is it that the hospital wants to learn from the motor racing pit stop? *Discipline* is the answer.

3 A effort   **B** aim   **C** action   **D** operation

This tests your knowledge of fixed phrases. Which of the above follows *in*; is followed by a full infinitive; and fits with the meaning? The answer is A: *in an effort to*. The others do not fit.

4 A clinic   **B** room   **C** ward   **D** theatre

This tests your knowledge of fixed collocations. What is the area in a hospital where operations are carried out? It is an *operating theatre*. Nothing else is possible.

5 A disease   **B** surgery   **C** therapy   **D** remedy

This tests your knowledge of collocations and your appreciation of the meaning of the text. Two of the above form possible collocations. Which are they? Which is correct in the context? B is the correct answer, as *critical minutes* are only likely to follow heart surgery, not heart disease.

Motor racing experts to give advice on speedy transfers of sick children

Britain's top children's hospital has turned to the world of motor racing for help in moving sick babies at maximum speed and with minimum risk.

Great Ormond Street Hospital in London has **(1)** ..... in experts from the MacLaren Formula One motor racing team to bring the **(2)** ..... of the pit stop into the sphere of medical care in an **(3)** ..... to learn how children might be transferred more quickly and safely out of the operating **(4)** ..... during the critical minutes that follow complex heart **(5)** ..... .

David Ryan, the MacLaren team manager, has visited the hospital and **(6)** ..... doctors how to shave seconds off a tyre change. Doctors hope to **(7)** ..... the method to help medical teams to **(8)** ..... lines, tubes and syringes and begin **(9)** ..... vital functions as soon as possible after a baby who has had surgery arrives in the **(10)** ..... care unit.

Specialists at the hospital, led by Martin Elliott, a cardiac surgeon, believed the speed and efficiency **(11)** ..... by motor racing teams at pit stops offered the **(12)** ..... parallel for the improvements they were seeking to **(13)** ..... and so contacted MacLaren for advice.

(14) ..... of the MacLaren team will return to the hospital later this month to examine a plan **(15)** ..... up by doctors to improve the transfers.

The Independent

TASK 3 For questions 6–15, read the remaining paragraphs and then decide which word best fits each space.

	A	B	C	D
6	educated	guided	instructed	lectured
7	adapt	adjust	turn	vary
8	introduce	insert	inject	enter
9	watching	guarding	nursing	monitoring
10	high	continuous	intensive	additional
11	displayed	noted	produced	mentioned
12	nearest	shortest	briefest	closest
13	put	make	form	do
14	members	owners	tenants	holders
15	done	taken	drawn	written

For each question decide what is being tested and why the incorrect options are wrong.

→ **Check your answers on p.122.**

Listening

(spend about 25 minutes on this section)

Paper 4 Part 4 Multiple matching

> ℹ **Exam information** In Paper 4 Part 4 you are often asked to interpret what is happening. You may have to identify the speakers or the topic, to decide what the context is, or recognize people's attitudes or motives.

▶ **Exam technique**

In interpreting what is happening, you will often have to find the answer from clues rather than from the exact words used in the options. For example, in task 2 below, for E *a presidential election,* you will probably not hear the words *presidential election* but you might hear about *people voting,* about *different candidates* and about *results* and *polls.* Task 1 practises this.

TASK 1 Look at the situations in the chart below and list some words that you think you might hear in a conversation about each situation.

a presidential election	vote, candidates, results, poll, winner, loser, speech
a flight in an aeroplane	
a weather forecast	
a football match	
a demonstration	
a lesson in a school	
a royal wedding	
a trip up a mountain	

→ Check your answers on p.122.

TASK 2 🎧 8.1 Listen to the recording twice and do both tasks below.

You will hear five short extracts in which various people are talking about situations in which they had problems.

TASK ONE

What situation is being talked about? For questions **1–5**, match the extracts with the situations, listed **A–H**.

A a demonstration

B a flight in an aeroplane

C a royal wedding

D a football match

E a presidential election

F a lesson in a school

G a weather forecast

H a trip up a mountain

Speaker 1 [1]
Speaker 2 [2]
Speaker 3 [3]
Speaker 4 [4]
Speaker 5 [5]

TASK TWO

What caused a problem in each situation? For questions **6–10**, match the extracts with the problems, listed **A–H**.

A people threw food at each other

B people got wet

C there were too many people

D there was not enough food

E people had drunk too much

F there was too much noise

G people couldn't hear the speeches

H people weren't very enthusiastic

Speaker 1 [6]
Speaker 2 [7]
Speaker 3 [8]
Speaker 4 [9]
Speaker 5 [10]

→ Check your answers on p.122.

Language development

Expressions of positive and negative thinking

Look at these expressions from the recording.

*I worked hard at **keeping everyone's spirits up.***

*Then suddenly **all hell broke loose.***

Put the words in *italics* in sentences 1–8 in the right order to make more expressions of positive and negative thinking. Mark each one P for positive thinking and N for negative thinking.

1 Good luck at the interview, Jack. I'll *crossed for fingers keep my you.*

2 I don't know what to do about Jenny. She just sits around all day watching TV. I've tried everything to get her to go out with her friends but she won't do anything. I'm *wit's my at end.*

3 Don't worry if you fail your driving test the first time. *It's world the not the of end.*

4 He just never washes up his coffee cup. And he never makes coffee for anyone else. He's so selfish. He *me bend the drives round.*

5 Three months ago I really thought we would go bankrupt, but we've had a lot of orders recently and at last there seems *light be the the to at tunnel of end.*

6 You really think he'll pay you back the money he owes you? *That day the be 'll.*

7 First the car broke down. Then I lost my briefcase. And then I dropped my phone and it broke. Never mind! I suppose *better things get only can.*

8 I answered the first two questions OK. The next two were more difficult. But when I got to the last two I realized I was *out my completely of depth.*

→ Check your answers on p.122.

Speaking

🕐 (spend about 25 minutes on this section)

Paper 5 Part 3 Negotiation

ℹ Exam information While doing the problem-solving task, you may have to negotiate a decision with your partner. If you can't agree, you can agree to differ, but you should try to reach agreement first.

▶ **Exam techniques**
- Think of some ideas before you start speaking. You don't have to mention all your points; just start with something that interests you and that you feel confident talking about. Task 1 practises this.
- It is important to know the kind of language that is useful when negotiating a point of view with someone. Task 2 practises this.

TASK 1 🎧8.2 Read the question below and make a list of ideas you might hear when two people discuss this problem. Then listen to the recording and tick the ideas you hear mentioned.

Work together. Look at the picture and make a list of eight to ten proposals to encourage people to use their cars less and public transport more in order to cut down pollution. Discuss the proposals and decide which three you think are the most effective.

➔ **Check your answers on p.122.**

TASK 2 Listen to the recording again. Make a note of the language the speakers use:

1 to compliment each other when they have a good idea (three expressions)
2 to give reasons for their arguments (two expressions)
3 to express an opposite point of view (three expressions)
4 to express their preference (two expressions)
5 to clarify what the other person has said (three expressions)

➔ **Check your answers on p.122.**

TASK 3 Work in pairs. (If you are working alone, look at p.4.) Read and discuss the question below. Try and use some of the language in task 2. If possible, record your discussion. Then play it back and think about how you might improve it.

Look at this list of different ways of getting people to do what you want. Check you understand the vocabulary. Then discuss them and agree on an order from the most acceptable to the least acceptable. Give reasons for your decisions.

persuade	request	order
flatter	bribe	blackmail
torture	threaten	beg

Note In the exam, candidates will be given a set of visual prompts to discuss. The task, however, will be similar to that in tasks 1 and 3.

How well are you doing?

Look back at the different sections in this unit and assess your performance for each one. Choose from A–C below.

Reading (gapped text)	...
Writing (article)	...
English In Use (multiple choice cloze)	...
Listening (multiple matching)	...
Speaking (negotiation)	...

A No problem; I feel quite confident about this type of question.
B OK, but I need some more practice.
C I definitely need more practice. I find this type of question difficult.

Reading

(spend about 30 minutes on this section)

Paper 1 Part 4
Multiple matching

ⓘ Exam information Remember you only have 15 to 20 minutes for each part of Paper 1. Time is very important. Part 4 will have between 12 and 22 questions.

▶ **Exam techniques**
- First it is important to get a general idea what the text is about. How can you do this? Check your answer on p.123. Task 1 practises this.
- This part of the paper often comprises a number of short texts (look back at Unit 1); but sometimes there is just one longer text. To make it easier to find the answers, you can underline or highlight important parts of the text. Task 2 practises this.

TASK 1 Read the first sentence of each paragraph in the article opposite and answer these questions. (Take only two minutes.)

1 What do many British athletes do before they compete?

2 What difference does this practice make?

3 Do all the athletes do exactly the same thing?

4 Which sports company is interested in this?

→ **Check your answers on p.123.**

TASK 2 Look at the names A–I in the exam task. Underline those names in the article opposite.

TASK 3 Now do the exam task.

→ **Check your answers on p.123.**

For questions **1–13**, choose your answers from the list of names (**A–I**). Some of the choices may be required more than once. When more than one answer is required, these may be given in any order.

Who

has been studying the connection between sport and music?	**1**	
listens to music purely to relax and stay calm before an event?	**2**	**3** . . . . .
listens to music purely for stimulation before an event?	**4**	
listens to music for both relaxation and stimulation?	**5**	
listens to music to take their mind away from the outside world?	**6**	**7** . . . . .
found some music too stimulating?	**8**	
listened to the same song repeatedly before an event?	**9**	
recommended one athlete should listen to something different?	**10**	
played a piece of music to a group of athletes?	**11**	
believes music is vital for a good performance?	**12**	
believes each athlete should make an individual choice of what to listen to?	**13**	

A Dr Karageorghis

B James Cracknell

C Katharine Merry

D Darren Campbell

E Audley Harrison

F Iwan Thomas

G Linford Christie

H Dwain Chambers

I Tony Jarrett

Music – the drug of choice for Britain's Olympians

BY JONATHAN THOMPSON

Psychologists believe they have discovered why Britain won so many medals at the Sydney Olympics: not drugs but music.

Dr Costas Karageorghis and his team of researchers at Brunel University in West London say that athletes can improve their performance by as much as 18 per cent by listening to the right sort of music.

Last night a host of medal winners – including rowing gold James Cracknell, sprinters Katharine Merry and Darren Campbell, and boxing gold Audley Harrison – confirmed that music had helped them to win. Dr Karageorghis has been researching the psychological effects of music in sport and exercise for over a decade, and has worked with some of the UK's top athletes. 'Essentially, it comes down to brainwave activity,' he said. 'The human mind produces brainwave responses to music, increasing its alpha activity. This pushes athletes into what is commonly referred to as "the zone" – almost a semi-hypnotic state where they perform on auto-pilot without any conscious effort. Being in "the zone" is absolutely necessary for a peak performance, and music helps to induce it.'

Dr Karageorghis says different athletes need different music. 'Some need songs that will relax them; others need songs that will stimulate them. Either way, the music should leave them feeling inspired.'

The key, he says, is the heart rate. Athletes who need to wind themselves up before an event will listen to a song which is the same speed, or faster, than their heart rate. Those who feel anxious before competing will choose music with a tempo below their heart rate, to calm them down and help them focus. Dr Karageorghis illustrated this by referring to two of his protégés: 'Audley Harrison will listen to Japanese classical music before a fight, to avoid burning off nervous energy, but Iwan Thomas (relay) will psyche himself up to *Firestarter* by The Prodigy before he races. It is a very individual process.'

James Cracknell, who rowed to Olympic glory and into the record books last month with Steve Redgrave, Matthew Pinsent and Tim Foster, said yesterday that listening to the Red Hot Chili Peppers' album *Blood Sugar Sex Magik* was a crucial part of the preparation for the race.

'I was listening to that CD on my Discman until about an hour before we competed,' he said. 'The music's vaguely aggressive and powerful, but it's also familiar, so it serves a joint purpose. It makes you relax a bit, but also winds you up at the same time. It keeps you going, which is very important.'

Katharine Merry, the 400m runner who won bronze at the Olympics, also cited music as a powerful influence on the quality of her performance. 'I listen to soft soul and R&B music like K-Ci and Jo Jo on the way to the track. It helps me to feel comfortable, relaxed and positive. In many ways, it is essential to a good performance. You have to lock off the rest of the world, and music helps you do that.'

Olympic 200m silver medallist Darren Campbell agreed. 'For an hour-and-a-half between the Olympic semi-final and the final I just lay on a couch and listened to the same Craig David song, *Rendezvous*, over and over again. It helped me to focus. I could get into my own little world so I couldn't hear or be distracted by other people on the track.'

Campbell also revealed that his coach, Linford Christie, is a convert. 'Linford always plays inspirational music to us,' he said. 'Last year at the world championships he sat us down, gave us a last little speech and told us to believe in ourselves, then played R Kelly's *I Believe I Can Fly*.'

Fellow international sprinter Dwain Chambers, the second-fastest Briton ever, is a firm believer in gospel music, which he began listening to on the advice of Olympic hurdler Tony Jarrett. 'I channel everything into the music, to avoid the nervous energy on the track,' he said. 'I listened to UK garage before races last year, but that psyched me up too much. Listening to gospel has really helped me to improve my performances this season. It's my legal drug.'

Dr Karageorghis is now working with Nike to make his research available to everyone. The sportswear company has adopted his concept to create the PSA (Personal Sports Audio) player, a tiny ergonomically designed device which plays digital music files downloaded from the internet. Athletes can visit the web site www.nike.com/nikedigital and download a musical package that is relevant to their workout before playing it on their PSA while exercising.

The Independent

Writing

(spend about 20 minutes on tasks 1 & 2; about 30 minutes on task 3)

Paper 2 Part 1 Notes and messages

ⓘ Exam information As *part* of the task in Part 1 of the Writing Paper, you may be asked to write a note or message.

▶ **Exam techniques**
- The purpose of your note may affect the language. For example, if you are asking someone a big favour you may be more polite than if you are asking a small favour. The purpose of a note is therefore important. Task 1 practises this.
- Think about who you are writing to. You can be less formal with friends but you will probably be more formal with acquaintances. Task 2 practises this.
- It is important to keep your note brief. But don't leave out any essential points. Task 2 practises this.
- Why is it a good idea to underline important parts of the question when you first read it? Check your answer on p.123.

TASK 1 Match each pair of notes to its purpose below.

• warning   • giving information   • request   • thanking

A1

Julia
Here's your CD back.
Thanks for lending it to me. It's great.
See you on Friday.
Rob

A2

Julia
Here's your CD.
Thanks.
Rob

B1

Alan
Won't be back till late.
All Stars concert on Channel 5 tonight 7.30.
Could you set the video?
Felicity

B2

Dear Alan
I'm afraid I won't be back till late – probably about 11.00. I'm going to the cinema with Evie. Just noticed there's an All Stars concert on TV tonight (you know I love them!). Could you be a sweetie and video it.
Ciao, darling!
Fizz

C1

Please don't touch the piano.
Repair not finished.

C2

Keep off!!

D1

Have gone to return the video.
Back in ten mins.

D2

I've gone up to the video shop to return The Yards.
I should be back in about ten minutes.

TASK 2 Look again at the notes. Answer these questions.

A1 / A2:
1 Which note is more polite?
2 What makes it more polite?
3 What would be the effect of leaving out *It's great* in A1?

B1 / B2:
1 What is the difference between B1 and B2?
2 Is B1 polite enough as it is?
3 What information in B2 is unnecessary?
4 How much can you leave out before the note starts to become less polite?

C1 / C2:
1 Is C1 too long?
2 Is C2 acceptable or is it rude?
3 Is the explanation in C1 essential information?

D1 / D2:
1 Which note would you write if you were in a hurry?
2 Who would you write D2 to rather than D1?
3 Is there any information in these notes that is not essential?

→ **Check your answers on p.123.**

TASK 3 You had planned to go and see the Peter Van Essen concert on Saturday 11th November with your friend, Sophie. As you live in Bristol, you had also arranged for both of you to stay with your sister in London. Unfortunately, when you ring up to buy tickets, both the concerts at the Piccadilly Hall are sold out. However, you manage to get two tickets for the Sunday.

Write a **note** to Sophie explaining what has happened and saying that you hope she will be able to come to the Sunday concert. Write approximately 50 words.

Write a **note** to your sister thanking her for her offer, explaining the situation and saying that you won't now stay the night after the concert because you will have to get back to Bristol to go to work on Monday morning. Write approximately 75 words.

Peter Van Essen
IN CONCERT

November dates
Mon 6th Tue 7th
MANCHESTER ROSE BOWL
0161 538 7777

Thu 9th Sat 11th
LONDON: PICCADILLY HALL
0207 980 4000

Sun 12th
CENTRAL ACADEMY OF LONDON
0207 848 6501

All tickets £22.50
24 hour C/C hotline 01273-458763 or online at
www.tickettout.com
Latest album 'Essen-tials' out Thu 16th November

Note Remember that a note will only form *part* of the Part 1 writing task in the exam, and you will not have to write two notes. You will only need to spend *part* of the time for the Part 1 task writing a note.

English In Use

(spend about 35 minutes on this section)

Paper 3 Part 4 Word formation

ⓘ Exam information There are two texts in Part 4. Time is therefore very important. You have about 15 minutes for the two texts: 7–8 minutes per text.

▶ **Exam techniques**
- Look at task 3. What should you do before you start trying to complete each space? Why? Check your answer on p.123. Task 1 practises this.
- In this part of Paper 3 it is useful to think about what part of speech is needed to complete each space. This will help you decide which form of the word to choose. Tasks 2 and 3 practise this.
- At least one of the words in this part will require a prefix. Tasks 2 and 3 practise this.
- As you get nearer the exam it is important to practise doing individual exercises in the correct time. Task 4 practises this.

TASK 1 Read the article in task 3 through quickly and tick the best summary below.

1 ☐ The Beatles are going to re-form for one concert on the Internet.

2 ☐ The Beatles' new album is selling extremely well.

3 ☐ The Beatles will never sell as many albums as today's bands.

TASK 2 Read the article again. Put a circle around the correct part of speech for each gap. Look at the words on the right of the text if it helps you.

0 (noun (person)) / verb / noun
1 noun (person) / verb / noun
2 noun / verb / gerund
3 verb / adjective / noun (person)
4 noun / adjective / verb
5 noun / verb / adjective
6 verb / adjective / prefix + verb
7 adjective / verb / noun

→ **Check your answers on p.123.**

TASK 3 Use task 2 to help complete the task below.

For questions **1–7**, read the text below. Use the words on the right of the text to form one word that fits in the same numbered space in the text. The exercise begins with an example (**0**).

THE BEATLES' NEW ALBUM

The first Beatles album to include all the band's number one hits amazed music (**0**) *analysts* by taking more than £10 million before its release.

Simply called '1', the (**1**) .... of 27 songs will be released in a fortnight but has already achieved a record number of Internet (**2**) .... These figures have helped the band to defy their (**3**) .... who have said that the Beatles can no longer sell albums in large volumes. More than one million copies of their album have been pressed in (**4**) ....

Although there have been a number of (**5**) .... since they split up in 1970, the new release has (**6**) .... interest because it brings together all of their transatlantic hits. Chris Windle, of EMI, said the (**7**) .... of '1' is in part due to a new marketing strategy using the World Wide Web.

Sunday Telegraph

0	*ANALYSE*
1	COLLECT
2	SELL
3	CRITICIZE
4	ANTICIPATE
5	COMPILE
6	AWAKEN
7	SUCCEED

→ **Check that one word has a prefix. Then check your answers on p.123.**

▶ **Exam technique**
Think about the techniques you have just practised in tasks 1, 2, and 3 and use them now to complete task 4.

TASK 4 Allow yourself only eight minutes to complete this task.

For questions **8–15**, read the text below. Use the words on the right of the text to form one word that fits in the same numbered space in the text.

MADONNA ON STAGE AND SCREEN

Madonna took to the stage in London last night to sing a (**8**) .... of songs in possibly the most (**9**) .... show in music history so far. Brixton Academy was packed to witness her first London concert in seven years. But the focus was really on the millions more watching on the Internet as a result of an (**10**) .... broadcasting deal with Microsoft. The Internet broadcast started (**11**) .... with many people (**12**) .... to receive pictures because of the rush to connect. However, the link improved as the support band, Texas, took the stage.

Apart from the income from website 'hits' and (**13**) ...., Microsoft forced (**14**) .... to download special player software. Before the concert, Madonna said the act was a (**15**) .... run for a full tour, her first since 1993.

The Daily Telegraph

8	HAND
9	PROFIT
10	EXCLUDE
11	BAD
12	ABLE
13	ADVERTISE
14	USE
15	TRY

→ **Check your answers on p.123.**

Listening

(spend about 25 minutes on this section)

Paper 4 Part 2 Note taking

ⓘ Exam information In Paper 4 Part 2 you will usually hear one speaker only, i.e. a monologue. There may be prompts from a second speaker.

▶ **Exam techniques**
- It is useful to get as much information as you can about the recording before you hear it. How can you do this? Task 1 practises this.
- In Part 2 you hear the recording once only. It is important that you don't miss any information. What should you do as you listen to the recording? Task 2 practises this.
  ➜ **Check your answers on p.123.**

TASK 1 Look at the information in task 2 and answer these questions.

1 Where is the festival?
2 How many bands have been booked already?
3 How long is the festival?
4 How much would it cost to go for Saturday and Sunday?
5 Can you camp there?

➜ **Check your answers on p.123.**

TASK 2 🎧9.1 You will hear the telephone information line of a summer music festival. As you listen, complete the notes for questions 1–10.

WESTBEACH SUMMER POP EXTRAVAGANZA

now in its [_____ 1] year

Venue:	Wilson's Fields at the [_____ 2] of Westbeach town
Bands already booked:	Inspiring Tide Perfect Harmony Green Metal – from [_____ 3]
Dates:	13th – 16th [_____ 4]
Tickets and full [_____ 5] of bands available from: – Westbeach Extravaganza website – Westbeach Community Theatre	
Ticket prices:	Thurs & Fri £20 per day Sat & Sun £30 per day 4 days [_____ 6]
Camping:	£10 per person per night full washing & toilet facilities available but limited [_____ 7]
Food stalls:	fish & chips, Mexican, Thai, Westbeach's special [_____ 8]
Travel:	extra [_____ 9] and [_____ 10] services will run to Westbeach.

➜ **Check your answers on p.123.**

Language development

Collocation *facilities*

1 Look at these sentences from the recording.

Camping facilities will be available.
*Full toilet and **washing facilities** will be provided.*

Cross out the three words below which you are unlikely to find with the word *facilities*.

adequate	excellent
definite	poor
state-of-the-art	serious
modern	old-fashioned
splendid	strong

2 Cross out the unlikely answers.

What would you expect to find at …

1 a five-star hotel?

adequate splendid excellent	facilities

2 a small and very cheap guest house?

poor state-of-the-art adequate	facilities

3 a new £80 million football stadium?

adequate modern state-of-the-art	facilities

4 a gymnasium built in the 1950s?

adequate old-fashioned splendid	facilities

5 a new, but not very large, sports centre?

adequate modern old-fashioned	facilities

➜ **Check your answers on p.123.**

Speaking

⏱ (spend about 25 minutes on this section)

Paper 5 Part 3 Opinions

ⓘ Exam information Each part of the Speaking Paper will last roughly three to four minutes.

▶ **Exam techniques**
- As well as giving your own opinion in Part 3, it is important not to dominate your partner. Ask their opinion, if necessary, and listen carefully to what they say. Task 1 practises this.
- Remember there are many different ways of giving your opinion in English. Try to use a variety. Task 2 practises this.
- You don't necessarily have to agree with your partner's opinion. You can agree to have different opinions. How can you do this politely? Task 3 practises this.

TASK 1 🎧 9.2 **Look at this task. Then listen to the recording and look at sentences 1–6 below. Write M if the man agrees and W if the woman agrees. Some sentences may be both or neither.**

Compare a number of different types of music and discuss what role these types of music play in society today. Use the pictures and the ideas below to help you.
- relaxation • spirituality • politics
- a social role • popular culture

TASK 2 Listen to the recording again. Write M if the man says it and W if the woman says it.

1 ☐ 'As far as I'm concerned he serves no purpose at all.'
2 ☐ 'To be perfectly honest, I rarely give money to buskers.'
3 ☐ 'It seems to me that they do brighten up the streets.'
4 ☐ 'As I see it, pop doesn't have much to recommend it.'
5 ☐ 'To my mind this is the most spiritual form of music.'
6 ☐ 'In my opinion some pop music is spiritual.'
7 ☐ 'With all due respect, I really can't agree.'

Which two phrases above are often used before criticism or slightly negative remarks?

➔ **Check your answers on p.124.**

TASK 3 What phrase does the woman use when she decides they cannot agree?

➔ **Check your answer on p.124.**

TASK 4 Work in pairs. (If you are working alone, look at p.4.) Read and discuss the question below. If possible, record your discussion. Then play it back and think about how you might improve it.

Decide on a type of background music that could be played in each of the following situations. Look at the pictures below which illustrate some different kinds of music, discuss the suitability for each situation, and try and agree which type would be best in each case.
- a wedding • a school concert • a football match
- a local festival • a party • working in an office

1 ☐ ☐ Buskers are annoying.
2 ☐ ☐ Orchestras have a social function.
3 ☐ ☐ Folk music has a spiritual role.
4 ☐ ☐ Some pop music is political.
5 ☐ ☐ Classical music is spiritual.
6 ☐ ☐ Pop music can never have a spiritual role.

➔ **Check your answers on p.124.**

How well are you doing?

Look back at the different sections in this unit and assess your performance for each one. Choose from A–C below.

Reading (multiple matching)	...
Writing (notes / messages)	...
English In Use (word formation)	...
Listening (note taking)	...
Speaking (opinions)	...

A No problem; I feel quite confident about this type of question.
B OK, but I need some more practice.
C I definitely need more practice. I find this type of question difficult.

Reading

🕐 (spend about 35 minutes on this section)

Paper 1 Part 1
Multiple matching

ℹ️ **Exam information** In Paper 1 you get one mark for each correct answer in Parts 1 and 4; two marks for each correct answer in Parts 2 and 3.

▶ **Exam techniques**
What should you do before you look at the questions? Why should you do this? Task 1 practises this.
➡ **Check your answers on p.124.**

TASK 1 This question gives you practice in *skimming* the text to get a general idea of the meaning. Look at the first two and the last two lines of each of the guidebook reviews. Mark each review 1, 2, or 3: 1 – good, worth buying; 2 – not too bad; 3 – not very good.

➡ **Check your answers on p.124.**

TASK 2 Answer the exam task by referring to the reviews of guidebooks to San Francisco.

➡ **Check your answers on p.124.**

For questions **1–16**, answer by choosing from the list (**A–F**). Some of the choices may be required more than once. When more than one answer is required they can be given in any order.

Which book is being described?

The beginning of this guide is not very good.	**1**	**2** .....
This guide has poor hotel and restaurant listings.	**3**	**4** .....
This guide has only one photo.	**5**	
This guide has one very unnecessary photo.	**6**	
The photos in this guide look very old.	**7**	
The writer thinks this is the best guide.	**8**	
This guide has some interesting stories in it.	**9**	
This guide does not capture the real feeling of the city.	**10**	
This guide is written in an amusing style (though not deliberately).	**11**	
This guide was written in a foreign language first.	**12**	
You should get this book if you are interested in:		
architecture.	**13**	
outdoor activities.	**14**	
interior design.	**15**	
visiting museums.	**16**	

A Eyewitness

B AA Explorer

C Time Out

D National Geographic

E Rough Guide

F Insight Guide

Ⓐ Eyewitness

£12.99

Like many highly-illustrated design-heavy guides, this is a triumph of presentation over content. With its lavish graphics, 3-D cutaways, room-by-room guides to museums and details of San Francisco cable cars, this is the book to have if you are planning a military invasion. How much it will tell you about the spirit of the place is another matter. The writing is rather routine and the tone insulting at times – do we really need a photo to explain what a cup of espresso is? That said, Dorling Kindersley does a good job of stimulating the appetite. Photos are generally excellent, and the strong visuals come into their own in the architecture chapter. The sightseeing section is thorough but makes no critical distinction between the tourist trap that is Fisherman's Wharf and the excitement of, say, the Mission. One to look through before buying something else.

B AA Explorer

£14.99

The AA does its best to show San Francisco as an outdoor sports destination, with much detail on cycling, in-line skating and snowboarding (for which you'd have to drive three hours to Lake Tahoe). The author admits that he prefers the unspoiled coast to the north to the city streets. Sadly, the guide never recovers from this start. The sights are listed alphabetically, which kills any atmosphere you might get moving around a particular area; the guide then tries to make up for this problem with feature inserts which fail to bring the corpse back to life. That just leaves the handy downtown map, which seems a little pricey at £14.99. Dull.

C Time Out

£10.99

This book tries hard to be cool and knowledgeable about the city, but too frequently falls into incomprehensibility and laughably simplistic generalizations about local issues that will be of little or no interest to most visitors. You'd never know from the self-important introduction that this is one of the world's most beautiful cities; the authors seem to want to list every sight without giving you a hint of why you'd want to go there. The book often neglects to mention the basic practical details. Yet when it does give them, it's all out of balance: endless references to pleasant but minor Hayes Valley, and a seemingly peculiar desire to send visitors on a long trip to the Tenderloin, epicentre of prostitution and petty crime. Get your hotel and restaurant information from the free alternative weekly newsheets when you arrive (they will be just as informative), and seek your guidebook advice elsewhere.

D National Geographic

£12.99

A thorough, intelligently-presented, well-illustrated guide, the National Geographic won't teach you anything you couldn't learn elsewhere, but it will probably give you the basics of what you need more clearly and concisely than any other book. It combines design-heavy graphics and photos with much more convincing bits of writing, and streamlines its information rather than packs everything in. There is detailed and interesting information about some of San Francisco's stunning hotel interiors; it also gives the best overview of sights in the wider Bay Area. Hotel and restaurant listings are thankfully short and well chosen. What lets it down is some unintentionally hilarious expressions. In North Beach, "you can let your gusto off the leash". Or "What a rush! What freedom! What a beautiful city!" What rubbish.

E Rough Guide

£8.99

Written with the authority of someone who actually knows the city, this is probably the best textual guide overall. It gives a balanced picture of each area and tells many of the city's best stories, frequently illustrating them with colourful quotations from famous San Francisco authors. It is up to date on city politics and understands – as others don't – that the architectural attractions of the new Main Library cover up the fact that there is little space for the books. But the guide could be livelier in places: far too much space is devoted to uninteresting destinations like Benicia, Vallejo and San José; and the hotel and restaurant listings are a bit unreliable. There are no photos, either, except for the front cover shot of the Golden Gate Bridge. Despite some reservations, definitely the best of the bunch.

F Insight Guide

£14.99

This one starts badly, with a cover illustration of a girl and her dog (with the Golden Gate Bridge seen only hazily in the background). Inside are more clumsy, uninspiring photos, seemingly ripped from a 1950s tourist brochure, along with a long and uninteresting introductory section on San Francisco's history, people and culture. There's a reactionary flavour to the descriptions of hippies and beatniks as well as a slightly paranoid reference to the 'gay landslide' overtaking the city. Maybe something got lost in the translation (the Insight series' home language is German). The guide to the city itself – after about 100 pages – gives pride of place to Fisherman's Wharf (boring) and continues in a similarly uninspired manner. The hotel and restaurant listings are equally uninteresting. Forget it.

Independent On Sunday

Language development

Adjectives

The reviews are rich in adjectives which describe writing and different features of writing.

1 What are the opposites of these adjectives?

reliable	comprehensible
practical	convincing
interesting	inspired

2 Look at these adjectives that can be used to describe a piece of writing. Put them into the appropriate column below depending on their meaning.

dull	insulting
thorough	balanced
up to date	lively
knowledgeable	simplistic
concise	detailed
clumsy	cool
repetitive	humourless

POSITIVE	NEGATIVE

→ Check your answers on p.124.

→ Check your answers on p.124.

Close up

List all the words in the reviews to do with books and check that you understand what they mean.
For example:
highly-illustrated, design-heavy, guide, presentation, content, graphics, writing, tone, …

→ Check your answers on p.124.

Writing

(spend about 20 minutes on tasks 1 & 2; about an hour on task 3)

Paper 2 Part 2 Informal letter

ⓘ Exam information In Paper 2 you may be asked to write an informal letter.

▶ **Exam techniques**
- An appropriate informal style is very important in an informal letter. Think about the person you are writing to and your reason for writing. Task 1 practises this.
- When you have finished writing, it is important to read through your work to check for mistakes. You can always improve what you have written. Task 2 practises this.

TASK 1 Read this letter ignoring any mistakes. Then choose the best sentence, A or B, to fill each gap.

> Dear Jack
>
> .....¹ We were delighted to hear that you got that job in Glasgow. It sound a great job and Glasgow is a wonderful city.
>
> We've just got back from our Caribbean cruise – you remember the one we'd always promised ourselves. What a nightmare! I mean, when you think to a cruise, you imagine beautiful sunshine, seas bright blue, lazing by the pool on board ship, great food, dancing the night away under a moonlit sky. .....²
>
> It was the end of the season hurricane and the weather was awful. In fact, we missed the worst of a hurricane by only a day or two. As a result, it poured with rain just about every day. The sea was unbelievably rough. .....³
>
> The boat itself didn't really lives up to expectations either. The food was really quite ordinary. I certainly expected better considering what we'd paid for the trip. .....⁴. And our fellow travellers – well, I know cruises appeal for the generation older but we hadn't expected everyone else to be old enough to be our parents!
>
> .....⁵ I've got an appointment with the bank manager this afternoon. I think he are going to want to know when we're going to pay to the cruise – that's the trouble with credit cards, isn't it!
>
> Write and tell us all about Glasgow and how you are all getting on. Hope to see you soon.
>
> Geoff.

1 A Thank you very much for your letter of the 15th June.
   B Thanks for your letter.
2 A Well, be warned – it's not like that at all.
   B You should note that the reality is somewhat different.
3 A And to cap it all, Elly was seasick for the whole of the first week.
   B Even more unfortunately Eleanor was indisposed for the first week.
4 A The cabins were OK – a bit small and dark, but OK.
   B Despite being a little small and dark, the cabin accommodation was adequate.
5 A Anyway, I've got to go now.
   B I am afraid I must draw this to a close now.

→ **Check your answers on p.124.**

TASK 2 Read through the letter again. Find and correct:

1 three word order mistakes
2 three mistakes with prepositions
3 three mistakes with verbs

→ **Check your answers on p.124.**

TASK 3 You have just come back from a disastrous holiday abroad. The hotel was not very good, there were delays on all your flights, and you also got ill. Write a letter to a friend telling them about your trip and how you intend to get a refund from the travel agent.

Write your letter in about 250 words.

English In Use

(spend about 30 minutes on this section)

Paper 3 Part 2 Open cloze

❶ Exam information In Paper 3 you have 90 minutes for six parts, an average of 15 minutes per part. You will not have much time to spare. Remember you can only fill a gap with *one* word in Part 2 but there may be more than one word which is acceptable for each gap.

▶ **Exam techniques**
- What should you do before you start trying to fill the gaps? Why? Task 1 practises this.
- What type of words does this part of Paper 3 test? How will this affect the way you do the task? Task 2 practises this.
- Don't leave any gaps empty. If you are not sure what word goes in a gap, make an intelligent guess. You might guess correctly. Task 3 practises this.
  → Check your answers on p.124.

TASK 1 Read the article without thinking about how to fill the gaps. Tick (✓) the true sentences below.

1 ☐ Hahn airport is not very busy.
2 ☐ Hahn is the closest airport to Frankfurt city centre.
3 ☐ Hahn is in a pleasant part of the countryside.

→ **Check your answers on p.124.**

TASK 2 Read through the article carefully and complete the first five gaps by writing one word in each space. Use the hints below to help you.

1 What preposition follows *consists*?
2 What conjunction can join the clause before the gap and the clause after it? Think about the meaning: is it a contrast? is it additional information?
3 Where is the countryside in relation to the airport? You will need a preposition in this space.
4 Note that the sentence gives the opinion of Ryanair and the International Air Transport Association. What phrase with *to* would make sense here?
5 Note that the word *indeed* indicates emphasis in this sentence. Note also that the text, so far, is in the present tense. The *-ing* form should give you a clue about the word which can fill the space.

TASK 3 Now complete the article by writing each missing word in the remaining gaps. Use only one word for each space.

HAHN AIRPORT

The airport for Frankfurt consists (**1**) .... a large shed. Three times a day, a plane arrives from Essex, (**2**) .... once daily another drops in from Ayrshire. Occasionally, a German charter flight takes off for sunnier shores. But otherwise the miles of rolling countryside (**3**) .... the airport remain blissfully undisturbed.

(**4**) .... to information from Ryanair and the International Air Transport Association, Hahn airport (**5**) .... indeed serving Europe's financial hub. But (**6**) .... Ryanair started flying there, some passengers have been alarmed to discover on landing that they are still a 90-minute bus ride away from the city of Frankfurt. (**7**) ...., few travellers have used the new no-frills flights (**8**) .... explore the peaceful backwater of Rheinland-Pfalz.

The small village of Hahn found (**9**) .... on the aviation map when the US Air Force built a large base there. With the end of the Cold War, the runway seemed likely to fall (**10**) .... disuse. The arrival of Ryanair has boosted its fortunes. Staff at Hahn's tourist office (**11**) .... point you towards some of the vineyards on the banks of the Mosel. Upstream it leads to the ancient Roman settlement of Trier; downstream, it meets (**12**) .... Rhine in the centre of Koblenz.

Should your final destination (**13**) .... Frankfurt, there is an alternative gateway: Frankfurt-Main International, 12 kilometres from the city centre, and the busiest airport in Continental Europe, (**14**) .... hundreds of flights each day. But it is not as cute (**15**) .... Hahn.

The Independent

→ **Check your answers on p.124.**

Listening

🕐 (spend about 25 minutes on this section)

Paper 4 Part 3 Multiple choice questions

ℹ️ **Exam information** The listening text in Part 3 will be the longest text in the Listening Paper. There will either be a sentence completion activity or multiple choice questions with four options to choose between.

▶ **Exam techniques**
- What should you do before you hear the recording? Why? Check your answer on p.124. Task 1 practises this.
- In this part of the Listening Paper you often have to interpret the speakers' feelings or attitudes. You should be able to do this from the actual words that the speakers use but you should also listen carefully to their intonation. This may help if you are unsure about an answer. Task 2 practises this.

TASK 1 Read through the multiple choice questions and options in task 3. Mark sentences 1–4 below T (true) or F (false).

1 Jane has been away on a trip.
2 Marlon might have missed some school to go on this trip.
3 There were beggars on the streets.
4 Jane thought the trip was just like a normal summer holiday.

➡ **Check your answers on p.124.**

TASK 2 🎧 10.1 Listen to the recording once and answer these questions.

1 The presenter sounds
A bored.
B doubtful.
C worried.
D disbelieving.

2 Jane sounds
A enthusiastic.
B unconcerned.
C worried.
D sad.

Did you base your answers to questions 1 and 2 above on the speaker's words or intonation?

➡ **Check your answers on p.124.**

TASK 3 Listen to the recording again and do the exam task.

For questions **1–8**, choose the correct option **A, B, C,** or **D**.

1 The presenter thinks that Jane's trip
   A is a trip everyone would want to do.
   B might have been a bit risky.
   C was a very sensible idea.
   D was an absolutely crazy thing to do.

2 How did Jane feel about taking her son to India?
   A She didn't want to take him.
   B She was worried about him missing school.
   C She had wanted to take him later.
   D She thought it was a good idea.

3 What was Jane's attitude towards inoculations for India?
   A Jane had all the inoculations but Marlon didn't.
   B She thought they did more harm than good.
   C She couldn't make up her mind.
   D She thought it would be too risky not to have them.

4 How did Marlon feel about the beggars?
   A He felt unhappy about them.
   B He wanted to give them sweets.
   C He got used to them.
   D He ignored them.

5 How did Jane feel about travelling by train?
   A It was always too crowded.
   B It was an experience not to be missed.
   C It was only OK if you travelled first class.
   D It was impossible to sleep on overnight journeys.

6 How did Jane feel about Marlon's friendship with Ram?
   A She was pleased about it.
   B She was surprised by it.
   C She thought it was a problem.
   D She thought Ram was a bad influence.

7 What health problems did they have while they were there?
   A They had a few problems.
   B They had trouble with their teeth.
   C They didn't have any problems.
   D The food and water gave them some stomach problems.

8 How does Jane feel about the trip now?
   A She thinks it was a mistake.
   B She's relieved that they got back OK.
   C She thinks it was a wonderful experience.
   D She thinks it was more expensive than it should have been.

➡ **Look at the transcript on p.125 and underline the words or phrases which helped you choose your answers. Then check your answers on p.125.**

Note In Part 3 of the Listening Paper, you will always hear the recording twice as you do the task.

Speaking

🕐 (spend about 30 minutes on this section)

Paper 5 Part 4 Discussion

ⓘ **Exam information** The whole interview will take about 15 minutes.

Exam techniques

- What should you be doing while your partner or the examiner is speaking? Why? Check your answer on p.125. Task 1 practises this.
- In this part of the interview it is important to be able to express your opinion and make points so that you keep the discussion going. Sometimes it may be necessary to make your point a second time in a different way so that people understand it clearly. Task 2 practises this.
- You will make your points more clearly if you illustrate them with examples. Task 3 practises this.

TASK 1 🎧 **10.2** Listen to the recording and answer these questions.

1 Where does the first speaker live?
2 Does he think there are too many tourists there?
3 How does the woman feel about tourism?
4 How do they all feel about theme parks?
5 Why does one of the men think car parks help?

→ **Check your answers on p.125.**

TASK 2 Listen to the recording again. Below are some phrases that can be used to show that you are going to explain your point again in a different way. Tick (✓) the ones you hear.

☐ Let me put it another way …
☐ What I meant was …
☐ Look at it this way …
☐ No, my point is that …
☐ Put it this way …
☐ What I'm trying to say is …

→ **Check your answers on p.125.**

TASK 3 Read the transcript of the recording on p.125. Find and underline five expressions used to illustrate a point or give examples.

→ **Check your answers on p.125.**

TASK 4 Look at questions 1–6 below. For each question think about

- what points you would make and how you would say them.
- how you could repeat each point in different words to make it clearer.
- how you could illustrate each point.

1 Has the way people take their holidays changed in your country over the last few years? If so, how? Why do you think this is?
2 How do people in your country spend their holidays?
3 What are the most popular holiday destinations in your country?
4 What problems does tourism cause in your country?
5 What solutions are there to these problems?
6 Does tourism bring any benefit to your country? If so, what?

TASK 5 Work in pairs. (If you are working alone, look at p.4.) Discuss the questions in task 4. If possible, record your discussion. Then play it back and think about how you might improve it.

How well are you doing?

Look back at the different sections in this unit and assess your performance for each one. Choose from A–C below.

Reading (multiple matching)	…
Writing (informal letter)	…
English In Use (open cloze)	…
Listening (multiple choice questions)	…
Speaking (discussion)	…

A No problem; I feel quite confident about this type of question.
B OK, but I need some more practice.
C I definitely need more practice. I find this type of question difficult.

Reading

🕐 (spend about 35 minutes on this section)

Paper 1 Part 2 Gapped text

ℹ️ **Exam information** Paper 1 Part 2 tests your understanding of how a text is structured and how the information, ideas, or opinions in the text are developed.

▶ **Exam techniques**

- Think about what you already know on the subject of the text. This information may help you understand the text. Task 1 practises this. Remember to answer questions according to what the text says, not what you think is correct.
- As well as getting a general idea of what the text is about, it is a good idea to decide what the purpose of the text is. This will help you when you do the task. Task 2 practises this.
- What will you look for in the text to help you decide how to reconstruct the article? Check your answer on p.126. Task 3 practises this.

TASK 1 **What do you already know about elephants? Tick (✔) the sentences you think are true.**

1 ☐ Elephants have a good memory.

2 ☐ Elephants live in family groups.

3 ☐ Elephants sometimes live for more than 50 years.

4 ☐ Elephants stay mainly in the same quite small area.

5 ☐ Numbers of elephants are decreasing.

TASK 2 **Read through the gapped text in task 3 quickly (four minutes maximum) and tick the best answer below.**

The main purpose of the article is to

1 ☐ show that elephants have extremely good memories.

2 ☐ explain how elephants are avoiding extinction.

3 ☐ explain how elephants use their memories.

4 ☐ compare memory in elephants and humans.

TASK 3 **Now read paragraphs A–G opposite. Use the underlined words and phrases to help you decide where the paragraphs go in the text.**

→ **Check your answers on p.126.**

For questions **1–6**, you must choose which of the paragraphs **A–G** opposite fit into the numbered gaps in the following article. Remember that there is one extra paragraph which does not fit in any of the gaps.

Why it is crucial that elephants have good memories

By Steve Connor, Science Editor

An elephant's memory is critical to the survival of its family, scientists have discovered, in a study that emphasises the importance of age and experience in the animal kingdom.

Elephants live in family groups of closely-related adult females led by a senior "matriarch", whose memory of other elephants in an area can ultimately decide on the breeding success of her family, the scientists found.

| 1 |

Karen McComb, of the University of Sussex and leader of the team, said yesterday that the findings will have an important effect on elephant conservation because poachers and hunters often kill the oldest females, thereby depriving the family of its wisest elder.

| 2 |

"Other large mammals, such as whales, dolphins and chimpanzees, also live in fluid social systems, 'socialising' with large numbers of their species, often in the course of roaming a large area of land or water. In this situation an ability to recognise friends amongst many acquaintances might be expected to have an effect on reproductive success," Dr McComb said.

| 3 |

The study, published in the journal *Science*, tested the ability of matriarchs to recognise the calls of other matriarchs recorded on tape. The scientists found that older matriarchs were better able to recognise the calls of the matriarchs and females they had already met and were friendly with.

| 4 |

Matriarchs who were older than 55 years were several thousand times more likely to group together defensively in response to calls from families they rarely met, compared with families which they often associated with.

| 5 |

The scientists also discovered that the older the matriarchs then the greater the chance of their families having the most success with rearing young elephants. "We believe this to be the first statistical link between social knowledge and reproductive success in any species," Dr McComb said.

| 6 |

A recent ban on the ivory trade had greatly helped to reduce poaching. There were signs, however, that killing for tusks was on the increase again. "Our research shows the unusual role that memory can play in the conservation of an endangered species," Dr Dunant said.

The Independent

A "The results highlight the disproportionate effect the hunting and poaching of mature animals might have for elephant populations," Dr McComb said. The findings also have implications for other social animals who rely on their elders for remembering and imparting information about the world around them.

B Younger matriarchs were less likely to recognise families they had already met, resulting in them adopting the defensive posture – with their family arranged in a circle with their trunks held high to smell any danger. This prevented them finding food and eating, which needs to be done almost continuously for the animals to eat enough to keep them in good health.

C The seven-year study in the Amboseli National Park of Kenya showed that the older the matriarch, the better her memory is of other elephants in the area and the better chance she has of passing on vital information about whether other elephants are potentially dangerous.

D Sarah Dunant, a member of the team from the Zoological Society of London, said African elephants were still under threat, with the population falling from an estimated 1.3 million individuals in 1979 to fewer than 500,000 in 1995.

E Elephants share with Man the distinction of being the longest-lived mammals, reaching an age of 60 to 70 years. Pregnancy lasts about 21 months, a young elephant suckles for nearly five years, and it becomes mature when about 15. Elephants' brains are larger than those of men, and the animals are very intelligent.

F Elephants roam many hundreds of miles and can meet up to 25 other families – representing some 175 adult females – for each year of roaming and searching for food. But the interaction between competing families can lead to serious quarrels with the loss of young elephants in extreme cases.

G In contrast, families with matriarchs aged 35 years were only 1.4 times more likely to respond to strangers than acquaintances. In fact the study found that older matriarchs had better social skills focused on recognising allies more easily.

Writing

⏱ (spend about 25 minutes on tasks 1–5; about an hour on task 6)

Paper 2 Part 2 Formal letter

ℹ **Exam information** You may be asked to write one of a variety of formal letters: making a complaint, applying for a job, requesting information, apologizing, etc.

▶ **Exam techniques**
- How should you organize your writing? Check your answer on p.126. Tasks 2 and 3 practise this.
- Make sure you use language appropriate to the formality and purpose of the letter. Tasks 1, 4, and 5 practise this.

TASK 1 Match the sentences below to an appropriate type of letter from the box. One has been done as an example.

> ~~job application~~ complaint apology reference
> explanation request for information letter of thanks
> request for advice

1 I would like to apply for the post of super-efficient personal assistant.   *job application*

2 As you can see, Mr Harrison has been a sound and hard-working member of staff and I would strongly recommend him for the post of Head of Computer Sciences.   ....

3 I am returning the watch together with a copy of the receipt and would be grateful if you would refund my money.   ....

4 I would be grateful if you would send me a brochure and details of your prices.   ....

5 Thank you very much indeed for organizing the guided tour of the museum for our delegates. They all enjoyed it very much and found it both stimulating and educational.   ....

6 I was wondering if you could recommend a suitable venue for our annual conference in September.   ....

7 Since so many people expressed interest in the scheme this year, we feel that it would be a good idea to run something similar next year.   ....

8 I would like to apologize for the poor service that you have experienced while travelling as a customer of our coach company.   ....

➔ **Check your answers on p.126.**

TASK 2 Read this question. Tick the ideas below which you think would be suitable topics for paragraphs in your letter of application.

You have seen the advertisement below and have decided to apply for the job.

WANTED
SUPER-EFFICIENT PERSONAL ASSISTANT

Dynamic, fast-moving, hard-working company director with poor memory and low organizational skills needs super-efficient personal assistant to take care of detail, make sure appointments are kept, and look after day-to-day office trivia. Do you have:

- charm, tact, and a good sense of humour
- excellent memory and organizational skills
- the ability to make independent decisions
- good word-processing skills

The post will also require considerable international travel and long, often anti-social, hours. An excellent salary and benefits await the right applicant.

Apply to: Matt Howard, Dotcommunications, Edgware Park, Hook, Hants.

Write your **letter of application** in 250 words. You must lay out your letter in an appropriate way but you do not need to include addresses.

- ☐ your word-processing skills
- ☐ your personality
- ☐ your desire for a high salary
- ☐ the skills required in your present job
- ☐ at university you went out with an Italian
- ☐ evidence of how you work independently

➜ **Check your answers on p.126.**

TASK 3 Now read the letter from Andi Bracewell and match the paragraph topics you ticked above to the middle three paragraphs in the letter. (Notice that at least one paragraph deals with two topics.) What are the topics of the first and last paragraphs? Complete the chart.

PARAGRAPH	TOPIC(S)
1	
2	
3	
4	word-processing skills
5	

➜ **Check your answers on p.126.**

Dear Matt

I would like to apply for the post of 'super-efficient personal assistant' advertised in yesterday's edition of 'The Independent'.

For the last five years I have been working as a personal assistant / number two to the manager of a small software company in Bristol. My work has mainly been concerned with organizing the life of my employer, making appointments, dealing with phone calls and correspondence, and looking after the office finances. I have an excellent memory and my employer often comments on how well his working life is organized. Furthermore, when he is away on business trips, I also have the responsibility in his absence for any decisions that may have an immediate effect on the business.

I believe I have a friendly, approachable personality and a good sense of humour. In a small company it is vital that the staff members have good relationships with one another and that the company maintains good relations with its clients. Over the five years I have been here we have had an extremely low rate of staff turnover and our client base has increased steadily, with very few customers taking their business elsewhere. These facts are evidence, I feel, of how our emphasis on the importance of good relations has worked.

I'm not bad at word processing. We always use the latest versions of the different packages and we've got all the good ones – Word, Excel, Powerpoint, that sort of thing. I'm also OK at shorthand, if you need to do any dictation. And I can also type from a cassette so if you record all your letters and things and give me the tape then I can type it out for you.

I am single with no family commitments and would welcome the opportunity to travel internationally. I have been happy in my present position but feel that the time has come to broaden my horizons and find a post that will be more challenging and develop my skills further.

I look forward to hearing from you.

Yours faithfully

Andi Bracewell

Andi Bracewell

TASK 4 One of the paragraphs in the letter above is written in an inappropriate register. Decide which paragraph it is and rewrite it.

TASK 5 Are you happy with the greeting at the beginning of the letter and the closing at the end of the letter? If not, how would you change them?

➜ **Check your answers to tasks 4 and 5 on p.126.**

TASK 6 Do the exam task below.

You see this advertisement and decide to apply for the job.

Well-known international management consultant requires

SUPER SECRETARY

Your duties will be: to make bookings with clients, organize travel arrangements and hotels, deal with phone calls and correspondence, and seek new business.

You will need: a good telephone manner, an excellent memory, good secretarial skills, a sense of humour, English and one other language, and a great ability to organize.

Good salary and benefits.

Write to: Rob Hanson, Excel, Thames St, Sutton KT23 4JT.

Write your **letter of application** in about 250 words.

English in Use

🕐 (spend about 30 minutes on this section)

Paper 3 Part 5 Register transfer

Exam information The two texts in Paper 3 Part 5 will have different registers or styles. They may also have different purposes.

▶ **Exam techniques**
- What should you do before you start trying to fill the gaps? Why? Task 1 practises this.
- Think about the purpose of each text. Ask yourself who will read each one and why. This information will help you identify the register when you fill the gaps. Task 2 practises this.
- What do you know about saying the same thing in English in more formal and less formal ways? Task 3 practises this.

→ **Check your answers on p.126.**

TASK 1 Read the first text in task 4 and answer these questions.

1 When must you pay for your tickets?
2 When are the tickets printed?
3 What is likely to happen if you amend your plans after you have paid for your tickets?
4 How long should your passport be valid for after your return?
5 Do you have to reconfirm onward and return flights?

→ **Check your answers on p.126.**

TASK 2 Read both texts in task 4. Answer these questions.

1 What is the purpose of the first text?
2 Who will read it and why?
3 Is the purpose of the second text the same or different?
4 Why is the style of the second text different from that of the first text?

→ **Check your answers on p.126.**

TASK 3 Match the more formal words and phrases on the left with the less formal equivalents on the right.

1 prior to	a the lot
2 to depart	b change
3 in full	c before
4 amendment	d to get in touch with
5 to ensure	e to leave
6 to contact	f to make sure
7 to return	g you don't need to
8 to allow entry	h at least
9 it is not necessary	i to let you in
10 a minimum of	j to get back

→ **Check your answers on p.126.**

TASK 4 Now do the exam task.

Read the airline information below and use it to complete the numbered gaps **1–13** in the informal note which follows. *Use no more than two words* for each gap. The words you need do not occur in the airline information. The exercise begins with an example (**0**).

PRE-DEPARTURE INFORMATION

Thank you for making a reservation with Flightfinders.

Payment in full is due eight weeks prior to departure. Please note that cheques take ten working days to process.

Tickets are printed when paid for in full. This means that after payment has been taken any amendments to your travel plans may mean that fresh reservations have to be made and your documents re-issued. In these circumstances, the full cancellation conditions may apply.

Please ensure that your passport will be valid for a minimum of six months upon your return to the UK. You may be refused entry to certain countries if your passport is near its expiry date.

Some airlines may tell you that reconfirmation of return flights is no longer necessary. Our experiences have shown otherwise. To avoid inconvenience and disappointment, we advise you to contact the airlines personally to reconfirm reservations and details of your return flight.

INFORMAL NOTE

Carol

I've just been reading the small print on the Flightfinders invoice and there are a few things I ought to tell you about our (**0**) *booking*.

Firstly, we have to pay the (**1**) .... eight weeks (**2**) .... leave. In fact, it would be a good idea to send them the money ten weeks before because they need ten days to process a cheque. Once we've paid, we can't make any (**3**) .... to our plans. Well, we can – but it's not a good idea. It would mean starting all over again and giving us (**4**) .... tickets.

Also could you (**5**) .... your passport is valid for (**6**) .... six months (**7**) .... we get back. They might not (**8**) .... in otherwise.

The other thing is: when we arrive, we must ring to (**9**) .... we have seats on the flight (**10**) .... Some airlines say you don't (**11**) .... to do this but Flightfinders reckon that we (**12**) .... We need to get in (**13**) .... the airline personally to do that.

Give us a ring if you've got any questions.

Sue

→ **Check your answers on p.126.**

Listening

(spend about 30 minutes on this section)

Paper 4 Part 3 Multiple choice questions

ℹ️ **Exam information** There will be between six and twelve questions in this part of the Listening Paper. If there are multiple choice questions, there will be four options.

▶ **Exam techniques**
- There may be two or three speakers in this part of the paper. It is important to work out quickly how many there are and who they are. This will help you to understand the conversation. Task 1 practises this.
- What should you do while you are waiting for the recording to start? Why? Check your answer on p.126. Task 2 practises this.

TASK 1 🎧11.1 Listen to four short recordings. For each one work out how many speakers there are. Decide what their relationship is to each other and who they are. Complete the chart below.

recording	no. of speakers	relationship between speakers
1	2	mother - son
2	2	boss - assistant
3	3	teacher - students
4	2	interviewer - interviewee

➜ **Check your answers on p.126.**

TASK 2 Read through the multiple choice questions and options in task 3 and tick (✔) the sentence which probably best describes the conversation.

☐ The effect of age on memory and what you can do about it.

☐ Why young people have better memories than old people.

☐ It is more important to exercise our bodies than our minds.

➜ **Check your answer on p.126.**

TASK 3 🎧11.2 You will hear part of a radio interview with two people talking about memory. Do the exam task below.

For questions **1–6**, choose the correct option **A**, **B**, **C**, or **D**. Listen to the recording twice.

1 Why is Reginald Potter on the show?
   A Someone else was late.
   B He wants to meet Sheila Matthews.
   C He wants to publicize his new book.
   D He wants to find out about memory improvement courses.

2 When Reginald Potter has appointments, he
   A often forgets which restaurant to meet people at.
   B is sure people will recognize him.
   C always knows what the person he is meeting looks like.
   D sometimes forgets people's names.

3 Sheila Matthews believes that as we get older our memory will
   A probably get a little bit worse.
   B inevitably get much worse.
   C sometimes get better.
   D stay the same.

4 Sheila Matthews explains that people often find that
   A names and places are the most difficult things to remember.
   B they have a good memory for some things and a bad memory for others.
   C it is more difficult to remember words than music.
   D the written word is the easiest thing to remember.

5 How does Sheila Matthews suggest that memory can be improved?
   A Losing weight can help improve your memory.
   B She can only improve people's memory for names.
   C There are lots of different ways of improving one's memory.
   D Repeating something is always the best way to remember it.

6 How does Reginald Potter feel about what he has discovered?
   A Surprised and enthusiastic.
   B Not very interested – he knew it already.
   C Interested – but it is not of use to him.
   D Worried.

➜ **Check your answers on p.126.**

Language development

Memory

Complete sentences 1–8 below with words from the box.

memo remind memorable remember
memoirs retrospect memory memorize

1 I know we decided to take the early train but in .... I think we should have waited for Jack.

2 She fell and hit her head on the pavement and now she's lost her ....

3 Can you .... what time the bus leaves?

4 You asked me to .... you to make a doctor's appointment this week.

5 Angela's phone number? That's easy. 494847. It's very ....

6 You must keep your PIN number secret. .... it. Don't write it down.

7 I don't think Astrid knows there's a meeting next week. I'll send her a ....

8 He retired from politics in 1996 and spent the next few years writing his ....

➜ **Check your answers on p.127.**

Speaking

🕐 (spend about 30 minutes on this section)

Paper 5 Part 4 Fluency

ℹ️ **Exam information** One of the things the examiners give you marks for is discourse management. This is the ability to express yourself in coherent, connected speech.

▶ **Exam technique**
In this part of the Speaking Paper it is important to try and speak fluently and keep up a coherent flow of language. One way of improving your fluency is to speak a lot! Whenever possible, practise speaking English with your friends and classmates. It also helps your fluency if you have a lot of things to say. Think of ways of making your answers longer but keeping them interesting. Tasks 1 to 3 practise this.

TASK 1 Look at the quiz below. For each question think of the answer you would give. Then think how you could extend your answer by giving a reason, or expressing an opinion, or telling a story.

The MEMORY QUIZ

1 How good do you think your memory is?
  A excellent
  B good
  C OK
  D awful

2 What things do you remember easily and which do you find difficult to remember?
  A names
  B faces
  C things you have to do
  D numbers
  E directions
  F …

3 How do you try and remember to do something? Do you …
  A write it down on a piece of paper?
  B write it on your hand?
  C tie a knot in your handkerchief?
  D do nothing – just remember it?
  E …

4 How do you remember a word in English?
  A I write it down with a translation.
  B I write it down in an English sentence.
  C I say it to myself a few times until I know it.
  D I write it on a piece of paper and keep it in my pocket.
  E …

5 Have you ever forgotten something very important?
  A Yes. (What was it?)
  B No.

→ Look at p.127 for some further ideas on what to say

TASK 2 Work in pairs. (If you are working alone, look at p.4.) Discuss the quiz above. If possible, record your discussion. Then play it back and think about how you might improve it.

TASK 3 🎧 11.3 Now listen to two native speakers discussing the first part of the quiz and answer this question.

Who do you think has the better memory? The man or the woman? Why?

Listen again and answer these questions.

1 Why does the man think he has an awful memory?
2 How does the man explain that he has a good memory for faces?
3 How is the woman affected by having a good memory for things she has to do?
4 Why does the man forget telephone numbers?
5 How easily does the man remember directions?
6 What do they think is wrong with writing something on your hand?

→ Check your answers on p.127.

How well are you doing?

Look back at the different sections in this unit and assess your performance for each one. Choose from A–C below.

Reading (gapped text)	…
Writing (formal letter)	…
English In Use (register transfer)	…
Listening (multiple choice questions)	…
Speaking (fluency)	…

A No problem; I feel quite confident about this type of question.
B OK, but I need some more practice.
C I definitely need more practice. I find this type of question difficult.

Reading

🕐 (spend about 35 minutes on this section)

Paper 1 Part 3 Multiple choice questions

ℹ **Exam information** This part of the Reading Paper tests a detailed understanding of the text, including opinions and attitudes. Remember: you are not allowed dictionaries in any part of the exam.

▶ **Exam techniques**
- What should you do first? Task 1 practises this.
- Do the questions follow the order of the text or not? What should you do when you have read a question? Task 2 practises this.
→ **Check your answers on p.127.**

TASK 1 Read quickly through the article (three or four minutes maximum). Tick (✔) the question below which the article answers best.

☐ Why has Super Mario been such a successful video game?

☐ How did Shigeru Miyamoto develop the Super Mario game?

☐ Why is Shigeru Miyamoto so important in the video game scene?

☐ What was wrong with video games before Shigeru Miyamoto came along?

→ **Check your answer on p.127.**

TASK 2 Read through the article slowly and carefully. The multiple choice questions require careful answering so it is a good idea to be familiar with the text before you read the questions.

TASK 3 Now read the multiple choice questions carefully. Mark the lines in the article where you think you will find the answer to each question.

→ **Check your answers on p.127.**

SUPER MIYAMOTO

Suits are heavily outnumbered by combat trousers and black T-shirts at the European Computer Trade Show. London's Olympia exhibition hall is filled with all manner of noises as expressionless twenty-year-olds race, hack, shoot and explode each other in virtual spaceships, enchanted forests, undersea kingdoms and the like. In the walkway
5 round the Nintendo stand there's a mass of people. What's going on? A small and modest middle-aged man is posing for photographs and signing autographs for a crowd of fans of all nationalities. Wherever they are from, they recognise him instantly. It is Mister Mario.

Mister Mario, better known as Shigeru Miyamoto, here on a rare visit to the UK, is an unlikely chieftain of cool. He's about 20 years older than most of the crowd at the show
10 for a start, and he is soberly dressed in a beige suit. But video developers refer to him, without any irony, as 'a god' and the video-gaming world is highly conscious of the debt it owes him. For 20-odd years ago, Miyamoto created not only Super Mario but Donkey Kong.

In the process he established the concept of the 'platform' game – the now-standard
15 format by which players progress from level to level, completing tasks as they go, copied in thousands of other games. He also invented the recognisable 'character', again now standard, and the forerunner of every screen face, from Sonic the Hedgehog to Lara Croft. As if this weren't enough, he is still at the cutting edge of video-gaming technology; his most recent creation, *Legend of Zelda: Ocarina of Time*, has been praised by gaming
20 experts as 'the greatest video game ever made' for its combination of originality and technical accomplishment.

Miyamoto's time is jealously guarded, and the interview room at the Nintendo stand was quite crowded, what with the translator, the PR lady, and the two company onlookers. So meeting him isn't a terribly intimate experience, which seems a shame, because he is

TASK 4 Now do the exam task.

For questions **1–6**, choose the letter **A, B, C**, or **D**. Give only one answer to each question.

1 According to the article, most computer game fans at the European Computer Trade Show
   A are wearing suits.
   B know what Shigeru Miyamoto looks like.
   C are at the Nintendo stand.
   D are middle aged.

2 Shigeru Miyamoto is highly regarded in the video game world because he
   A invested huge sums of money to develop the Super Mario game.
   B developed Sonic the Hedgehog and Lara Croft after Super Mario.
   C invented the idea of the platform game.
   D created the first Nintendo video game.

3 According to the article, the writer is disappointed because
   A he was not invited to the preview.
   B Miyamoto did not seem to be taking things seriously enough.
   C there were too many other people present when he met Miyamoto.
   D Miyamoto is not as creative as he used to be.

→ **Check your answers on p.127.**

remarkably smiling and friendly for such an exalted figure – even
rather jolly. At the pre-show guests-only preview, he staged an
impromptu air-guitar show on stage (playing the guitar is his main
non-game hobby).
   Back in the prehistoric 1970s, Miyamoto studied industrial design
at college, and joined Nintendo in 1977. Its main business back then
was playing cards and stationery, with a sideline in arcade games.
'While a lot of my friends were trying to make big stuff like cars and
consumer electronics, I rather wanted to work on concept work. I
thought toys and small stuff would be interesting. With these
commodities I can surprise the world, surprise the others,' he
explains. An enthusiastic reader of *manga*, the Japanese cartoon
comics, he took it in his stride when he was given carte blanche to
design a completely new game for Nintendo. 'When I was a kid I used
to draw cartoon comics myself. When you make *manga* you have to
decide what kind of characters, what kind of world you should draw,
and from the beginning to the end there have got to be scenarios. So
for me that kind of concept is taken for granted.'
   He decided to include these elements in his new project; elements
particularly absent in the popular video games of the time. 'I think the
reason why I was unique was that mainly there were programs made
by the technical types, the engineers who didn't have the artistic
background or design background. There were no artists or designers
in the field. I was boasting that I was one of the five best game
designers in the world because there were no game designers at that
point!'
   Whether you believe that Miyamoto is a creative giant on the level
of Steven Spielberg (who himself praises Miyamoto as a genius) or
whether you think the whole video-game scene is a sorry waste of
human ingenuity, it is unlikely that you are completely unaware of
Miyamoto's impact. The Super Mario series has sold more than 140
million games worldwide. A survey earlier this year found that 97% of
16- to 21-year-olds instantly recognised Super Mario, the cheerful,
moustachioed, princess-rescuing cartoon plumber, while only 24 per
cent were able to name the government minister in charge of finance.
The latest incarnations of Mario and his friend Donkey Kong (genial,
hairy, banana-collecting gorilla) have moved into state-of-the-art 3D
graphics, and are so realistic that Kong can be found distracting the
real gorillas at Longleat safari park on their own television set.

Independent on Sunday

4   Miyamoto enjoyed working for Nintendo because he
   A   wanted to develop something new and unexpected.
   B   had an industrial design background.
   C   was allowed to create a video game based on a
       Japanese comic.
   D   loved creating cartoon characters.

5   Miyamoto was so successful because
   A   he told everyone how good he was.
   B   he was a better technical engineer than anyone else at
       the time.
   C   the idea of having a story and different scenes was
       completely new.
   D   Steven Spielberg thought he was a genius.

6   Super Mario, Miyamoto's famous video game character,
   A   is recognized by 97% of the population.
   B   has not been updated by Nintendo.
   C   travels to a safari park in his newest adventure.
   D   is better known by 16–21 year-olds than some
       important politicians.

Language development

Adjective–noun collocations

1 Find the following adjective–noun collocations in the
article. Underline them, and notice how they are used and
match them to a definition below.

1   enchanted forest
2   recent creation
3   gaming experts
4   technical accomplishment
5   intimate experience
6   exalted figure
7   industrial design
8   artistic background

a   people who know all about computer games
b   highly-praised person
c   close, personal event
d   magic woods
e   scientific skill
f   something that has just been made
g   past experience in art
h   the planning of machines, factories, etc.

→ **Check your answers on p.127.**

2 Complete the review below with the appropriate form
of the collocations from exercise 1.

The Magic Kingdom

Videorama £39.99

This .... [1] by Jay Walls and Betty Hart for
Videorama is a masterpiece of .... [2] that
will have .... [3] reaching for their wallets.
The game play features a journey through an
.... [4] in which you meet the
.... [5] of the great magician, Mandrango.
With his help you enter the magic kingdom and perform a
number of intellectually stimulating tasks. Without giving away
any of the storyline or the amazing effects, it is enough to say
that this game brings together Walls' genius for
.... [6] and Hart's impressive
.... [7]. The result is both an
.... [8] and a mind-blowing array of
special effects. Buy it and enjoy!

→ **Check your answers on p.127.**

Writing

⏱ (spend about 25 minutes on tasks 1–3; about an hour on task 4)

Paper 2 Part 2 Report

> ℹ **Exam information** Examiners will give good marks for well-organized, accurate, and appropriate answers which show a range of vocabulary and structure. They will penalize irrelevance, repetition, illegibility, inaccuracy, and lack of organization.

▶ **Exam techniques**
- Give your report a clear introduction. Often this will state the purpose of the report and how the information was gathered. Task 1 practises this.
- If your report has a conclusion or summary, make sure it is clear and concise. If you intend to express a personal opinion or recommendation, where should you do this? Task 2 practises this.
- What should you do when you have finished writing? Task 3 practises this.
- ➜ Check your answers on p.128.

TASK 1 Read the question. Then look at the three introductions A, B, and C below. Which do you think is best? Why? What is wrong with the others?

You have been asked to produce a report on some clothes shops in your town. You need to consider the range and style of clothes, the prices, and the attitude of staff towards customers in each of the shops. Write your report in about **250** words.

A We visited shops in Netterton for this report. We looked at the clothes on sale and what they cost. We also talked to the staff in the shops. Some of them were quite friendly. I didn't think much of Woollens.

B This report looks at some of the clothes shops in Netterton. We list them by name and give information about each one which we hope will be useful to people shopping in the town.

C The aim of this report is to provide useful information about a number of the more popular clothes shops in Netterton. The clothes shops listed were all visited by our researchers, who rated them in terms of friendliness of service, range of clothes on sale, style and fashion consciousness, and price.

➜ Check your answers on p.128.

TASK 2 Look at the three conclusions A, B, and C below. Which do you think is best? Why? What is wrong with the others?

A **Recommendation**
Don't go to Woollens. It has cheap and nasty sweaters. Buckley's is OK – a bit on the expensive side. LBJ is good value. But Epic is definitely the coolest place in town.

B **Conclusion**
Older customers will find Woollens more to their taste, whereas the younger generation will probably head straight for Buckley's or Epic. Epic boasts the latest fashions at reasonable prices. Buckley's, on the other hand, is where people will go for something more expensive and unusual for a special occasion. LBJ has a wide appeal at affordable prices.

C We thought Woollens was rather old-fashioned. LBJ had reasonable clothes at reasonable prices. Buckley's had good stuff but was really rather expensive. Epic had great clothes and the prices were good too.

➜ Check your answers on p.128.

TASK 3 Read the two paragraphs below. Cross out four extra words in paragraph A. Correct six spelling mistakes in paragraph B.

A **Woollens**
34 High St
Woollens opened in Netterton High Street for twenty years ago. It stocks sensible clothes that do appeal to the middle aged rather than the young. It has a good range of both the men's and women's clothes: sweaters, comfortable skirts and trousers, and shirts and blouses. Prices are so reasonable and they have two sales a year. The staff are friendly and helpful.

B **LBJ**
16 Church St
LBJ is the shop for all your clothing needs. It has a very wide rainge of goods from coats and boots for outdoor wear, to shirts, sweaters, and trousers, right down to underclothes, socks, and hankerchiefs. Surprisingly you will find both up-to-the-minute desinger names as well as many more tradicional brands. Even more surprisingly perhaps, everything is reasonably prized. The staff are knowledgable, polite, and eager to please.

➜ Check your answers on p.128.

TASK 4 Answer the question in task 1 with reference to the clothes shops in your town. Write a report in about 250 words.

English In Use

Paper 3 Part 6 Gapped text

ⓘ **Exam information** In the exam you will have about 15 minutes to answer each part of Paper 3. Part 6 tests your understanding of how the different parts of a text are linked together.

▶ **Exam techniques**
- What should you do before you start trying to fill the gaps? Why? Task 1 practises this.
- How will you decide which option goes into each gap? What factors will influence your decision? Task 2 practises this.
- → Check your answers on p.128.

TASK 1 Read the article and answer these questions.

1 What is tram-surfing?
2 What is happening to the new trams?
3 What is train-surfing?
4 Where did it start?
5 What are rollerbladers doing?
6 Why are the authorities worried?

→ Check your answers on p.128.

TASK 2 Answer questions 1–6 below about the corresponding gap in the article in task 3.

1 Why are the outside ledges being removed? Do they want children to stand on these ledges?
2 Representatives have gone to the schools for a reason. What structure expresses that reason?
3 What do the children and teenagers hold? What parts of speech could follow *hold*?
4 What might Tom Cruise have done in *Mission: Impossible* that would have encouraged train-surfing?
5 What caused the arrival of tram-surfing? What phrase means *because of*?
6 What do you think the police have tried to do about rollerbladers? What word means the same as *stop*?

→ Check your answers on p.128.

TASK 3 Now do the exam task.

For questions **1–6**, read the following text and then choose from the list **A–J** the best phrase given below it to fill each of the spaces. Each correct phrase may only be used once. Some of the suggested answers do not fit at all. The exercise begins with an example (**0**).

TRAM-SURFING

A craze among young people for 'tram-surfing' – holding on to the outside of moving carriages – has forced a city to redesign its fleet of hi-tech vehicles.

Manchester decided to take this action on the new extension of their system after youngsters were spotted tram-surfing (**0**) *J* through the city. The 32 trams will be sent back to the workshop to have an outside ledge removed, (**1**) *B*.

'We're extremely concerned about this,' said Jane Neraney, a spokeswoman for the Greater Manchester Passenger Transport Executive. The executive has sent representatives to schools (**2**) *A* the dangers, and promises a new classroom campaign in the autumn.

The sport is a version of the deadly train-surfing craze that first started in Brazil, where it claims up to 200 lives a year. Children and teenagers hold (**3**) *F* the trains, often at high speed, ducking under bridges and electric cables.

Train-surfing came to Britain in the late 1980s with a series of horrific accidents and deaths on British Rail. A more recent outbreak was blamed on the hit movie *Mission: Impossible*, which had Tom Cruise (**4**) *H*.

Tram-surfing has arrived (**5**) *D* the rebirth of streetcar systems in Sheffield, Birmingham and Croydon as well as Manchester.

In Sheffield, managers said rollerbladers had joined the surfers, hanging on to the back of the trams at 45 kph. A police campaign seems (**6**) *I* that practice. In the latest outbreak in Manchester, children have been seen hanging on to vehicle mirrors. These examples of teenage bravado may appear gentler than the railway version, but the authorities are still extremely concerned at the prospect of death or injury.

Independent On Sunday

A to warn children of
B preventing children from gaining a foothold
C to be run over by a car
D thanks to
E travelling at only 35 kilometres per hour
F on to the top or sides of
G encouraging people to travel safely
H climbing over train roofs
I to have ended
J *as they sped*

→ Check your answers on p.128.

Listening

(spend about 30 minutes on this section)

Paper 4 Part 2
Sentence completion

ℹ Exam information Remember that you will hear Part 2 once only and that you will mainly hear just one person speaking. You will hear some of the information more than once because the speaker may paraphrase or recap on what he or she is saying. You will be listening for specific information. During this paper you write your answers on the question paper. You are allowed ten minutes at the end to transfer your answers to an answer sheet.

▶ **Exam technique**
- What can you do while you are waiting for the recording to start? Why? Tasks 1 and 2 practise this.
➜ Check your answer on p.128.

TASK 1 Look at the sentences in task 3 carefully. Think about these questions before you listen to the recording.

1 Do you think that what Charlie cooked last week has any relation to what he is going to cook this week?
2 What ingredients do you know that Charlie will be using?
3 Is he cooking a main course or a dessert?
4 Do you think he will be using an oven?

➜ Check your answers on p.128.

TASK 2 Think about what sort of words you are likely to hear in this type of programme. Tick (✔) the words you think you might hear.

☐ slice	☐ skin	☐ gently	☐ paper
☐ smash	☐ fur	☐ freshly	☐ match
☐ crush	☐ prescription	☐ softly	☐ shrimp
☐ saw	☐ recipe	☐ loudly	☐ leaf

➜ Check your answers on p.128.

TASK 3 🎧12.1 You will hear a cookery programme on the radio. For questions 1–9, fill in the missing information in the sentences. You will hear the recording once only.

Charlie demonstrated the way to make [_____ **1**] in the previous week's programme.

He is going to cook a [_____ **2**] in this week's programme.

He [_____ **3**] this recipe.

You should use [_____ **4**] to fry the onion and garlic.

You need to [_____ **5**] and chop the tomatoes.

You can add some water or [_____ **6**] if necessary.

You can buy [_____ **7**] olives to make things easier.

You should use [_____ **8**] parsley.

You can add some [_____ **9**] black pepper to taste.

➜ Check your answers on p.128.

76 UNIT 12

Speaking

⏱ (spend about 30 minutes on this section)

Paper 5 Part 2 Explaining

ℹ **Exam information** In Part 2 of the Speaking Paper you may be asked to explain or hypothesize about something you are given to look at. Remember that you will only have about one minute to do this.

▶ **Exam technique**
Remember there are no right or wrong answers in the interview. The examiner is assessing your English not your opinions or your general knowledge.

TASK 1 🎧 **12.2** You are going to hear a recording of someone discussing the picture above. Tick (✔) the different people you hear mentioned who are at the fashion show.

☐ models   ☐ ordinary people
☐ designers   ☐ film stars
☐ tailors   ☐ photographers
☑ buyers   ☐ journalists

TASK 2 Listen again and write down why the speaker suggests the different people may be at the fashion show.

➜ Check your answers on p.128.

TASK 3 Now look at the transcript on p.128. Find and underline the different expressions used to explain and give reasons why the different people are at the fashion show.

➜ Check your answers on p.128.

TASK 4 Work in pairs. (If you are working alone, look at p.4.) Look at the pictures below. Describe one each and discuss why you think the people are doing what they are doing. If possible, record your descriptions. Then play them back and think about how you might improve them.

How well are you doing?

Look back at the different sections in this unit and assess your performance for each one. Choose from A–C below.

Reading (multiple choice questions)	…
Writing (report)	…
English In Use (gapped text)	…
Listening (sentence completion)	…
Speaking (explaining)	…

A No problem; I feel quite confident about this type of question.
B OK, but I need some more practice.
C I definitely need more practice. I find this type of question difficult.

13 Conflict

Reading

(spend about 35 minutes on this section)

Paper 1 Part 4
Multiple matching

ⓘ Exam information Remember that time is one of the most important factors in Paper 1. Part 4 may contain the longest text. There is a lot to read in a relatively short time. It is therefore important to read quickly and to find the answers quickly.

▶ **Exam techniques**
Think about the different techniques you have used in the earlier units of the book. Select appropriate techniques for dealing with the exam question. Tasks 1 and 2 give further practice in useful techniques.

TASK 1 First look quickly at the texts in task 3 containing information about different types of martial arts. Read only the first and last two lines of each text. Then look at the questions below and tick (✓) the ones that you think you will be able to answer about some of the texts.

☐ Which country does it come from?
☐ Does it train the mind and the body?
☐ What techniques are involved?
☐ Where can I learn it?
☐ How old is it?
☐ Do you need a weapon?
☐ What time are classes?
☐ How popular is it?

➜ Check your answers on p.128.

TASK 2 Read through questions 1–15 in exam task 3 so that you know what information you are looking for.

Read the first two statements. Look quickly at each text and underline any relevant information.

➜ Check your answers on p.129.

TASK 3 Now do the exam task.

For questions **1–15**, answer by choosing from the list **A–H**. Some of the choices may be required more than once. When more than one answer is required, these may be given in any order.

Of which martial arts are the following stated?

You use weapons for this.	1 ..... 2 .....
This is neither Japanese nor Chinese.	3 ..... 4 .....
This is a mixture of different martial arts disciplines.	5 .....
This is very good for defending yourself against a number of people.	6 .....
This used to be illegal.	7 .....
You do not hurt your opponent.	8 .....
This requires you to wear special clothing and equipment.	9 .....
This is widely used by security personnel.	10 .....
You might see this as part of a performance.	11 .....
	12 .....
This relies on subtlety rather than strength.	13 .....
In this you concentrate on defeating your opponent as quickly as possible.	14 .....
	15 .....

A Aikido
B Shotokan Karate
C Capoeira
D Kenpo Karate
E Wing Chun Kung Fu
F Wushu
G Taekwondo
H Kendo

Ⓐ AIKIDO

Aikido originated in the centuries-old tradition of the Japanese martial arts and is a form of *budo* – a way of life that seeks to polish the self through a mixture of hard physical training and spiritual discipline.

Unlike other martial arts, with Aikido one does not seek to overpower an opponent. There is no attack in Aikido. Its uniqueness as a martial art lies in its awareness of a deep sense of harmony with all of creation. Training involves not only defending oneself but bringing the attacker under control without the necessity of causing injury.

Because of Aikido's noncompetitive, harmonious philosophy, men and women of all ages can help each other as they train together, at an energy level appropriate for each individual.

Ⓑ SHOTOKAN KARATE

Shotokan Karate is a weaponless martial art developed in Okinawa, Japan. It emphasizes power, speed and efficiency in combat. Skilled practitioners defeat their opponents with as few techniques and as little effort as possible. This is particularly useful when facing multiple opponents. Shotokan is distinguished from other martial arts by the lines and the strength of its punches, blocks, and kicks. Precise techniques, accompanied by mastery and focus of energy flows and a deep knowledge of the body's vital points, make this karate style a comprehensive system for self-defense and combat.

However, Shotokan Karate is much more than just a way to defend and fight – it is a complete system in which the training itself has profound effects on the trainee. It is an ideal way to become and stay fit, as it combines intense aerobic and anaerobic exercises. It is a way to increase self-discipline and the confidence to overcome everyday problems. Shotokan Karate encourages and helps in the exploration and understanding of both the physical and mental self.

➜ Check your answers on p.129.

C CAPOEIRA

Capoeira is a breathtaking Afro-Brazilian art which combines practical martial arts, dance, acrobatics, music, history and philosophy. The origin of Capoeira is obscure since its evolution during the Brazilian slave trade was not well documented. Most theories suggest that movements were adapted from traditional Angolan dance and this evolved into techniques for self-defense. When Capoeira was outlawed by slave owners, the fighting art then appeared in the form of a dance through the addition of music and acrobatic movements. In the 1930s Capoeira was legalized in Brazil and is now spreading throughout the world.

D KENPO KARATE

Kenpo Karate is an eclectic martial art, which seeks to take the most efficient techniques for self-defense from many other disciplines. Kenpo tends to be oriented toward self defence in modern attacker / defender situations, although students are encouraged to take part in competitions as a way of advancing their own personal growth in the martial arts.

Kenpo includes movements from both Chinese and Japanese martial arts styles. It emphasizes multiple strike defences, joint locks, evasions, pressure points, sweeps and kicks. Instructors typically have experience in multiple martial arts disciplines, and make use of this other knowledge in their teachings.

E WING CHUN KUNG FU

Wing Chun Kung Fu's roots can be traced from the Southern Shaolin Temple in China to the late Grand Master Yip Man. It is one of the few martial arts that does not attribute its origins to a man. Although popularized as Bruce Lee's "mother art", Wing Chun remains substantially different from his practice. Wing Chun is taught mainly as an internally-oriented style. It stresses technique, sensitivity, and subtle awareness instead of pure strength. It provides practical self-defence for men and women and a means for developing the mind and spirit.

F WUSHU

Modern Wushu is a martial art which combines a foundation in the traditional Chinese fighting arts with a modern emphasis on aesthetics, grace, and performance. It emphasizes a combination of strength and flexibility rarely seen in other martial arts or sports. Both a martial art and a performance art, Wushu is the national sport of China, and is practised throughout the world. Along with open-hand training, Wushu athletes spend considerable time training with weapons such as broadsword, staff, spear, and straight sword.

G TAEKWONDO

Taekwondo is a form of unarmed combat which originated in Korea over 2,000 years ago. Taekwondo's effectiveness is derived from the development of body flexibility and flowing movements, as well as pure strength. It involves the skilled application of punches, kicks, and blocks to bring about the rapid defeat of an opponent. Recently, Taekwondo has gained world-wide popularity for its simple and effective self-defence applications as well as a means of figure and weight control. Many police, armed forces, private security companies, and educational institutions have seriously adopted Taekwondo training.

H KENDO

Kendo is a Japanese style of fencing which developed during the Meiji period in Japan (1868–1912) from the two-handed sword fighting techniques of the samurai. Today Kendo, which means "way of the sword", is practiced with *shinai* (bamboo swords), and fighters wear protective equipment covering the target areas: the head, wrists, and abdomen. The *shinai* is approximately four feet in length and is made of four carefully formed bamboo pieces bound together. The protective equipment consists of a face mask, a breastplate, fencing gloves, and a kind of apron to protect the stomach and hips. Under this protection, *kendoka* (students of kendo) wear a wide split skirt, reaching the ankles.

Language development

Nouns and adjectives

1 Complete the chart below.

NOUN	ADJECTIVE	NOUN	ADJECTIVE
protection			popular
harmony			confident
	injured	tradition	
	efficient		sensitive
competition		effect	
spirit			flexible

→ Check your answers by finding the words in texts A–H. Then, if necessary, check on p.129.

2 Complete the sentences below using words from the chart in exercise 1.

1 He's in hospital with a very nasty .... He fell off a ladder and broke his leg.

2 Buy some aspirin. They're very .... at getting rid of headaches.

3 He's so .... He's answered all the letters and tidied the office.

4 You need to wear these headphones as .... against the noise of the engine.

5 The government's .... has decreased considerably since they raised taxes.

6 It's .... in Britain to wear white at weddings and black at funerals.

7 She's very .... that she's going to pass all her exams – but I'm not so sure.

8 I don't think we've ever argued. We have an extremely .... relationship.

9 You can't tell him off. He's so .... he just bursts into tears.

10 I don't know what time she's arriving so we'll just have to be .... about what time we have lunch.

→ Check your answers on p.129.

🔍 Close up

Find and complete these phrases from the texts, as in the example.
martial arts

.... training .... movements
.... discipline .... growth
.... effects .... combat
.... self .... strength
.... self .... equipment

→ Check your answers on p.129.

Writing

⏱ (spend about 25 minutes on tasks 1–4; about an hour on task 5)

Paper 2 Part 2 Review

ⓘ **Exam information** In the Writing Paper you may have to write a review of a book, film, play, or TV programme.

▶ **Exam techniques**
- The purpose of a review is to give information about the subject and an opinion on it. You need to think about the sort of things you should mention in a review and how to organize them. Tasks 1 and 2 practise this.
- By choosing your words carefully you can bring your description to life and also indicate your opinion. Tasks 3 and 4 practise this.

TASK 1 Tick (✔) the ideas that you would expect to find in a book review.

☐ the plot / story
☐ the writer's style
☐ the main characters
☐ strengths of the book
☐ other books by the same author
☐ the organization of the book
☐ the picture on the cover
☐ the development of the characters
☐ weaknesses of the book
☐ the theme / idea behind the book
☐ the opinion of the reviewer
☐ the number of copies printed

TASK 2 Look at the review below. Match each paragraph (A, B, C, or D) to one of the boxes below the review.

The Shape of Snakes
Minette Walters
Macmillan £16.99

A Minette Walters's seventh novel, *The Shape of Snakes*, is, quite simply, remarkable. An ambitiously-structured detective thriller, narrated by a woman, Mrs Ranelagh, who, in 1978, found a neighbour dying in the rain-soaked street in front of her house, it succeeds magnificently at almost every level. Walters's psychological thrillers have always combined compassion and a strong social conscience with a ruthless ability to create unease, suspense and, sometimes, horror.

B *The Shape of Snakes* is angrily concerned with racism and our attitude to mental conditions: the dying woman, Annie Butts, is black and suffers from Tourette's syndrome, whose symptoms include sudden body movements, talking to yourself and unwillingly swearing and using rude words. Those around her, seeing only the symptoms and ignorant of the cause, nickname her 'Mad Annie'.

C Although the court decided Annie's death was accidental, Mrs Ranelagh has spent 20 years while living abroad trying to prove she was murdered by racist neighbours. Now back in England to confront suspects and witnesses, she reveals that most people on whom her inquiry touches, including her husband, have guilty secrets and the reader finds the frightening reasons for Mrs Ranelagh's own strange psychology.

D Walters reconstructs Ranelagh's past investigation in the form of e-mails, letters, newspaper cuttings, transcripts of official reports and even, unusually, photographs, which I suspect come out of the Walters's family album circa 1978. There are perhaps a couple too many nasty but not-quite-convincing twists but otherwise this novel is a superb exploration of guilt and revenge.

The Observer

☐ The main themes of the book The victim	☐ The investigation The story
☐ A general description of the book The sort of books this author writes	☐ How the book is structured Opinion

➜ Check your answers to tasks 1 and 2 on p.129.

TASK 3 Underline all the words and phrases in the review which you think might be useful when you write other reviews.

➜ Check your answers on p.129.

TASK 4 Put the words below into the appropriate column.

remarkable	superb
unimaginative	predictable
dull	awful
humourless	dreadful
hopeless	magnificent
brilliant	amazing
witty	fascinating
boring	original

positive adjectives	negative adjectives
remarkable	

➜ Check your answers on p.129.

TASK 5 An international magazine has asked its readers to write reviews of books they have recently read or films they have recently seen. You decide to write a review. Say what was good and bad about it and make a recommendation as to whether readers should buy the book or see the film.

Write your **review** in about 250 words.

English In Use

(spend about 45 minutes on this section)

Paper 3 Part 1 Multiple choice cloze

❶ Exam information You write your answers to Papers 1, 3, and 4 on special answer sheets. For Papers 1 and 3 you must use a pencil.

▶ **Exam techniques**
Think about the different techniques you have used in the earlier units of the book. Select appropriate techniques for dealing with the exam questions. Task 2 gives further practice in useful techniques.

TASK 1 Try and do this exam task in ten minutes.

For questions **1–15**, read the text below and then decide which word best fits each space. The exercise begins with an example (**0**).

Grandmother has her day in court

When retired teacher Joan Meredith wanted to make a (**0**) _C_ about nuclear weapons she sat down in the roadway outside the Trident submarine (**1**) ..... on the River Clyde, near Glasgow in Scotland.

Yesterday magistrates responded in kind, (**2**) ..... her to find a comfortable spot in their courtroom and to sit for the entire day's (**3**) ..... as punishment for non-payment of a £100 fine.

Mrs Meredith, 70, from Northumberland, in the north-east of England, had been (**4**) ..... to spend a week in jail for refusing to pay the fine imposed after a peace (**5**) ..... at Faslane. She even packed a case for a (**6**) ..... in Low Newton prison near Durham. But magistrates in Alnwick chose to enact a little-used (**7**) ..... of the Magistrates Court Act and told her she must stay in the court precincts for the day.

Dressed in a purple T-shirt and (**8**) ..... socks, Mrs Meredith sat at the back of the court listening to (**9**) ..... and pronounced herself satisfied with her (**10**) ..... .

A grandmother of six, she was (**11**) ..... fined after joining a blockade of Faslane (**12**) ..... by an anti-nuclear group. A week-long jail term imposed in June was (**13**) ..... to give her another chance to pay. Mrs Meredith refused to do so because she does not believe her (**14**) ..... were morally wrong.

She would do it again, she said yesterday. "I can't see this (**15**) ..... any difference."

The Guardian

0	A fuss	B mark	C point	D statement
1	A base	B station	C place	D site
2	A calling	B forcing	C ordering	D threatening
3	A procedure	B proceedings	C process	D procession
4	A waiting	B intending	C allowing	D expecting
5	A crisis	B revolution	C protest	D objection
6	A season	B spell	C turn	D cycle
7	A section	B topic	C group	D detail
8	A matching	B fitting	C suiting	D joining
9	A episodes	B meetings	C circumstances	D events
10	A judgment	B sentence	C result	D decision
11	A primarily	B newly	C originally	D principally
12	A done	B forecast	C performed	D organized
13	A suspended	B reserved	C forgiven	D lost
14	A measures	B operations	C actions	D performances
15	A being	B making	C doing	D meaning

➜ **Check your answers on p.129.**

Paper 3 Part 4 Word formation

TASK 2 Read the article below and the article on p.82 carefully. Answer the questions for each one.

Workers denied right to paid holiday
1 Why are the workers unhappy?
2 What do they have a right to?
3 Why are they not getting this?

Mobile phones to carry health warning
1 What will you get if you buy a mobile phone before Christmas?
2 Which people in particular will this be aimed at?
3 Why is this happening?

➜ **Check your answers on p.129.**

TASK 3 For questions 1–7 use the words underneath the text to form one word that fits in the same numbered space in the text. The exercise begins with an example (0).

WORKERS DENIED RIGHT TO PAID HOLIDAY

Thousands of workers are being deprived (**0**) _unlawfully_ of their full holiday (**1**) .... because bosses are ignoring legislation that gives (**2**) .... four weeks' paid holiday a year.

Companies are using a wide (**3**) .... of ploys and 'excuses' to evade a law that came into force nearly two years ago.

Some (**4**) .... simply refuse to grant their workers any paid time off; tell them (**5**) .... that they do not qualify; or claim they cannot afford it. Other workers are threatened with (**6**) .... for trying to claim their rights and some have their wages cut so that (**7**) .... can finance the time off, according to a recent survey.

The Independent

0	LAW	4	ORGANIZE
1	ALLOW	5	CORRECT
2	EMPLOY	6	DISMISS
3	VARY	7	EMPLOY

Do the same for questions 8–15.

→ Check your answers on p.129.

MOBILE PHONES TO CARRY HEALTH WARNING

Mobile phones sold in the run-up to Christmas will carry a (8) .... health warning – despite the lack of firm evidence that they are (9) ....

Officials confirmed yesterday that they were (10) .... a leaflet that would warn buyers about (11) ....over mobile phones' potential health risks. The leaflets will warn (12) .... that children should not spend too long on their mobiles.

A report published earlier this year called for more research because there were (13) .... worries over the potential health risks of mobile phone use. The report said that mobile phone use among children should be (14) .... because their brains were more vulnerable than adults to (15) ....

The Independent

8	GOVERN	12	SPECIFY
9	HARM	13	CONTINUE
10	FINAL	14	COURAGE
11	CERTAIN	15	RADIATE

→ Check your answers on p.129.

Listening

(spend about 30 minutes on this section)

Paper 4 Part 4 Multiple choice questions

ℹ Exam information In Part 4 each multiple choice question has three possible options. One mark is given for each correct answer.

▶ **Exam techniques**
Think about the different techniques you have used in the earlier units of the book. Select appropriate techniques for dealing with the exam task. Tasks 1 and 2 give further practice in useful techniques.

TASK 1 Read questions 1 and 2 in exam task 3.

For question 1: decide if the words below are to do with buying a boat, a car, or a caravan. Some words will go with more than one of them.

condition	price	sleep	engine	road	river	old	wheel

For question 2: put the phrases below in the chart according to their meaning. Which are formal (F) and which are informal (I)?

to get a new one   to mend   to put things right
to exchange   to get your money back   to be reimbursed   to swap

to replace	to get an on	to exchange	to swap
to repair	to men	to put things right	
to get a refund	to get your new)		

→ Check your answers on p.129.

TASK 2 🎧13.1 Now listen twice to the first speaker on the recording and answer questions 1 and 2 of the exam task.

TASK 3 Now read the other questions. Then do the exam task.

For questions **1–10**, choose the correct option **A**, **B**, or **C**. Listen to the recording twice.

1 The first speaker bought a
  A boat.
  B car.
  C caravan.

2 The speaker eventually got
  A it replaced with a different one.
  B it repaired.
  C his money refunded.

3 The second speaker's boss doesn't tell her
  A when she's coming in late.
  B what to do.
  C about all her appointments.

4 The speaker
  A wants more money.
  B is looking for a new job.
  C doesn't do her job properly.

5 The third speaker's holiday was spoilt because
  A the plane was delayed.
  B his luggage was lost.
  C the hotel wasn't very good.

6 When he got home, the speaker felt
  A angry.
  B relieved.
  C happy.

7 The fourth speaker
  A stopped when he saw his neighbour.
  B waved at someone he knew.
  C did not set off as soon as the lights changed.

8 The speaker felt
  A angry.
  B frightened.
  C apologetic.

9 The fifth speaker thinks that the person she is talking to should
  A find a new job.
  B make an official complaint.
  C talk to her colleague.

10 The speaker thinks that the person she is talking to is
  A being sensible.
  B not taking the right action.
  C overreacting to the situation.

Speaking

⏱ (spend about 25 minutes on this section)

Paper 5 Part 3 Evaluation

ℹ **Exam information** In Part 3 of the Speaking Paper you may be asked to look at different ideas with your partner and then choose the best, after discussing their good and bad points.

▶ **Exam techniques**
- Use appropriate language to talk about the value of different ideas and express preferences. Tasks 1 to 3 practise this.
- What should you do if you cannot reach an agreement with your partner? Check your answer on p.130. Task 4 practises this.

TASK 1 Put the phrases below into the correct column in the chart.

I'd go for …

My choice would be …

The problem with … is …

What I like about … is …

The good thing about … is …

The advantage of … is …

That would be my preference.

If it was up to me, I'd choose …

The disadvantage of … is …

The drawback with … is …

Saying what is good about something	Saying what is bad about something	Expressing a preference

➡ **Check your answers on p.130.**

TASK 2 Read the exam question in task 3. Look at the phrases in task 1 above. Think about what you might say.

TASK 3 🎧13.2 Listen to two people discussing the question and tick the phrases in task 1 that you hear.

You have been given the use of a large indoor stadium in your country to raise money for charity. You can use this for up to 12 hours for an event of your choice. Look at the suggestions for what you might organize. Discuss the advantages and disadvantages of each one and decide which would be the best and why.

➡ **Check your answers on p.130.**

TASK 4 Listen to the recording again. What do the pe[ople] decide?

TASK 5 Work in pairs. (If you are working alone, look at p.4.) Discuss the question below. If possible, record your discussion. Then play it back and think about how you might improve it.

Your course has come to an end and your class want to buy your teacher a present. Look at the suggestions below. Discuss each of them. Then decide which would be best and why.

TASK 6 🎧13.3 Now listen to two native speakers discussing the question.

1 Listen to the first part of the recording and note down the reasons the speakers give for and against each idea.

PRESENT	FOR	AGAINST
wine		
pen		
CD		
book		

2 Listen to the second part of the recording and answer these questions.
  a What two expressions does the woman use to show that she wants to stop discussing each item and make a decision?
  b What does the man think they should do?
  c What does the woman think they should do?
  d What do they decide to do?

➡ **Check your answers on p.130.**

How well are you doing?

Look back at the different sections in this unit and assess your performance for each one. Choose from A–C below.

Reading (multiple matching)	…
Writing (review)	…
English In Use (multiple choice cloze)	…
English In Use (word formation)	…
Listening (multiple choice questions)	…
Speaking (evaluation)	…

A No problem; I feel quite confident about this type of question.

B OK, but I need some more practice.

C I definitely need more practice. I find this type of question difficult.

Reading

🕐 (spend about 40 minutes on this section)

Paper 1 Part 2 Gapped text

▶ **Exam techniques**
Think about the different techniques you have used in the earlier units of the book. Select appropriate techniques for dealing with the exam question. Tasks 1 and 2 give further practice in useful techniques.

TASK 1 You are going to read an article entitled *More than just talk, talk, talk*. What do you think it is about? Tick (✔) the most likely summary below.

☐ How to be a politician.

☐ Conversation involves skills other than just talking.

☐ Why I won't buy a mobile phone.

→ Check your answer on p.131.

TASK 2 Read through the gapped text in task 3. Match a sentence below to each paragraph (a–i) in the gapped text.

1 Dealing with interruptions.

2 In a conversation people need time and respect.

3 Starting a conversation.

4 We use conversation skills a lot.

5 The importance of choosing the right time for a conversation.

6 Be patient.

7 Conversation is more than just speaking.

8 Don't bore people by talking too much.

9 Be honest – or your body language will give you away.

→ Check your answers on p.131.

TASK 3 Now do the exam task.

→ Check your answers on p.131.

Choose which paragraphs (**A–G** opposite) fit into the numbered gaps in the text below. There is one extra paragraph which does not fit in any of the gaps.

More than just talk, talk, talk

(a) There are few aspects of working life which don't involve listening and talking to others. Conversation is used to form and maintain relationships, give and take instructions, seek and impart information, and provide and get feedback.

(b) However, conversation is much more than an exchange of words. We are not logic machines but are influenced by our emotions. Consequently, how something is said can be just as influential as what is said. What a listener hears and understands is influenced by prior knowledge, situation, timing and the speaker's choice of vocabulary, intonation and body language.

1 [ ]

(c) If a conversation is to work each person must have the opportunity to express their opinion, make their thoughts and feelings clear, and to be listened to seriously. None of us likes to be lectured to, patronized, put down, not given proper attention, denied a chance to finish, or have our opinions ignored or trivialized.

2 [ ]

(d) If we bounce a new idea off a colleague trying to finish a report against a deadline, ask someone to discuss a staff appraisal ten minutes before they go into a client meeting, or raise a sensitive personal issue in front of others, this will rarely lead to a constructive dialogue.

3 [ ]

(e) The person initiating the conversation also needs to engage the attention of the other. The most effective way is to start with the main point one wishes to make or to state the reason for the conversation. It is easier for the listener to focus their mind if they know roughly what's coming.

4 [ ]

(f) Don't go on at length without giving the other person the chance to respond. If the subject is complex, you need to know the listener has fully understood what has been said. It can help to ask if you have made yourself clear and how they see things. There are a number of signals which will tell you that you have gone on too long and are losing attention – such as surreptitious glances at a wall clock or wrist watch, eyes wandering, slumped posture and fidgeting.

5 [ ]

(g) Sometimes they are seeking clarification, or have spotted a factual error. But if the point is relatively trivial, or they have anticipated something you were going to say, you can quickly get back to your main thread by saying 'that's a good point which I'll be coming to in a moment'. How you handle a potential interruption can weaken or strengthen the value of a conversation, as indeed can your method of dealing with difficult topics – such as giving a reprimand, rejecting a colleague's proposal, chasing a late payment or delivery, or explaining an unfavourable assessment.

6 [ ]

(h) Facial expression and body language of both speaker and listener contribute to the conversation. Although one can hide the truth in what one says, it is very hard to control one's face or body language. Most people can sense whether someone is being honest in their opinions and feelings. So, to maintain trust, it is better to be honest both in what one says and in giving feedback to what is said.

(i) We all make mistakes during conversation. Consequently we should be tolerant, curbing our impatience, annoyance or irritation at the failings of others, and work with them to achieve a constructive outcome.

Independent On Sunday

A It may be irritating if the other person wants to interrupt while you are in the middle of a complicated explanation. But, having decided they want to say something, they will not give you their full attention until they have said it. Rather than show impatience, it is better to stop, invite their contribution and give them your full attention than to try and continue regardless.

B We need to create the right climate for conversation. Those involved should be free to talk and not preoccupied with something else. And there should be no needless distractions. The person initiating a conversation should ask, 'Is this a good time to talk about … or would you prefer me to come back later?'

C In cases such as these, although you may be telling people things they don't want to hear, respect their feelings. Whenever possible avoid the language of blame. Blame leads to resentment and hostility. If you want co-operation and a change in behaviour, avoid attack. It is better to say: 'we have a problem' than 'you have a problem', and ask 'how are we going to solve it?' rather than 'what are you going to do about it?'

D The high-stress office culture of today seems to be based on a culture of long working hours and little or no time for social activity. However, that environment is going to change. Pleasure will become as important as business. This will have a positive effect on families. People will have increased leisure time, lower stress levels. And enhanced communication between family members will lead to fewer marital breakdowns.

E Although the importance of 'oral communication skills' in the workplace is highly publicized, this phrase suggests that it is talking rather than listening that is important. However, most people want a genuine two-way exchange in which both feel they are being heard and understood. So it is perhaps better to think of 'conversation skills'.

F If you have lots of ideas to put over, it helps to list them and organize them into a logical sequence beforehand. People generally grasp facts and specific information more easily than generalizations. However, the facts and information must be relevant to the main argument. Do not overload the listener. Moreover, because the listener is having to absorb each statement while listening to the next, brief but regular pauses can help comprehension.

G Few people, except tyrants and bullies, do these things consciously to others. However, most of us are guilty of some of them from time to time, perhaps because we have other things on our mind, we have been approached at an awkward moment, or we are tired and impatient.

Language development

Being negative

1 Match the verbs on the left (from the text) with the meanings on the right.

	to make something appear unimportant
to patronize	to make continual (often annoying) small movements
to ignore	
to put down	to behave in a superior way towards someone
to trivialize	to sit in a tired manner
to be impatient	to pay no attention to something or someone
to fidget	
to slump	to make someone appear stupid or silly
	to be intolerant of delay and eager for something to happen

→ Check your answers on p.131.

2 Complete the sentences below with appropriate forms of words from exercise 1.

1 This is an important issue. It would be dangerous to .... it and, what's more, we mustn't .... it.

2 I hate teaching that class. If they're not .... in their chairs with their heads down, they're .... with their pens and pencils.

3 He always .... his students – just because he knows the subject and they don't.

4 Don't .... so ....! I'll give you the answers when everyone's finished.

5 I know he's behaved stupidly but don't .... him .... in public. He'll never forgive you.

→ Check your answers on p.131.

Writing

⏱ (spend about 25 minutes on tasks 1–3; about an hour on task 4)

Paper 2 Part 2 Letter of reference

ⓘ **Exam information** You may have to write a letter of reference in Paper 2.

▶ **Exam techniques**

Think about the different techniques you have used in the earlier units of the book. Select appropriate techniques for dealing with the exam question. Tasks 1, 2, and 3 give further practice in useful techniques.

TASK 1 Read the exam question below. Underline the important parts of the question. Then read the answer below. Is the answer complete? If not, what is missing?

➜ **Check your answer on p.131.**

Question:

A friend has sent you this note.

> I've applied for a job as a youth organizer at a summer camp in the States this year. They'd like a letter of reference from someone who knows me well. They want to know how long you've known me, what my personality is like, what experience I have with young people (teenagers), and how well I am likely to adapt to living in an English-speaking environment. I'd be really grateful if you could write to them for me. The address is Vermont Summer Camps, Stowe, Vermont, USA. Thanks.
> Carlos

Write your **letter of reference** in about 250 words.

Answer:

> Dear Sir or Madam
>
> **Carlos Lacerda**
>
> (a) I have known Carlos Lacerda all my life. We grew up together and went to school together near Valencia in Spain. We have also been colleagues on a number of weekend expeditions with youth groups from the town where we live.
>
> (b) Carlos has considerable experience of young people, especially teenagers. He was a member of a local youth group for many years, taking up a position of responsibility within it from the age of 16, and eventually taking it over and running it for two years before he went to university.
>
> (c) The group was small with about 15–20 members. When Carlos was in charge, he was responsible for the weekly organization of activities, for collecting group subscriptions and running the finances, and also for planning the programme of events from month to month. These events included fund-raising for local charities, helping the elderly in the local community, leisure evenings and discos for members and their families and excursions to places of interest, both local and further afield.
>
> (d) Carlos has travelled widely throughout Spain and Europe, living for six months in Austria as part of his degree course. I feel sure that he would adapt well to living in an English-speaking environment.
>
> (e) I have no hesitation in recommending him as a youth organizer on your summer camps.
>
> Yours faithfully,
>
> **Monica Sanchez**
>
> Monica Sanchez

TASK 2 The missing paragraph from the answer in task 1 concerns Carlos's personality. Decide which paragraph below is best and why.

A Carlos is a pretty cool guy. He's always there for his friends. Teenagers think he's pretty cool too. They're on the same wavelength. On the organization front he's pretty much got his act together. He's streetwise and he knows what he likes, but he's aware that other people have their needs.

B Carlos has an engaging personality. He is friendly and sociable and always willing to listen as well. He gets on particularly well with teenagers, who seem to warm to him and appreciate his sense of humour. In addition, he is well-organized and responsible but always tempers his enthusiasm with the interests and feelings of those around him.

C Carlos is friendly and sociable. Teenagers seem to like him. He knows how to make them laugh. He is well-organized, responsible, and enthusiastic.

➜ **Check your answer on p.131.**

TASK 3 Read the answer in task 1 again. Match these headings to the paragraphs in the answer.

☐ what experience Carlos has with young people

☐ how I know Carlos and how long I've known him

☐ my recommendation

☐ how I feel Carlos would adapt to an English-speaking environment

☐ what experience Carlos has of organizing groups

➜ **Check your answer on p.131.**

TASK 4 Answer the exam task below.

A friend leaves you this note.

> I've applied for a job as a tour guide for an English travel company taking English people and Americans round our town. They'd like a letter of reference from someone who knows me well. I was hoping you could do it! They want to know how long you've known me, how good my English is, how well I know the local town (history, sights, etc.), and how well I get on with people. I'd really appreciate it if you could do it. Thanks.
>
> Victoria

Write your **letter of reference** in about 250 words.

🕐 (spend about 45 minutes on this section)

Paper 3 Part 3 Error correction

▶ **Exam techniques**
Think about the different techniques you have used in the earlier units of the book. Select appropriate techniques for dealing with the exam question. Tasks 1, 3, and 4 give further practice in useful techniques.

Error correction

TASK 1 Find one extra word in five of the sentences below. Be careful! One is correct.

1 Many people are rejecting the traditional medicine and turning to homeopathy.
2 After a short time I found that dieting had no effect on my weight.
3 Within the next and twenty years electric cars will have become standard items for every household.
4 I cannot stress over enough the importance of getting good exam results.
5 Governments are so worried about the threat to many of the world's coral reefs that they are already making up plans for dealing with the crisis.
6 The icecap at the North Pole has been melted for the first time in 50 million years, increasing fears about global warming.

➜ **Check your answers on p.131.**

TASK 2 Now do the exam task below.

Paper 3 Part 5 Register transfer

TASK 3 Read through both texts on p.88 and make four correct sentences.

	is formal.
Text 1	is very informal.
Text 2	is a suggestion.
	is an advertisement.

➜ **Check your answers on p.131.**

TASK 4 Decide if the sentences below are true (T) or false (F). Read the two texts again if necessary.

1 Sir Jeremy Mallins is the present Director of Hope Thring.
2 The company is moving to Australia.
3 Zak would like to change jobs.
4 Zak does not quite have the right qualifications for the job.
5 Jake thinks Zak should apply for the job.

➜ **Check your answers on p.131.**

In most lines of the following text, there is one unnecessary word. It is either grammatically incorrect or does not fit in with the rest of the text. Find the word and write it in the space at the end of each line. Some lines are correct. Indicate these with a tick (✔).

Internet shopping too slow

SHOPPING on the Internet was condemned yesterday so as too troublesome, too
expensive, and too slow by a Trading Standards Institute report which revealed that
the consumer e-commerce is not living up to its reputation.

More than a third of Internet shoppers experienced such late deliveries, wrong orders,
and companies that had disappeared with their money, the report said. Problems
that included a firm which took credit card details from customers then vanished, a national
flower delivery chain which took away payments but did not deliver the bouquets, and
a company which charged £10 to dispatch off a computer mouse 15 miles away.

Other of websites were accused of offering goods or services that did not live up to
their advertising. They included an 'idyllic' beach resort that did not mention how it was
beside a lorry park and had been severely damaged by a hurricane. A Trading
Standards Institute spokesperson said many large and well-known businesses
were delivered a disappointing level of service.

Late or non-delivery of goods was a far typical problem, with many companies leaving
consumers to spend the extra time and money chasing round their goods, he said.
'Though it is extremely convenient it has pitfalls, which we must to seek to avoid.
Some of the big names in retailing are not getting customer service right.'

0	*so*
1	....
2	....
3	....
4	....
5	....
6	....
7	....
8	....
9	....
10	....
11	....
12	....
13	....
14	....
15	....
16	....

➜ **Check your answers on p.131.**

Use the information in the advertisement to complete the numbered gaps in the informal note from Jake which follows. Use no more than two words for each gap. The exercise begins with an example (**0**).

1 ADVERTISEMENT

DIRECTOR

Hope Thring is now welcoming applications for the post of Director to succeed Sir Jeremy Mallins, who is leaving the company to take up a new appointment in Australia.

Under Sir Jeremy's leadership, the company has recently achieved major success in establishing itself as a market leader in the chemical manufacturing industry.

Applicants will have considerable experience in manufacturing, not necessarily chemicals, a proven track record of success, and the ability to motivate a staff of around 100.

The post will require a considerable amount of overseas travel.

Benefits include a generous holiday entitlement of 35 days p.a. and a company car. Salary is negotiable.

For an informal discussion, please contact Dr Robin Cousins on 0131-225-3647.

Written applications with full career details to: j.mayall@hopt.com by 15th July.

Note: candidates must be available for interview in Edinburgh on 30th July.

2 INFORMAL NOTE

Zak

I know you're interested in changing jobs so I thought I'd let you know that our company is
(**0**) ....*looking for*.... a new director. Sir Jeremy Mallins has been (**1**) .... a new job in Australia.

The company has really grown while he's been in (**2**) .... We're now one of the top companies in the industry. We (**3**) .... chemicals – but I think you know that.

Anyway, they want someone who's (**4**) .... manufacturing for a while. But you (**5**) .... to know anything about chemicals – don't worry! They want someone who's done (**6**) .... in their present job – and you certainly have. You'd have about 100 people (**7**) .... you – and you'd have to keep them keen!

If you get the job, you'd have to make quite a few (**8**) .... But the holidays are really (**9**) .... and you'd have a company car. If you want to have (**10**) .... with someone, get (**11**) .... with Robin Cousins on 0131-225-3647. Or just get your application (**12**) ....by 15th July.

One other thing – you have to be able to (**13**) .... here for interview on 30th July.

Go for it!

Jake

→ **Check your answers on p.131.**

🕐 (spend about 25 minutes on this section)

Paper 4 Part 2 Note taking

ℹ️ **Exam information** Don't forget, you hear Part 2 once only.

▶ **Exam techniques**
Think about the different techniques you have used in the earlier units of the book. Select appropriate techniques for dealing with the exam question. Task 1 gives further practice in useful techniques.

TASK 1 Look at the notes in task 2 and think about these questions and comments.

1 Mail UK is a postal delivery service. What kind of driving jobs is it likely to be offering? Think of two or three possibilities.

2 What do you need to be good at to deal with people?

3 & 4 In what way might people involved with a postal service have to be flexible?

5 What will they have to move?

6 Why might the staff need to be enthusiastic?

7 Look at the jobs you thought of in question 1 above. What areas of responsibility might each job be given?

8 You might have to apply to a person or a position within the company. If it's a position, what position(s) could it be?

TASK 2 🎧**14.1** You will hear a recorded message on the employment hotline for Mail UK, a postal delivery service. For questions 1–8, complete the notes about the type of job on offer. Listen to the recording once only.

MAIL UK

Type of job: [___ | **1**] drivers

We are looking for people who are:

good [| **2**] – able to deal politely with all sorts of other people

flexible – willing to do [| **3**]
          or [| **4**]

reasonably fit – you have to move heavy [| **5**] in the course of your work

enthusiastic – the job requires work of a [| **6**]

conscientious – you have responsibility for looking after [| **7**]

Send letter of application to: [| **8**], Mail UK, Romford, Essex

→ **Check your answers on p.131.**

Speaking

🕐 (spend about 25 minutes on this section)

Paper 5 Part 3 Revision and practice

ℹ️ **Exam information** You are expected to negotiate and collaborate with your partner in this and the following part of the exam. It is not essential to complete the task set in the time given, but you should try to do so.

▶ **Exam techniques**
Think about the different techniques you have used in the earlier units of the book. Select appropriate techniques for dealing with the exam question. Task 1 gives further practice in useful techniques.

TASK 1 🎧14.2 Listen to the recording and tick (✔) the expressions you hear in the chart below.

ASKING FOR AN OPINION	☐ What do you think?
	☐ What about you?
GIVING AN OPINION	☐ It seems to me that …
	☐ I also think …
CLARIFYING	☐ You mean …
	☐ How do you mean?
AGREEING	☐ Absolutely.
	☐ I'd agree with that.
EXPRESSING AN OPPOSITE IDEA	☐ Wouldn't you say that …
	☐ Don't you think …?
COMPLIMENTING	☐ I hadn't thought of that.
	☐ That's a good point.
EXPRESSING PREFERENCE	☐ I'd go for …
	☐ My choice would be …
DISAGREEING	☐ Do you really think so?
	☐ I see what you mean, but …
GIVING AN EXAMPLE	☐ Take … for example.
	☐ For instance …
SUPPORTING AN ARGUMENT	☐ The point is …
	☐ The main reason is …

Think of one more expression for each section.

➡ **Check your answers on p.131.**

TASK 2 🎧14.3 Work in pairs. (If you are working alone, look at p.4.) Look at the pictures below and follow the examiner's instructions on the recording. If possible, record your discussion. Then play it back and think about how you might improve it.

TASK 3 🎧14.4 Now listen to part of a conversation between two native speakers doing the same activity.

1 Listen to the conversation and note down the qualities needed for each job.

secretary	artist	construction worker

2 Listen to the conversation again. Match a function from the box to each of the phrases or sentences below from the conversations.

> giving an example   agreeing   giving a reason
> expressing preference   asking about preference

Secretary
Definitely!
My mum used to be a secretary.
I certainly have never wanted to be a secretary.
I can't say I have either.
Too much running around.

Artist
That's something I would like to be.
What kind of artist would you like to be?
Sculptor? Painter? Sketcher?
Cartoonist or something … or graphic design.

Construction worker
My uncle's a construction worker.
Is it for you?
It's not for me.
I'm too artistic.
I'm a bit scared of heights.

➡ **Check your answers on p.132.**

How well are you doing?

Look back at the different sections in this unit and assess your performance for each one. Choose from A–C below.

Reading (gapped text)	…
Writing (letter of reference)	…
English In Use (error correction)	…
English In Use (register transfer)	…
Listening (note taking)	…
Speaking (revision and practice)	…

A No problem; I feel quite confident about this type of question.
B OK, but I need some more practice.
C I definitely need more practice. I find this type of question difficult.

15 Behaviour

Reading

(spend about 35 minutes on this section)

Paper 1 Part 3 Multiple choice questions

ℹ Exam information The texts in the Reading Paper will be between 450 and 1,200 words long. Texts in Part 3 are between 450 and 850 words long.

▶ **Exam techniques**
Think about the different techniques you have used in the earlier units of the book. Select appropriate techniques for dealing with the exam question. Task 1 gives further practice in useful techniques.

TASK 1 Spend 2–3 minutes getting an idea what this article is about, using one of the techniques practised earlier in the book. Decide if the sentences below are true (T) or false (F).

1 Al Capone's home city was Chicago.
2 Al Capone was jailed for murder.
3 Al Capone always felt that he was an honest businessman.

→ Check your answers on p.133.

TASK 2 Now do the exam task.

→ Check your answers on p.133.

AL CAPONE

Al Capone was to crime what JP Morgan was to Wall Street, the first man to exert national influence over his trade. When Capone came to crime in Chicago in 1920, his home city was split up into groups of quarrelling gangs. Like any ruthless businessman, he first took over the centre of the city, then its suburbs, then the whole State of Illinois. Next, he called one of the first international gangland conventions at Atlantic City, New Jersey in 1929; and, as chief of the trade, he divided up the United States into territories with defined borders for rival gangs. Crime was now run by a few people, with agreements on fixed prices, and one man its acknowledged leader. The small-time crook, like the small-time businessman, was nearly eliminated, for the organized gangs co-operated with the police to get rid of him. In the suppression of competition, the big gangs were a positive benefit to society.

It was Capone who, in the six years before the Atlantic City convention, had risen to the position of America's most feared criminal. The newspapers had blown up his reputation from murk into myth, the Chicago Crime Commission had given him the name of Public Enemy Number One, and the federal government had given him the opportunity of making more than $60m yearly solely from the illegal sale of alcohol, known as bootlegging, all because of the amendment to the Constitution which prohibited the sale of alcohol. Soon the newspapers were to destroy him through the same method of publicity, the Crime Commission was to push President Hoover himself into a campaign against Capone, and federal agents and federal tax laws were to catch and jail the monster that federal tax law had created in the first place.

Capone was born a Neapolitan in the Brooklyn slums. Had he not been, he might have used his ruthlessness and powers of organization to make a fortune in legitimate business. Instead he grew up in quarters where, as one famous

---

Read the text carefully. Look at questions **1–5** below. Choose the best option **A**, **B**, **C**, or **D** for each question.

1 How did Al Capone become so powerful?
   A He co-operated with the police.
   B He ran legitimate businesses.
   C He gradually took over crime in the state of Illinois.
   D He organized the Atlantic City convention.

2 Al Capone became so well known because
   A he invited America's biggest criminals to Atlantic City.
   B the newspapers printed a lot of stories about him.
   C the President spoke out against him.
   D he sold bootleg alcohol.

criminologist pointed out, 'the neighbourhood criminal gang opened up a form of gainful occupation and of adventurous life to the hopeless young.' Always open-handed towards charity and a good family man, Capone offended none of the peasant taboos of his childhood.

The fact that he was notorious as a killer and a corrupter of society did not disturb his opinion of himself as an honest, if tough, businessman – he was, after all, one of the few people who always paid the hundreds of thousands of dollars he lost in gambling debts. And his chief business, he felt, was legitimate in human terms, even if it was against the strict letter of the law. 'They call Al Capone a bootlegger,' he complained. 'Yes, it's bootleg while it's on the trucks, but when your host at the club or in the locker room hands you a drink on a silver tray, it's hospitality. They say I break the prohibition law. Who doesn't?' Capone did not mention that he also broke the law against extortion and murder to control bootlegging, and few others were allowed by him to compete.

Al Capone was certainly the wickedest man of his time, and one of the richest. Crime seemed – briefly – to pay. Like other great empire builders, Capone left a legacy to his heirs. He had pioneered the use of the truck and the telephone and the tommy-gun to unify American crime; even after the end of prohibition, organized criminals moved into other fields to keep up their profits. Capone had already begun takeovers in Chicago in the communications and cleaning businesses. Later criminals followed his example, and legitimate businessmen found themselves unable to fight back against this new competition.

In a curious way, however, it was legitimate business as well as corrupt State governments and the prohibition law, which had given American gangsters their chance. For the criminals had often been called in to break strikes and to terrify the newly-founded unions; in return the unions called in other criminals to fight those hired by the bosses. Violence breeds violence, and thus, in a country where violence was not uncommon, the well-organized family gangs of Southern Italy were allowed to intimidate and exploit, and eventually hold a nation to blackmail. Their opportunity was prohibition; and their greatest representative was Capone.

The consequences are still with us; the children of the gang chiefs still get their hands on billions of dollars a year from the American public through percentages on slot-machines or juke-boxes or trucks or a hundred more of the services of daily life. Capone set the pattern for crime to be big business and for business to use the method of crime. He made up the rules and he laid out the tools. His name still reaches to every household, as do the fingers of his greedy followers.

Al Capone by FD Pasley

---

3 According to the writer, Al Capone believed
   A he could have made a fortune in legitimate business.
   B competition was good for business.
   C people should not pay their gambling debts.
   D selling bootleg alcohol was legitimate even if it was illegal.
4 Why did criminal gangs become powerful at this time in the United States?
   A They had trucks, telephones, and tommy guns.
   B They started running legitimate businesses.
   C The unions called them in to fight.
   D A unique situation allowed them to exploit prohibition.
5 The writer feels that
   A despite all his faults Capone benefited American society.
   B we can still see Capone's influence in American society today.
   C Capone was a great and generous man.
   D Capone was misunderstood.

Language development

Verb–noun collocations

1 Cross out one verb in each box which does not go with the noun on its right.

1	break change enforce ~~prohibit~~ respect	the law
2	do look for ~~reach~~ drum up go into	business
3	condemn ~~apply for~~ prevent provoke stamp out	violence
4	~~confirm~~ belong to join build found	an organization

2 What did these people do? Write sentences as in the example, using verb-noun collocations from exercise 1.

He took something from a shop without paying. *He broke the law.*

1 She became a member of the National Union of Teachers.
2 They wrote to a newspaper saying they believed violence was wrong.
3 He advertised his restaurant in the local paper.
4 She started a video rental shop.
5 He told the driver not to park on a double yellow line.
6 They stopped two people who were about to start fighting.
7 They started the United Nations.
8 They agreed a deal.
9 He insulted the man standing next to him and pushed him.
10 They decided to stop people smoking in public places.

➔ **Check your answers on p.133.**

Writing

🕐 (spend about an hour on this section)

Paper 2 Part 1 Brochure

ℹ Exam information Part 1 of the Writing Paper is compulsory. The task may be divided into more than one section / type of writing. One section may ask you to write a contribution to a brochure.

▶ **Exam techniques**
Think about the different techniques you have used in the earlier units of the book. Select appropriate techniques for dealing with the exam question.

Complete this exam task.

You have received the memo below and some entries from the current edition of the Staff Brochure at the company where you work. Read the memo carefully and then revise the entries for the Staff Brochure as instructed.

memo

FROM: *the Managing Director*

As you know, I've been keen to make some changes to the Staff Brochure for some time but I just can't seem to fit it into my schedule. I'd be grateful if you could do it for me. I've selected the bits from the old brochure that need changing and written some comments for each one about what needs doing. I'd like to see a new version by the end of next week.

Thanks

Jim

⬤ STAFF DEVELOPMENT

There is a very limited budget for staff development. As a result, staff will only be financed to attend courses, conferences and other events for which they are specifically recommended by their managers.

– *more money available*
– *encourage staff to develop skills and knowledge*

⬤ HOLIDAYS

Staff are required to give three months' notice of requests for holiday. It cannot be guaranteed that staff will be able to take holiday at any particular time even if the request is made three months in advance.

– *three months' notice = guaranteed dates*
– *one month's notice OK*
– *company will be as flexible as possible*

⬤ WORKING FROM HOME

Working from home is not permitted.

– *OK with manager's approval*
– *need contact phone number*
– *let reception know*

⬤ COMPLAINTS AND IMPROVEMENTS

Any member of staff who has complaints about the company or any member of its staff, or suggestions for the improvement of procedures within the company, should communicate with their direct superior.

– *complaints & suggestions welcome*
– *my door always open*
– *good suggestions rewarded*

Write new entries for the Staff Brochure in about 250 words.

English In Use

🕐 (spend about 30 minutes on this section)

Paper 3 Part 2 Open cloze

ℹ Exam information Remember that in Part 2 you must put *only one word* in each space. Sometimes there may be more than one word which is acceptable for a gap. However, you should only write one word. You must also spell correctly.

▶ **Exam techniques**
Think about the different techniques you have used in the earlier units of the book. Select appropriate techniques for dealing with the exam questions. Tasks 1, 2, and 4 give further practice in useful techniques.

TASK 1 Read through the article opposite and answer these questions.

1 When do people most often lose things?
2 Do people lose things more or less often than they used to?
3 When they lose something, what do 20% of women do?
4 What do 25% of men do?
5 What do British people lose most of all?
6 What would a lot of British people like to lose?

→ **Check your answers on p.133.**

TASK 2 Look at the first four gaps in the article opposite. Use clues 1–4 below to help you find the first four answers.

1 What phrase (... *to*) can be used to indicate a direct contrast?
2 Think carefully about the meaning of the sentence. How will the contrast early in the sentence affect the meaning? What do you think people believe about technological advances?
3 How can adverbs (e.g. *easily*) be qualified? Look carefully at question 2 in task 1 for help with this one.
4 What tense is the verb *increase*? What is the subject? Singular or plural?

TASK 3 Now complete gaps 5–15. Try and do this in ten minutes.

You'll lose a year of your life looking for missing possessions

The average person in Britain spends a year of their life looking for lost items, with Mondays being the most likely day **(0)** *to* misplace vital possessions.

Research published today shows that **(1)** .... to popular belief, technological advances have **(2)** .... helped people find, file and organize things **(3)** .... easily but **(4)** .... increasing the likelihood **(5)** .... people losing money, handbags, wedding rings and **(6)** .... important possessions.

The fast pace **(7)** .... stress of modern life is also causing people to overreact when they cannot find something, **(8)** .... more than one in five women saying they cried **(9)** .... they lost something and more than one quarter of men swearing in frustration. The findings showed that women were more likely than men to resort **(10)** .... violence when they lose things.

Britons most commonly lose money, followed **(11)** .... keys, the remote control of the television, and underwear. Take-away menus, wedding rings and reading glasses also fell **(12)** .... the top 10 of 'most frequently lost' items.

Of things people wanted to lose, over half of **(13)** .... from Yorkshire, London and the Midlands **(14)** .... keen to lose boring friends, with one in 12 people in Britain saying they would like to lose **(15)** .... current partner.

The Independent

→ **Check your answers on p.133.**

Paper 3 Part 6 Gapped text

TASK 4 Read the article in task 5 and answer these questions.

1 Why is the stone important?
2 How did scientists prove this?
3 What is the figure?
4 What parts of the body were identified?
5 What had academics previously thought about the stone?

→ **Check your answers on p.133.**

TASK 5 Now do the exam task.

For questions **1–6**, read the following text and then choose from the list **A–J** the best phrase given below it to fill each of the spaces. Each correct phrase may only be used once. Some of the suggested answers do not fit at all. The exercise begins with an example (**0**).

'Lump of rock' turns out to be world's first sculpture

A stone dismissed by experts as no more than a lump of rock has been identified as the world's first sculpture and the oldest piece of figurative art ever seen.

New scientific data suggests (**0**) *that early humans were producing representations of life* 220,000 years ago, 170,000 years earlier than previously thought. It is a discovery which could revolutionize our understanding of human development.

Italian and American archaeologists used powerful microscopes to prove (**1**) ....., deliberately chiselled and shaped by human hands.

The data from their examination suggests (**2**) ...., probably a woman. Yet, since its discovery 15 years ago, the rock has been disregarded by most academics.

The archaeologists' examination also demonstrated (**3**) ..... to produce roughly symmetrical grooves on either side of the object to produce arms, and that other areas had been deliberately abraded to make what may have been intended as breasts. The base had also been flattened so (**4**) .....

It is the first time (**5**) ..... But although the findings confound the majority of academics who had dismissed the object as purely natural, the research vindicates the Israeli archaeologist Professor Nama Goren, who discovered the stone and who first suggested that it was a primitive sculpture of a woman.

Depending on what further discoveries are unearthed, archaeologists may have to start rewriting the origins of human thought. "We hope (**6**) ..... on the evolution of the human mind," said Dr d'Errico of the French National Centre for Scientific Research.

David Keys, Archaeology Correspondent, Independent On Sunday

A that the sculpture could stand upright
B that probably took between 15 and 30 minutes to make
C that the prehistoric object was intended to portray a human being
D that our research will help change currently accepted views
E that it has been widely ignored
F that a volcanic stone from the Golan Heights in Israel is a primitive sculpture
G that a stone tool had been used
H that it will be studied further
I that the object has been given detailed scientific examination
J *that early humans were producing representations of life*

→ **Check your answers on p.133.**

Listening

Paper 4 Part 3 Sentence completion

ℹ Exam information You may get a sentence completion exercise in this part of the Listening Paper.

▶ **Exam techniques**
Think about the different techniques you have used in the earlier units of the book. Select appropriate techniques for dealing with the exam questions. Tasks 1 and 3 give further practice in useful techniques.

TASK 1 Read through the sentences in task 2 to get an idea of what you are about to listen to. Tick (✔) the words and phrases below which you think you might hear in the recording.

- ☐ the lowest possible price
- ☐ a fair price
- ☐ cultural background
- ☐ Third World countries
- ☐ western countries
- ☐ simple rules
- ☐ football
- ☐ friendly
- ☐ experience
- ☐ negotiation
- ☐ respect
- ☐ reasonable
- ☐ tourists
- ☐ introduce
- ☐ magazine

➜ **Check your answers on p.133.**

TASK 2 🎧 **15.1** You will hear a discussion between two people who have different opinions on the subject of bargaining. For questions 1–9, complete the sentences. Listen to the recording twice.

Geoff Haynes thinks it's OK for [**1**] to bargain.

He thinks that bargaining sometimes forces local shopkeepers to [**2**] and suffer hardship.

Tricia believes the point of bargaining is to get a [**3**].

Experienced shopkeepers sometimes get [**4**] than they should.

In poorer countries, we should pay a fair price to [**5**] the shopkeeper.

Tricia thinks you should bargain in a [**6**].

She once spent [**7**] buying a carpet.

During the negotiation she also met the [**8**].

Geoff is very much [**9**] Tricia's bargaining experience.

Look back at your answers and check that they fit grammatically.

➜ **Check your answers on p.133.**

Paper 4 Part 4 Multiple matching

TASK 3 In the multiple matching question you are sometimes asked to identify function: how the language is used in order to do something or get something done. Match speech bubbles (1–6) to the functions (A–F) below.

1 In those days, of course, life was very different. We had no money for materials and people rarely bought paintings, but there was a great feeling of community among local artists.

2 I always admired Jackson. I thought his work was better and more polished than Waldheim. Waldheim, of course, had more sense of colour but not the depth of feeling.

3 I was wondering whether to buy this sculpture or that one. I like them both very much but … well, what should I do?

4 I'd like you all in a group, please. Move in a bit on the right. That's it. Further, please. I can't get you all in the picture. Come on, move up. OK, good.

5 Good? Of course I am. The first album went straight to platinum. Good? I'm just amazing. You wait. You haven't seen anything yet. In five years' time you won't even remember why you doubted me.

6 Oh, that's a pity. I mean, I just love the design and the cut. And I think it looks fabulous on Kate. But that colour is really just not me. It's such a shame.

A asking advice
B remembering
C comparing
D expressing disappointment
E boasting
F ordering

➜ **Check your answers on p.133.**

TASK 4 🎧15.2 You will hear five artistic people talking about their work. Listen to the recording twice. While you listen you must complete both tasks.

TASK ONE

For questions **1–5**, match the extracts with the people listed **A–H**.

A sculptor

B painter

C musician

D novelist

E journalist

F photographer

G poet

H dress designer

Speaker 1	1
Speaker 2	2
Speaker 3	3
Speaker 4	4
Speaker 5	5

TASK TWO

For questions **6–10**, match the extracts with each speaker's intention listed **A–H**.

A expressing regret

B boasting

C complaining

D apologizing

E ordering

F asking advice

G comparing

H remembering

Speaker 1	6
Speaker 2	7
Speaker 3	8
Speaker 4	9
Speaker 5	10

➡ **Check your answers on p.133.**

Speaking

🕐 (spend about 25 minutes on this section)

Paper 5 Part 4 Reporting

ℹ **Exam information** At the beginning of Part 4 of the Speaking Paper you may have to report to the examiner the results of the discussion you had with your partner in Part 3.

▶ **Exam technique**
It is important to know how to report in English. Learn some different ways of reporting in English. Tasks 1 to 3 practise this.

TASK 1 🎧15.3 Listen to the recording and answer the question.

What have Maria and Carlos been deciding?

➡ **Check your answer on p.134.**

TASK 2 Listen to the recording and complete the sentences with the reporting verbs you hear.

1 I .... we should get him a bottle of wine.
2 I .... that once he'd drunk it, it was gone.
3 I .... about a CD.
4 He .... that he'd had a really nice pen.
5 I .... we could have his name engraved on it.
6 She .... you it was a good idea, did she?
7 I .... it was a good idea.
8 You reluctantly .... it was a good idea.
9 You .... to give him a pen.

➡ **Check your answers on p.134.**

TASK 3 Work in pairs. (If you are working alone, look at p.4.) Listen to Unit 13 transcript 13.2 again. Then report to each other what you heard. Use some of the reporting verbs in the activity above. If possible, record your discussion. Then play it back and think about how you might improve it.

How well are you doing?

Look back at the different sections in this unit and assess your performance for each one. Choose from A–C below.

Reading (multiple choice questions)	...
Writing (brochure)	...
English In Use (open cloze)	...
English In Use (gapped text)	...
Listening (sentence completion)	...
Listening (multiple matching)	...
Speaking (reporting)	...

A No problem; I feel quite confident about this type of question.
B OK, but I need some more practice.
C I definitely need more practice. I find this type of question difficult.

Paper 1 Reading answer sheet

Candidates use the answer sheet for all parts of this paper.

UNIVERSITY of CAMBRIDGE
Local Examinations Syndicate

Candidate Name
If not already printed, write name
in CAPITALS and complete the
Candidate No. grid (in pencil).

Candidate Signature

Examination Title

Centre

Supervisor:
If the candidate is ABSENT or has WITHDRAWN shade here ☐

Centre No.

Candidate No.

Examination
Details

SAMPLE

Multiple-choice Answer Sheet

Use a pencil.

Mark ONE letter for each question.

For example, if you think C is the right answer
to the question, mark your answer sheet like this:

0 A B ▮ D E F G H I

Rub out any answer you wish to change with an eraser.

DP306/080

CAE1

Paper 1 Reading (1 hour 15 minutes)

Part 1

Answer questions **1–18** by referring to the reviews of computer programs on p.97.

For questions **1–18**, answer by choosing from the list (**A–F**) below. Some of the choices may be required more than once.

A touchMe 1.1   **C** Poetry Ink   **E** DietSleuth
B Let's Go Fishing **D** Ski3D   **F** Eliza 6.0.1 and Azile 4.5

The reviewer thinks this program is a waste of money.	1 …
You can use this program to correct mistakes in your files.	2 …
This program would be useful for a lazy schoolchild.	3 …
There is a large amount of factual information contained in this program.	4 …
The reviewer thinks this is the most exciting program.	5 …
This program could help you become better known.	6 …
You can choose 'night' on this program.	7 …
This program is the most expensive.	8 …
You need to visit a shop in this program.	9 …
The reviewer thinks this program lessens the appeal of its content.	10 …
This program might be rude to you.	11 …
You can compete against other people in this program.	12 …
This program helps solve a problem that is not really a problem.	13 …
You will probably find this program amusing.	14 …
This program will help you if you are bad at mathematics.	15 …
This program has an educational aspect to it.	16 …
There is a limit to the length of time this program will run.	17 …
You can add information to this program.	18 …

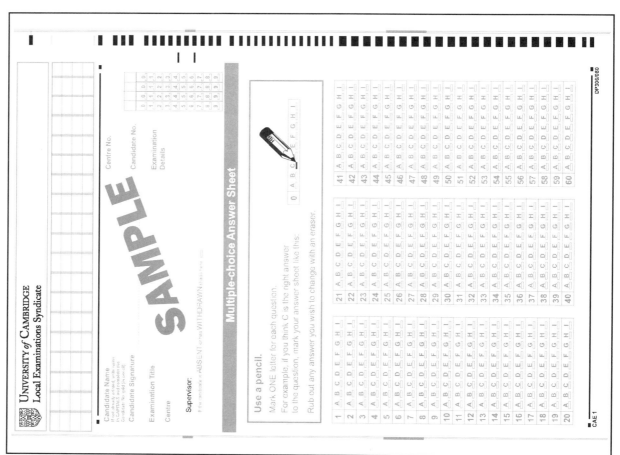

A touchMe 1.1
Date changer
Freeware

I used to work in a school, and once there was a case where a pupil had got permission to write his homework on his computer at home. When the teacher asked for the homework on the day it was due, the pupil informed the teacher that the floppy disk he had brought it in on had broken and he would bring his homework in the next day. This he did. After a couple of minutes with the disk, the teacher told the pupil he was going to punish him for lying and doing his homework late.

How did he know? He simply found out the date that the homework document was created, and the day it was last altered. However, this cute little free program *touchMe* enables you to set these dates to whatever you wish.

This can aid you in pulling the wool over your teacher's eyes, but more importantly, you can use it to correct any errors that creep into your files. You could, of course, always ignore *touchMe* and just change the Date and Time settings on your computer and resave your work. But isn't finding a complex solution to a simple problem what computer programming is all about?

B Let's Go Fishing
Fishing game
Shareware $10

Fishing is probably the most popular participation sport in the country. That's if you can call sitting around on a riverbank, occasionally waving a rod about, either participation or sport. This game captures all the excitement and more (sorry to be rude!) in a black and white game.

You start with a trip to the fishing shop to buy rod, line and small live wiggly things as bait. Then it's off to the lakeside for a spot of fishing and a great deal of sitting.

Each time you land a fish you have less time to catch the next one. Once you have used up all your bait, it's back to the fish market to sell some of your fish for cash, which you can then spend in the fishing shop on more bait and equipment.

You can only visit the shop three times, so once you run out of bait, your score is the total weight of fish you have left at the end. It's not terribly exciting, but there's a whole hour of fun to be had. It's definitely not worth paying the fee for this program, so save your money and do some real fishing instead.

C Poetry Ink
Poetry
Freeware

This file is issue ten of *Poetry Ink*, a magazine about poetry. It contains general articles about poetry, reviews of poetry multimedia, tips on writing and poetry contributions.

It's clearly created by enthusiasts and they are probably extremely talented writers as well. However, call me pedantic, call me elitist, call me whatever you like, but a computer screen just isn't the correct place to read poetry. I'm not sure why but it somehow cheapens the written word and makes it hard to fully appreciate it. In the same way that red wine requires a different shaped glass from white wine and fish demands different cutlery from steak, so it is with poetry – the medium is nearly as important as the message.

However, if you're hoping to be a poet and you want your voice to reach a wider audience, then using this free software will be your best chance – assuming you have Internet access in your bare and lonely poet's corner.

D Ski3D
Skiing game
Shareware $15

It's so real you can almost smell the Austrian wine and feel the snow on your cheeks. *Ski3D* brings the thrills of skiing to the screen of your computer.

There's a choice between downhill and slalom skiing as well as a selection of courses for you to race against your opponents. Make sure you take those turns neatly or else you'll find yourself taking a heavy fall. As you launch off downhill, the ski course presents itself to you in a detailed picture with barriers down the side of the course and fir trees for you to try to miss.

If this doesn't create enough problems for you, then you can edit the program to make up your own twisting and turning courses. And if that isn't dangerous enough, you can even turn on the night sky and watch the stars as you ski. If you can't make it to the dry-ski slope or you haven't been able to book up for a winter holiday, this highly entertaining piece of shareware is the next best thing.

E DietSleuth
Diet Analysis
Shareware $20

If you've ever tried to go on a calorie-controlled diet, you'll know what a pain it is to work out the intake from all the different foods you take in each day. *DietSleuth* goes a long way towards helping you keep track of what's going in by calculating the details of your diet. At its heart, *DietSleuth* has a database with over 5,000 different foods listed in 21 different categories. Rather than just watching the calories, *DietSleuth* has a breakdown of calories, carbohydrates, protein, fibre and grammes of fat for each food listed.

All you have to do is add the foods you eat to a daily intake section and *DietSleuth* adds up all the key categories. If a food type is not available from the database, just key in details from the food packaging.

Using *DietSleuth* is undoubtedly easier than trying to calculate all the values by hand; it does rely on accurate weighing of the various foods you eat, but if you want to monitor your diet closely, this software will certainly help.

F Eliza 6.0.1 and Azile 4.5
Psychoanalysis
Shareware $5 each

Eliza is a novelty program which, as well as being a text editor, can conduct psychoanalysis sessions! It's actually pretty good at interpreting what you type in. Occasionally it does make mistakes, but that just adds to the fun.

All the options you'd expect to find in the average text editor are here – fonts, colours, styles and so on – but you can also choose whether *Eliza* appears as a male or female face at the top of the screen.

Azile (that's *Eliza* spelt backwards, of course) is a nasty version of *Eliza*, which delights in insulting you and making fun of your problems. Its style comes about halfway between Sigmund Freud and a mass murderer. Strangely, you can't select a female version of *Azile*.

Of course, you'd really have to be mad to believe anything *Eliza* or *Azile* says but give them a try anyway. People do say that laughter is the best medicine.

Part 2

For questions **19–24** you must choose which of the paragraphs **A–G** fit into the numbered gaps in the following newspaper article. There is one extra paragraph which does not fit in any of the gaps.

Warning: exercise can damage your health

By Roger Dobson

People starting fitness programmes often think they can do more than they should.

Getting fit can seriously damage your health. Exercise may be all very well for keeping the heart and lungs in shape, but other parts of the body are losing out in the sprint to get fit.

19

Participants also risk getting a variety of specific problems including jogger's nephritis, runner's knee, golfer's groin, parachutist's ankle, runner's claw toe, and thrower's elbow. And even worse, there are the diseases waiting to be caught from fellow enthusiasts, from conjunctivitis to legionella. New research on the effects of exercise has found that there are hidden dangers in having too much of it, and sports medicine specialists now want the emphasis to be on quality rather than quantity.

20

'If the Government is propagating healthy exercise for everyone, the message must be taken in the context that some people will take health advice to an extreme,' says Professor Michael Horton, head of the bone centre at University College, London, and the organiser of a conference on the impact of exercise on the skeleton. While the density and strength of bones is boosted by exercise, too much of it can lead to a weaker skeleton as people become older. Women are particularly at risk: evidence from the USA shows that as many as 70 per cent of young women students who took part in college athletics had irregular menstrual cycles caused by exercise and poor diet and as a result were building up problems of osteoporosis in later life. Bones grow and adapt to pressure by increasing the strength in those areas where it is needed. Football players have a very dense ankle structure and leg bones as a consequence both of running and of impact.

21

'Swimming can increase muscle mass and help with the respiratory system, but it has no effect on the skeleton. Squash on the other hand is good because the rapid changes of movement increase bone mass. Activities with high impact and big changes in movement are best for the skeleton. Every time we put a foot on the floor the physical effect is sensed by the skeleton and it will adapt,' says Professor Horton.

22

Prof John Davies, professor of sports medicine and medical adviser to the Welsh Rugby Union, says that 90 per cent of sports injuries involve damage to soft tissue, including sprains and strains. 'We see a lot of pulled muscles and stress fractures and a lot of it is down to poor technique and people going at it too hard without any graduated regime,' he says. 'Choosing the right activity is important. Some people, for instance, are built for running and others are not. There are alternatives to running and there is now evidence that power walking is as beneficial but without the jarring effects.'

'Here people are in close proximity to each other in a crowded, moist atmosphere, and the situation lends itself to the transmission of a whole range of respiratory infections – sore throats, colds, fungal infections, verrucae and so on,' says Prof Greg McLatchie, professor of sports medicine at Sunderland University.

24

So if you're thinking it's time to get fit, take care. Exercise does indeed have its benefits but consider the drawbacks too. If you ever needed an excuse to put your feet up in front of the television and watch other people struggle at sporting endeavours, you've got one now!

A 'One of the main problems is that if you take someone who is sedentary and put them in a training regime, then a substantial number may be at risk of injuries like stress fractures because of their immature skeleton. The message is that exercise is good for you, but your initial health has to be taken into consideration and you need to be aware that at extremes it can cause damage, particularly when taken without any preparation.'

B A major problem only now being recognised is that many people embark on fitness programmes with an over-optimistic enthusiasm and assume that the body is far fitter than it really is. Some experts are urging a more cautious approach.

C Backs and necks are getting strained, knees damaged, ankles twisted and bones cracked by the stresses and strains of running and jogging and thousands of other activities that have become popular over the last 20 years in the fight against flab.

D The danger of side effects from too much exercise is not the only problem facing those who want to get fit. There are risks associated with exercising while the skeleton is unfit and unprepared, and there is also the problem of choosing the right exercise.

E And his research shows that the most unlikely places can be the source of infection. After several swimmers and curlers at a Scottish leisure complex went down with a form of legionellosis, investigators eventually found that the airborne infection had travelled all the way along the pipes and vents of the ventilation system from a contaminated jacuzzi.

F Clare MacEvilly, a sports scientist at the British Athletics Foundation, said: 'The study is really good, you probably couldn't get a better design. But as the paper says, it is very much a preliminary study. It was only for two weeks and there were only ten people.'

G Over time, these can have a serious impact on the cartilage of the knee leading to arthritis, and urban joggers running on hard surfaces are thought to be most at risk. Apart from the risk of trauma and long-term bone problems, there is also the danger of picking up an infection from other enthusiasts. These infections are known collectively as changing-room syndrome.

The Independent

23

Part 3

Read the following newspaper article and then answer questions **25–31**. Choose **A, B, C,** or **D** for each question. Give only one answer to each question.

These animals are dying out. And all because of consumer demand for a fine wool called shahtoosh.

The men who make it can spend months weaving a single shawl out of a wool so fine it strains the eyes to work with it. They then need a holiday to restore their eyesight. It is the world's most sophisticated symbol of wealth: weight for weight, the wool is more valuable than gold, or platinum, and in an exclusive central London store that shawl, which may cost the weaver his eyesight, can cost the consumer £11,000.

The expanding trade in shahtoosh is leading to the extinction of the remaining herds of Tibetan antelope, or chiru, from which it comes.

But although the trade has been illegal in most of the world for 22 years – that £11,000 shawl was one of 138, worth more than £300,000, seized in a police raid on the shop 'Kashmir' in central London in February 1997 – it remains legal in the Indian state where it originates.

The state of Kashmir lent its name to shahtoosh's humbler but ecologically friendly relative, cashmere, and it is the immensely skilled workers of the state who spin and weave both wools.

Last week, confronted by legal moves from the Wildlife Protection Society of India to shut down the trade for good, the chief minister of Jammu and Kashmir, Dr Farooq Abdullah, was defiant.

'As long as I am the chief minister,' he declared, 'shahtoosh will be sold in Kashmir.' The campaign to ban the trade, he went on, 'maligns the people of the state', and he claimed that there was 'no evidence of Tibetan antelope being reduced in number or their being shot to acquire wool for shahtoosh.'

For centuries shahtoosh has been a highly prized item throughout India. But for a long time confusion has reigned about its origin. Even today a website in the United States puts out the notion that twice a year the Tibetan antelope moult, leaving their wool on rocks or bushes. Wind blows the hair into little balls. Tibetans and Nepalis trek through the mountains for weeks to return with little handfuls of wool. But this is pure invention.

As Dr George Schaller, director of America's Wildlife Conservation Society, discovered during long expeditions on the bleak and dry Tibetan plateau in the past few years, the antelope are trapped and shot, usually during the winter months, when the undercoat, where the shahtoosh comes from, is at its thickest.

This is the only verified way in which shahtoosh can be obtained. Tibetan herdsmen pull the wool from the skins of the dead animals to sell to local dealers. 'In the courtyard of one such dealer,' Dr Schaller reported in 1988, 'were sacks of wool ready for smuggling into western Nepal and from there to Kashmir, where the wool is woven into scarves and shawls.'

Shahtoosh has been culled, spun and woven in this way for centuries. But in the past ten years it has finally arrived in the West as the ultimately wealthy fabric. This huge new demand has been answered by ruthless and large-scale killings of antelope by organised gangs driving on to the Tibetan plateau and shooting the antelope from vehicles, killing as many as 500 animals in a hunt.

The Chinese estimate that between 2,000 and 4,000 antelope are illegally killed every year. Enforcement of the ban on killing, which China has signed, is especially difficult because of the huge area of the plateau, its remoteness and the bitter cold of the winter months when most of the hunting takes place.

There have, however, been impressive Chinese successes. In 1996 the director of the Arjin Shan Reserve, Song Binqian, received information about a gang of poachers at work on the plateau and confronted them. After a lengthy gunfight more than 20 poachers surrendered. In their possession were seven rifles, 10,000 rounds of ammunition and 1,100 dead antelope. The leader of the gang was jailed for seven years.

An additional nasty twist to the illegal trade in the antelope is its connection to the illegal trade in tiger bones. This was uncovered in 1993 when three shahtoosh traders confessed to investigators in India that tiger bones and skins were bartered for raw shahtoosh, yielding vast

profits on both sides; on the Kashmiri side, it was claimed, the profits were used to buy arms for militants in the state's long-running rebellion.

Another trader revealed that for one bag of tiger bones – the result of poaching in India's game reserves, and immensely prized in Chinese traditional medicine – he would receive two bags of pure shahtoosh.

The Wildlife Protection Society of India, which was founded by the wildlife photographer and film-maker Belinda Wright in 1994 in response to the new threat from the Chinese medicine trade to India's decreasing number of tigers, has been fighting the shahtoosh trade every way it can.

According to Ms Wright, who was born in India of British parents, the people with most to lose from a successful blocking of the shahtoosh trade are about a dozen wealthy businessmen.

The workers who spin and weave it would continue with their customary trade in cashmere, which is produced from a domestic goat.

And for those who long for fine shawls but will not support the killing that is needed to produce shahtoosh, she recommends 'shahmina': a wool that has been developed recently in India, with virtually the same weight, texture and warmth as shahtoosh, produced from pure strains of high-altitude goats. With no bloodshed involved and no danger to the survival of any species.

The Independent

25 The men who weave shahtoosh
   A commit a crime when they do this work.
   B are experts at what they do.
   C are paid £11,000 for a single shawl.
   D are all blind.

26 What is the attitude of the Kashmiri chief minister?
   A He thinks the courts should decide whether to ban the shahtoosh trade.
   B He is worried about the number of antelope that are killed.
   C He feels there are good arguments for limiting the sale of shahtoosh.
   D He sees no reason to ban the sale of shahtoosh.

27 How is shahtoosh traditionally obtained?
   A The animals are killed and the wool is pulled from the skin.
   B The wool is taken from the live animal in the winter.
   C The wool is taken from the animals after they die naturally.
   D The wool falls from the body naturally and then people collect it in bags.

28 According to the writer, why is it particularly difficult for the Chinese to enforce a ban on hunting?
   A The gangs of hunters are now organized by people in the West.
   B The poachers are armed and dangerous.
   C The animals are hunted in a remote and inhospitable area.
   D The poachers are well organized and have vehicles.

29 What is the connection between trade in shahtoosh and trade in tiger bones?
   A They are both very important in traditional Chinese medicine.
   B People who hunt for antelope often hunt tigers too.
   C Shahtoosh can be exchanged for tiger bones.
   D Antelope bones have become very popular too.

30 The shahtoosh trade continues because
   A a small number of rich people want it to.
   B the people who spin and weave the wool need jobs.
   C antelope numbers have to be controlled.
   D there is no alternative material of the same quality.

31 What is the writer's opinion of the shahtoosh trade?
   A It is a Kashmiri tradition that should be allowed to continue.
   B It is unnecessary and should be banned.
   C If it is banned, shahtoosh weavers will lose money.
   D There is no evidence that antelope are killed for their wool.

Part 4

Answer questions **32–49** by referring to the magazine article about the singer, Sophie Ellis-Bextor's, week.

For questions **32–49** choose your answers from the list **A–F**. Some of your choices may be required more than once.

When more than one answer is required, these may be given in any order.

A	Sunday	C	Tuesday	E	Thursday
B	Monday	D	Wednesday	F	Friday

On which day or days did the following happen?

She got up later than usual.	32 …
She went shopping with some of her family.	33 …
She spent the evening talking business.	34 …
She travelled by plane.	35 …
She had lunch in a restaurant.	36 …
She read about herself in the newspaper.	37 … 38 …
She hurt herself.	39 …
She answered questions from the press and the public.	40 … 41 … 42 …
She prepared for a TV programme the following day.	43 …
She spent all or some of the day with members of her family.	44 … 45 … 46 …
She had her dinner delivered to her flat.	47 …
She spent the evening with some friends.	48 …
She stayed out later than she wanted to.	49 …

My week

Sophie Ellis-Bextor

Vocalist on 'If This Ain't Love', which is vying with Victoria Beckham for the Number 1 spot

A Sunday

I'm taking it easy at my dad's cottage in Sussex. We're celebrating the birthday of my twin brother and sister, who have just turned two, and we've organised a big party with about 70 guests and an entertainer, who blows enormous balloons and makes balloon animals. I spend the majority of the day on the bouncy castle with lots of kids, but pay the consequences by getting burnt knees after chasing them round on my hands and knees. The overall effect is very relaxing; when you're doing something as crazy as pop music, it's good to have something to bring you back to earth.

B Monday

I get up at seven, because the children wake me. We wander into a local department store, where the children and I have fun playing on a games machine, and my dad buys my single. This afternoon I catch the train home and get back to my flat in north London in the early evening. I've been reading some of today's papers and have been finding the comments about Victoria Beckham and me rather amusing. She's actually been very decent to me; who knows, one day we may work together. My only criticism is that she claims that she wants her song to do the talking. Yet she hasn't stopped promoting it and pointing it in the right direction. Still, I'm not going to get upset about who'll be at Number 1 and Number 2 this weekend. So my flatmate and I order some take-away sushi from Yo sushi: I love sushi and they can bike it round …

C Tuesday

My day is dominated by press interviews, although one takes place in a pub in Camden Town, which made quite a change. This evening I have been invited out to dinner by a couple of guys from a record company, who could potentially be signing me. They take me to a Thai restaurant called Silks and Spice on Chalk Farm Road. I feel that it's important to get to know your business partners on a personal level, so being wined and dined by them is a great excuse. I recorded the single in Thailand, so I know a bit about Thai cuisine and the dishes I like. I order some delicious Tom-cha-kai – a soup with lemongrass, ginger and chicken – and some fish cakes. It's a very relaxed evening, we have a great laugh and the business we discussed looks promising.

D Wednesday

I have a lie-in and get up at about nine, then go to EMI, my record label, to record an interview. Afterwards I meet my dad for lunch at Carluccio's new place on Oxford Street. I then have an appointment with Premier, my model agency; after getting on the underground and boiling to death, I arrive in a melted state. I've only been modelling since January, but because of the single there are now a few projects in the pipeline. After some phone interviews, I go round to my mum's in west London for dinner. She makes a fantastic seafood pasta dish with salad. It's been an Italian cuisine day for me.

E Thursday

I leave the flat at seven to do the breakfast show at Kiss FM. I'm only on for about half an hour, but it's great fun. At about 10.30 a.m. I go to do a radio link-up in a west London studio. I do about 20 regional radio interviews at the same time, but I'm on the air with very enthusiastic people who keep my energy up. At 3.00 p.m., I go to a record store at Oxford Circus for some interviews with BBS News and Channel Five. It was great to see people buying the single, and I sign quite a few on request. Then I look at the papers and read some hysterical nonsense that I am having a romantic encounter with someone from a popular TV show. There is some romance in my life but I won't comment on it. When I get home I talk to a researcher from Woman's Hour, which I'm appearing on next week – I'm really looking forward to it.

F Friday

I fly up to Glasgow to do a rehearsal for FBI, the BBC's Saturday morning show, along with the band and some people from the record company. The show goes out live tomorrow, which I'm looking forward to – it's always good to play live. We're finished rehearsing by 12.00 and so we jet across to Edinburgh to visit some close friends of mine. The idea is to get an early night and not to party too long as we have to get back to Glasgow and get up really early tomorrow – but what with the late opening hours our intentions get rather lost. As for the weekend – well, I don't really care if the single gets to Number 1 or not. So we'll just have to wait and see.

The Independent

Paper 2 Writing (2 hours)

Part 1

You must answer this question.

1   You work at the Eccleston Theatre, a new theatre which is about to open very soon. You have received the note below from the theatre manager.

Read the note, the proposed leaflet about the opening night, and the cutting from the newspaper. Then, using the information provided, write the **two letters** listed below.

> *Jo*
>
> *Bad news I'm afraid! I've just heard from Hugh Dalton's agent that he can't make it on the 15th. Shooting starts on his new film in California at the end of June and there's no way he'll be able to get back for the opening. He was very apologetic but that's not much use to us. I've been racking my brains trying to think of who else we could ask. How about Julia York? You know, she was nominated for an Oscar last year for 'A Girl Like Me', and she's done lots of television. She's also always in 'Hello!' magazine but perhaps we'd better not mention that! Anyway, I spoke to her agent who said she's free then and would probably love to do it but could we write to her and formally ask her? So could you write and ask her? Tell her a little bit about the theatre and explain what the programme will be that evening. By the way, the schools organizer has told me that they've put together an hour–long programme (much better than half an hour, I think) so we'll move the buffet back to 8.30. Could you also drop Sir Terence a line and let him know about these changes?*
>
> *Thanks a lot*
> *Andi*

GRAND OPENING
of
THE ECCLESTON THEATRE
South Street, Harpenden, Herts
on
Friday 15th July at 6.30 p.m.
by
Oscar-winning actor, director, and producer
HUGH DALTON

6.30 drinks and snacks in the foyer
7.00 formal opening by Hugh Dalton
7.15 speech by Sir Terence Hanley, director of the theatre building programme
7.30 a programme of song and dance performed by local schools
8.00 buffet dinner backstage

R.S.V.P.

THEATRE TO OPEN NEXT MONTH

Next month will see the opening of the Eccleston Theatre on South Street. This valuable new addition to the cultural life of Harpenden has been almost entirely the work of Sir Terence Hanley, who has lived in the area all his life. He raised the money for the project, bought the site and oversaw the building. 'I am delighted to announce that we will be up and running from the middle of next month with an exciting production of "Romeo and Juliet" starting on Saturday 16th July', he told our reporter.

a) Write a short **letter** to Sir Terence Hanley explaining the changes to the programme (approximately 100 words).

b) Write a **letter** to Julia York, asking her to open the theatre. Tell her a little bit about the theatre and explain what the programme will be on that evening (approximately 150 words).

You do not need to include addresses. You should use your own words as far as possible.

Part 2

Choose **one** of the following writing tasks. Your answer should follow exactly the instructions given. Write approximately 250 words.

2   An English language magazine published in your town contains a regular feature entitled 'My favourite English-language film'. You decide to write a short review of your favourite film in English for the magazine including a brief summary of the plot and the main characters, a comment on the acting and direction, and saying why you particularly like this film.

3   An international publisher is collecting articles for a book entitled 'Global Creativity – a personal view'. The book will comprise a collection of articles on different creative, but not necessarily famous, people from all over the world. You have been asked to write a short article on someone from your country saying something about their life and work, why you have chosen this person, and why you find their work important.

4   There have been severe storms in your country causing flooding and some damage to property but no loss of life. Reports of these events have been greatly exaggerated in the newspapers and on TV and an English friend of yours has written to you to find out what is happening and if you are OK. Write a letter to your friend, reassuring him / her that you are all right, explaining what has happened and what the situation is now.

5   You have done some freelance work for an international organization which is now considering the possibility of setting up a branch in your town or region. They have asked you to write a report on whether this is a good idea or not.

Write your **report** for the organization. Discuss factors such as geographical position, communications, staff recruitment potential and salary expectations, and any other important issues, and make a recommendation as to whether opening a new branch in your area would be a sensible course of action.

Paper 3 English in Use answer sheets

Candidates use the answer sheets for all parts of this paper.

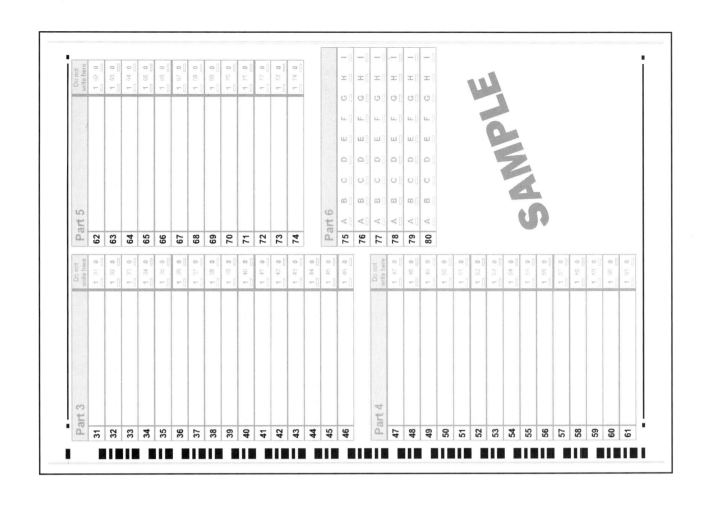

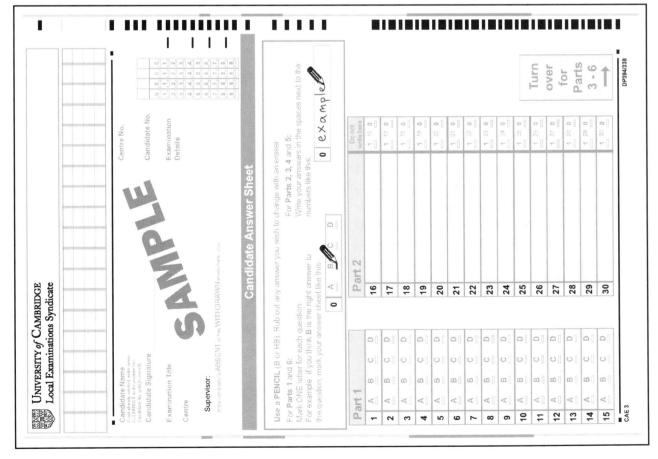

Paper 3 English In Use (1 hour 30 minutes)

Part 1

For questions **1-15**, read the article and then decide which word opposite best fits each space. The exercise begins with an example (**0**).

FAST LANE FOR PEDESTRIANS

Get ready for the next transport ..B.. (**0**). A group of London businesses are so annoyed with the tortoise-like ... (**1**) of walkers down Britain's busiest shopping street that they have ... (**2**) the world's first pedestrian fast lane.

Under their plans, lodged (apparently) in all ... (**3**) with Westminster City Council, one-way fast lanes would have a minimum speed limit of 5 kph, and would be ... (**4**) by speed cameras. Anyone caught dawdling in the fast lane, reading maps, using a mobile phone, or carrying bulky shopping bags would be ... (**5**) to a £10 on-the-spot fine. This, ... (**6**), is after they have been pulled over into the slow lane for a reprimand.

Andy Kourpas, spokesman for the West End businesses behind the ... (**7**), said: 'Overcrowding of the pavements on Oxford Street is ... (**8**) problems and delays for shoppers and for people who work in the area. It can take ages to get anywhere, and ... (**9**) become frayed when people are ... (**10**) up by slow walkers or window-shoppers.'

A ... (**11**) of pedestrians in the two-kilometre-long street has found that nine out of ten had ... (**12**) some form of 'pavement rage', with more than half ... (**13**) on a daily ... (**14**). Most say they are regularly bumped into, nudged or elbowed. A quarter said tourists were the chief ... (**15**), particularly when they stop to look at maps or street signs.

Independent On Sunday

	A	B	C	D
0	rebellion	revolution	outbreak	resistance
1	travel	increase	progress	passing
2	proposed	intended	argued	voted
3	gravity	attention	resolution	seriousness
4	monitored	tended	guarded	served
5	guilty	liable	responsible	risking
6	unfortunately	hopefully	sadly	presumably
7	demonstration	manifestation	campaign	deed
8	making	doing	starting	causing
9	tempers	characters	personalities	moods
10	taken	held	put	done
11	research	measure	scan	survey
12	become	approached	experienced	occurred
13	suffering	feeling	bearing	troubling
14	reason	way	routine	basis
15	culprits	criminals	suspects	defendants

Part 2

For questions **16–30** complete the following article. Use only one word for each space. The exercise begins with an example (**0**).

A DNA fingerprint ..of.. (**0**) every active criminal in Britain will be taken ... (**16**) part of government plans ... (**17**) a wide-ranging overhaul of the criminal justice system, the Prime Minister said yesterday.

In his first public announcement ... (**18**) returning from holiday, Tony Blair promised to deliver a courts system fit for ... (**19**) 21st century. Addressing police officers in Kent, in southern England, he accused the courts of being run for ... (**20**) own convenience and promised to ensure that victims, witnesses and police giving evidence would receive more respect.

Mr Blair declared the justice system archaic, saying it hindered police efforts to keep up ... (**21**) organised crime, and announced ... (**22**) £107m package to expand the DNA database. According to a government spokesman, the database should hold ... (**23**) than three million samples – equivalent ... (**24**) almost the whole criminal class of the UK.

'I think we ... (**25**) effectively got a 19th century justice system in a 21st century world,' the Prime Minister said.

'We have totally failed to keep ... (**26**) to date with the fact that we have got major organised crime operating in a completely different way to 50 ... (**27**) 60 years ago,' he said.

In a clear attempt to go one better ... (**28**) crime than the previous government, Mr Blair stressed that he was ... (**29**) favour of so-called zero tolerance and wanted a law-abiding society based on courtesy ... (**30**) others.

The Independent

Part 3

In **most** lines of the following text, there is **either** a spelling **or** a punctuation error. For each numbered line **31–46**, write the correctly spelled word or show the correct punctuation. **Some lines are correct**. Indicate these with a tick (✔). The exercise begins with three examples.

The carpets in the glass lifts that go up and down in the middle	✔
of the worlds biggest cruise ship are changed every 24 hours to	world's
display the currant day of the week. The crew say that losing	current
track of time is easy on the £410m floting superhotel, *The*	... **31**
Explorer of the Seas. With the casino, theatre, pools, and malls	... **32**
of bars, restaurants, and shops, it is easy to loose track of	... **33**
everything, including the sea, aboard this city.	... **34**
Last night *The Explorer* sailed from the port that long ago saw	... **35**
the *Titanic* off. In three weeks 5,000 poeple will board this	... **36**
magnificient cruise ship for her first trip around the islands.	... **37**
'This is not really something for the independant tourist,' said	... **38**
a company spokeswoman Kate Selley, with massive	... **39**
understatement. However it is something for those who want	... **40**
every need catered for. From the pagers given to parents who	... **41**
leave there children in one of its five creches, to the immaculate	... **42**
pool table that alters to counter the ships movement, every	... **43**
touch has been considered.	... **44**
Passengers on a one-week cruise of the caribbean will pay	... **45**
from £929 each up to £13,000 for two if they want the Royal	... **46**
Suite. With it's marble bathroom and jacuzzi, the suite will suit	
those who cannot possibly travell without having a piano next to	
the bedroom.	

Part 5

For questions **62–74**, read the following informal note. Use the information in it to complete the numbered gaps in the formal letter which follows. **Use no more than two words** for each gap. The words you need do not occur in the note. The exercise begins with an example **(0)**.

INFORMAL NOTE

Jack,

Sorry you weren't able to come along to the usual get-together the other night but, as promised, here's a brief note of what happened.

- The new members all told us a bit about themselves.
- We voted on the new secretary. As you know, Chris Knight and Verity Lambert were both up for the post. Chris got it by 9 votes to 6.
- Hermione told us all about her trip to Connecticut. Sounded great – she's going to write it up and send it round to anyone who's interested.
- There was a lot of talk about what to do with all those books that Reg Foulkes picked up over the years and gave us just before he died last year. We couldn't make up our minds!!!
- We agreed to have the usual summer disco to raise money for the association. Tom Smith is in charge this year.

Hope to see you at the next one.

Best wishes

Len

FORMAL LETTER

Dear Mrs Gresham

I am sorry you were unable to attend the last *meeting*. **(0)** of the Letchford Association but I thought you would be interested to know what happened.

First of all, the new members all … **(62)** themselves. We then proceeded to … **(63)** a new secretary. Mr Knight and Mrs Lambert had both been … **(64)** for the position. Mr Knight received nine votes to Mrs Lambert's six and was therefore … **(65)**.

Following that Mrs Hermione Greville gave … **(66)** about her trip to Connecticut. She intends to write up what she said and … **(67)** it to members who are interested.

There was then … **(68)** about what to do with Mr Foulkes' … **(69)** of books. You may remember he made a generous … **(70)** to the association just before he died last year. No decision … **(71)**.

As is our … **(72)** there will be a … **(73)** disco this summer. Mr Smith will … **(74)** it this year.

We look forward to seeing you next month.

Yours sincerely,

Leonard Finlay

For questions **47–61**, read the two texts below. Use the words in the boxes to the right of the two texts, listed **47–61**, to form **one** word that fits in the same numbered space in the text. The exercise begins with an example **(0)**.

NEW PLAN TO PUSH VEGETABLES

A ……………… **(0)** scheme will start in schools across Britain this autumn as a result of … **(47)** research into that most difficult piece of childhood diplomacy: how to persuade youngsters to make the right … **(48)** when offered fruit and vegetables or chocolate and chips.

With the use of a … **(49)** video and some old-fashioned … **(50)**, psychologists at the University of Wales managed to increase by five times the number of fruit and vegetables eaten by groups of primary-age school children whose previous eating habits had been labelled as 'most … **(51)**'.

… **(52)** projects in three schools last year produced huge increases in the … **(53)** of fruit and vegetables with children still eating their greens six months after the end of the study.

Independent on Sunday

0	nation
47	succeed
48	choose
49	promote
50	bribe
51	health
52	try
53	consume

CHILDREN LACK PROTECTION

Pushy parents are often more … **(54)** about seeing their children on television than the children themselves, according to research published yesterday.

Independent … **(55)** might be needed to intervene and protect children against parents and directors who may not always act in their best interests.

The research was commissioned after … **(56)** from viewers about the use of children in a … **(57)** of programmes from news and current affairs to late night … **(58)** comedy shows. The research included an examination of how children were used, what … **(59)** took place and whether the children were capable of giving … **(60)** consent.

'Viewers need some … **(61)**,' said one of the researchers. 'It may be necessary to extend the current guidelines, which cover child actors, to include all children.'

The Independent

54	enthusiasm
55	arbitrate
56	complain
57	vary
58	satire
59	consult
60	inform
61	assure

Paper 1 Listening answer sheet

Candidates use the answer sheet for all parts of this paper.

Part 6

For questions **75–80**, read the following text and then choose from the list **A–J** the best phrase given below it to fill each of the spaces. Each correct phrase may only be used once. **Some of the suggested answers do not fit at all.** The exercise begins with an example **(0)**.

Hebridean island gets first roundabout

The island of Tiree in the Inner Hebrides is to get its first roundabout; not to ease traffic flow but to show the inhabitants what one looks like.

Parents among Tiree's population of just 730 are worried their children's lack of experience will put them in danger when they leave the island, which is 11 miles long and five miles wide.

Islanders live a life virtually free from traffic on the quiet, single carriageway B-roads of Tiree. Now the grounds of the island's only school will be transformed ...J.. **(0)** boasting the island's only roundabout, traffic lights and zebra crossing.

Jessie Gray, 50, the deputy head of the school, which has 120 pupils, said: "Children do get to the mainland now a lot more than my generation did at the same age. This seemed like a great idea ... **(75)** there."

A group of volunteers will also be brought in to help make mini-traffic lights and road signs. Those helpers include the island's telecom engineer, John Gorman, 50, who helped start the ball rolling by winning a £500 grant ... **(76)**.

Mr Gorman, who moved to Tiree from Glasgow eight years ago, said: "We will be able ... **(77)** about two-way traffic. On the island you don't pass another car unless one or other vehicle is stopped in a passing place. It must be very difficult for children ... **(78)** when they see two-way traffic for the first time."

James Christie, 36, is an approved driving examiner for light goods vehicles at the airstrip. He voluntarily helps teenagers on the island ... **(79)**.

Mr Christie said: "It would be possible for a teenager ...**(80)** on the island only ever having experienced the single-lane roads here, then fly to London, hire a car and drive round a big city without ever having seen a roundabout or a set of traffic lights."

The Independent

A to prepare for their driving test
B to start getting them used to the roads
C to develop the island's driving test
D to teach them
E to widen roads throughout the island
F to pass their test
G to help pay for the work
H to receive a new driving licence
I to judge speeds
J to include its own small, tarmac strip

Paper 4 Listening (approximately 45 minutes)

Part 1

🎧 **PT1** You are going to hear an antiques dealer talking about his work. For questions **1–8**, fill in the missing information. You will hear the recording twice.

The speaker started buying and selling antiques in order to add to his [1] .

His wife was angry because he sold a [2] .

At first it's essential to have [3] so that you can build up some stock.

Being friendly with [4] is a very good idea.

It can be less risky to start trading in [5] rather than in your own shop.

The speaker believes that having a particular [6] makes good financial sense.

The speaker finds it [7] when people want to bargain.

Sometimes people think an antique is [8] just because it's more expensive.

Part 2

🎧 **PT2** You are going to hear the traffic and travel news on Bartlebury Local Radio. As you listen, complete the sentences for questions **9–16. Listen very carefully as you will hear the recording ONCE only.**

On the ring road to the north of the town there will be [9] for a little longer because of [10] .

The High Street is closed because of a [11] which has caused flooding.

You should use Walton Street and [12] if you want to go through the town centre.

All trains are [13] .

Flights to Italy have been [14] by two airlines because Italian [15] are on strike.

For flight information for the rest of the week you should phone the [16] .

Part 3

🎧 **PT3** You will now hear a discussion between a publisher and a nutritionist. For questions **17–24** complete the sentences. You will hear the recording twice.

Nero Varley publishes a magazine about [17] .

Nero Varley hopes that his 'experiment' will be seen as [18] by his readers.

The most recent issue of his magazine was unusual because it had [19] showing pictures of very different looking women.

On the cover of the magazine there is usually [20] to make it stand out.

Nancy Allbright thinks that [21] probably don't buy the magazine.

Nancy Allbright feels it is [22] that readers chose the woman with the fuller figure.

Both the speakers feel that [23] causes women to worry about their body shape.

Nancy Allbright feels that [24] is OK if it is done for medical reasons.

Paper 5 Speaking (approximately 15 minutes)

You are now going to work through all the stages of a complete speaking test. Work in pairs. (If you are working alone, look at p.4.) If possible, record the speaking test. Then play it back and think about how you might improve it.

Part 1

With your partner, take it in turns to ask and answer the questions below.

Where are you from?
Can you tell me something about where you live?
What do you do?
What do you do in your free time?
How long have you been learning English?
What do you enjoy about learning English?
What are your future plans?

Part 4

🎧 PT4 You will hear five short extracts in which people talk about influences on their lives and work. **Remember that you must complete both tasks as you listen. You will hear the recording twice.**

TASK ONE

For questions **25–29**, match the extracts with the people, listed **A–H**.

A	an architect	Speaker 1 [25]
B	an artist	Speaker 2 [26]
C	a writer	Speaker 3 [27]
D	a sculptor	Speaker 4 [28]
E	an actor	Speaker 5 [29]
F	a politician	
G	a film director	
H	a dancer	

TASK TWO

For questions **30–34**, match the extracts with the main influence on each speaker's life and work, listed **A–H**.

A	death	Speaker 1 [30]
B	coastal scenery	Speaker 2 [31]
C	a grandfather	Speaker 3 [32]
D	the human body	Speaker 4 [33]
E	people in general	Speaker 5 [34]
F	a father	
G	a drama teacher	
H	going to the cinema	

Part 3

Work in pairs. Discuss the task below. Try and reach an agreement if you can.

You work at a college which would like to expand the number of courses that it offers. You can afford to run two new courses in the Humanities (Arts) Department. Look at the possibilities below. Discuss the advantages and disadvantages of each type of course and decide which two new courses you would run.

· fine art
· sculpture
· music
· creative writing
· photography
· journalism
· architecture
· film studies

Part 4

Work in pairs. Discuss these questions.

Discuss the following statements in pairs. Decide if you agree or disagree with them and give reasons for your answers.

· Many arts courses are of little practical value and should not therefore be offered at universities and colleges.
· Access to all exhibitions of art (museums, art galleries, etc.) should be free.
· The amount of money spent on making mediocre movies would be much better spent on projects of real artistic value.
· No piece of art can ever be worth as much as £37m.
· Much modern art looks as if it was done by a five-year-old and has about as much artistic merit.
· Popular art and music will never become as great as the classical art and music of the past.

Part 2

Take it in turns. One person look at the pictures in A and discuss the questions below. The other person look at the pictures in B and discuss the same questions. When your partner finishes talking you should comment briefly on his / her pictures.

A

Compare and contrast the three pictures you have been given.
What is your first impression of each photo?
What atmosphere do they convey?
Why do you think the photographer took each photo?
Is there a message in the photo? If so, what?
Which do you prefer? Why?

B

Answer key

Level The exam tasks in Units 1–4 are not as difficult as those you will find in the CAE exam. These tasks aim to prepare you for exam level tasks by providing useful practice in the style of the exam.

1 Influences

Reading p.6

TASK 1 1 books (the texts mention *novels, fiction, writers, stories, writing, volume, readable, exciting reading*); 2 *Shackleton* (there is no hint that it is fiction, unlike in the other reviews); 3 *A Star Called Henry* (1916 and later) and *Shackleton* (his first Antarctic expedition was in 1900).

TASK 2 1 / 2 / 3 – A / B / D (in any order); 4 – C; 5 – B; 6 – C; 7 – D; 8 – A (*they live quietly in central London … and inflict their loneliness on each other. Nearby*); 9 – B (*she was adopted, returned, fostered, returned … with no father … (her) search for her real mother*); 10 – C (*uncomfortable in middle age, confused by their life decisions*); 11 – D (*a cop-bashing Republican hero*); 12 / 13 – D (Henry's activities are exciting: *the narrative rockets along*) / E (*the adventures of this complex character make exciting reading*); 14 – E (the book tells the story of Shackleton's life and adventures).

In the multiple matching activities you should be able to answer the questions without understanding every word of the texts. When you have finished the task, you will be aware that there are quite a few words in the text that you do not know. Do **not** get out a dictionary and look them all up. If you want, choose five or six words (at the most) to look up and learn.

Language development p. 7

1 1 d; 2 a; 3 b; 4 f; 5 c; 6 e.

2 1 fallen off; 2 fell for; 3 fallen out; 4 fallen out; 5 fall for; 6 falling off.

Phrasal verbs are important. Learn them in small numbers; five or six at a time at the most. A useful way of trying to remember any new vocabulary is to write a sentence that is true and about yourself, and that includes the new item of vocabulary. Do that for these phrasal verbs.

Writing p.8

TASK 1 1 D (*Simpson*); 2 B (*publishing*); 3 the 'p's in B and the 's's in D are repeated at the beginning of words; 4 This is a matter of taste but I prefer B. It contrasts Penge (a rough area in the 1940s) and publishing (a profession that is not considered rough at all). *Simpson's start* does not arouse interest in the same way.

TASK 2

1 Where I grew up	2 Nursery school	3 Primary school	4 Secondary school and my inspiration
A C E H	G D I	J L N	B K F M

TASK 3

Make notes on each of the paragraphs before you start to write. Organize your notes into some sort of logical order. Then write your article. Try and give your finished article to a teacher (or a friend) to correct.

Model answer

DEATH GIVES NEW LIFE

Can a detective novel change someone's life? You probably think the answer is no. But you'd be wrong. I discovered *Too Many Cooks* by Rex Stout in a secondhand bookshop two years ago, and I haven't been the same since!

Rex Stout's detective is Nero Wolfe, an enormously fat eccentric, who lives in New York, cultivates orchids, eats and cooks gourmet food, and for a living solves seemingly unsolvable crimes. Even more eccentrically, he never leaves his house on business, preferring to send his secretary / sidekick, Archie Goodwin, to interview suspects and do all the legwork.

Too Many Cooks is unusual in that the story finds Nero Wolfe away from home, though not, it has to be said, on business. He has gone to West Virginia where he will be guest of honour at a convention of fifteen master chefs. There

is considerable professional jealousy between the chefs and before long one of them is found dead with a knife in him. From there the story develops along the lines of classic detective fiction with Wolfe providing the ingenious solution in the closing pages.

Various things struck me about the story the first time I read it. The first was the main characters: although unusual, they were realistically portrayed. The interplay between them was as fascinating as the story itself. Second, was the plot: how cleverly it was worked out and how it perfectly fitted the psychology of the different suspects.

The final effect was that not only did I want to read more Nero Wolfe books (there are forty-two altogether) but I wanted to write detective stories. I started planning and plotting right then and there – and I've already had a couple published.

English In Use p.9

TASK 1 1 T (*she … fire to it*); 2 F (Mr Hanley's descendants may get £1,500 for it).

TASK 2 a 1 judged (the only word that fits here); 2 threw (*put* is possible, though if you put something *into* a fire you might burn your hands!).
b 1 described (you describe something *as* …); 2 lit (you light a fire *with* something).
c 1 decided (the only word that fits here); 2 set (*to set fire to something* is a fixed expression).
d 1 examined (the only word that fits here); 2 put (if you put something *on* the fire rather than *into* it you probably won't burn your hands!).

TASK 3 3 revealed (none of the other words can be used with regard to the ending of a book)
4 forgotten (*to lie forgotten* is a fixed expression)
5 descendants (your children and grandchildren are your descendants)
6 protective (sympathetic *to*; preserving *of* and defensive *of* are incorrect English)
7 critic (someone who comments on literary work is a critic)
8 Fortunately (this is the only word which can satisfactorily link the previous sentence to this sentence)
9 work (this is the word used for artistic achievement)
10 expected (*intended* does not fit with the idea of an auction; you would have to say 'it is hoped that the letter will … '; or 'Phillips guess that the letter will …')
11 auctioned (*traded* or *exchanged* are not words used in this situation; to *bid* is what you do at an auction when you offer a sum of money for something)
12 department (the different areas of expertise in an organization – business, shop, auction house, etc. – are called departments)
13 speculation (*speculation* includes the idea that there are *different* opinions held or assumptions made; *imagination* does not fit here with the meaning)
14 creates (*to create a mystery* is a common expression)
15 indeed (with the meaning of *really*. The other words do not fit)

Think about how you record vocabulary that you want to remember. Do you translate the word into your language? Do you write an explanation in English? Do you write an example sentence in English? Do you use two of these methods or all of them? There is no right way to record and learn words. Try out some new ways and use the method that works best for you.

Listening p.10

TASK 1 In the first column you will find numbers; in the second column sums of money; and in the third column adjectives describing the phones.

TASK 2

Phone	Price	Comment
Motorola 3788 (**1**)	£39.99 (**2**)	least cool
Nokia 8850	£329.99 (**3**)	coolest and *smallest* (**4**)
Nokia 8210	£149.99 (**5**)	*lightest* (**6**)
Ericsson T28	–	*thinnest* (**7**)
Nokia 5110	–	*most popular* (**8**)

🎧 1.1

P presenter; R Rachel Hickson

P   And now over to Rachel Hickson, who's been looking at the mobile phone market with the intention of buying one for her teenage son. Rachel, I know teenagers are very style and fashion conscious. What sort of things influence their choice of mobile phone?

R   Thanks, Peter. Yes, you're right, teenagers are fussy and if you thought buying a phone for one might be simple, think again. The first major decision to make is about tariff or fees – in other words how do you pay for the calls? Do you pay a monthly fee which gives you free calls or do you pay as you go? But that's very much the easy decision. The really difficult decision is which phone to buy. And for teenagers at any rate, it's not the features of the phone that are the most important thing – how many games does it have? how many rings does it have? – the important thing is how 'cool' the phone is. So, for example, it would be an act of unimaginable cruelty to give your child a Motorola 3788 because that is the least cool phone in the world. It would just be so embarrassing to be seen in public with it. For parents, though, it has obvious attractions. Initially priced at £59.99, retailers are now well aware of its standing amongst the young and as a result you can pick it up from shops now for £39.99. However, it is worth bearing in mind that it will never leave your child's bedroom. Of course, if you're going to really spoil your child and you've got money to burn, you would have to get the Nokia 8850. This is quite simply the last word in phones at the moment – the smallest and coolest phone there is. Though wait … before you rush out and buy one, you need to know how much it is. £59.99? £99.99? Keep going. £199.99. Keep going again. This phone sells at a staggering £329.99. So yes, you might want to consider something else. The problem is that whatever you buy – if it's for a teenager – has to be a superlative. The best, the smallest, the lightest, even the most expensive. But, if you think the coolest is too expensive, you could try the Nokia 8210 which is the lightest phone around at the moment. I'm afraid it'll still make a hole in your wallet and costs a penny off £150 at a mere £149.99. Still too much? Then why not go for the Ericsson T28? It's not the most expensive, nor is it the lightest – it's the thinnest. Or, if like me, you are completely confused by all the different choices, why not just get the Nokia 5110, which is, without doubt, the most popular. It won't break the bank and it'll keep everyone happy. And with that advice back to you, Peter.

P   Thank you, Rachel. And I'm glad my children are old enough to buy their own phones …

The Spectator

Speaking p.11

TASK 1 1 C; 2 B; 3 E; 4 G; 5 A, F; 6 H; 7 I; 8 D, J.

TASK 2

This answer …	A	B	C	D	E	F	G	H	I	J
is longer	✔			✔	✔		✔	✔	✔	
gives an opinion		✔					✔			
gives a reason	✔	✔					✔		✔	
is personal	✔	✔		✔	✔		✔	✔	✔	
gives extra information	✔				✔	✔	✔	✔	✔	
opens up other topics for discussion		✔			✔		✔		✔	
tells how the speaker feels / felt	✔	✔					✔		✔	

The answers above are a guide only. One could argue, for example, as to whether B is a longer answer or not. The point is clear, however, that C, F, and J may be factually correct but from the point of view of satisfying the examiner, of demonstrating good communication skills, and of contributing to the conversation, they are very poor answers.

C   could be improved by saying more about Alicante: where it is, what size it is, what most people do there, whether the speaker likes it or not; and the speaker could ask the examiner or their partner if they have been there.

F   could be improved by saying more about what is difficult: why the speaker finds prepositions difficult, what can be done to learn them. The speaker could mention other aspects of English that he or she finds difficult and (if

the subject has not been raised already) move on to talking about things that they find easy.

J   could be improved by giving reasons. The speaker could say what they like about flying, whether they have flown an aeroplane or not, what they will need to do to become a pilot.

🎧 1.2

A   I find it really difficult that there are so many words that mean almost the same thing. For example, you can say you like something, or you love it, or you're fond of it, or you adore it, or you're keen on it, or you are partial to it. I know some of them are different but some are more or less the same. It's very confusing sometimes.

B   The climate is just wonderful. It's almost always warm and sunny. And I like the food too. It's really tasty. Have you ever tried Spanish food?

C   Alicante, Spain.

D   I'm hoping to get into university to study medicine. And if I manage to do that then at some point in the future I will specialize in a particular area of medicine. But I don't know what that is likely to be at the moment.

E   About ten years. I started when I was in primary school and I've been learning it ever since. Then, when I left school I went to Australia and spent six months at a language school in Melbourne.

F   Prepositions.

G   I just love being able to listen to music and understand the words. And I love to watch British and American films and understand what's happening without having to read the subtitles. And sometimes I buy books in English too.

H   I went to a fantastic party last week. It was my friend's birthday and a big group of his friends got together and we went out for a meal and then we went on to a disco. We got back at about four in the morning.

I   Probably winning a music competition when I was at school. It was nice to win it, of course, but it was the first time I realized I was any good at music. It motivated me to continue playing and now it's a big part of my life.

J   I want to be a pilot.

How well are you doing?

This is a chance to look back over each unit and think about what you have achieved. Make a note of things you have done well, and things which need more work and improvement.

2 Infernal machines

Reading p.12

TASK 1 C. Not A – there is no family living there at the moment. Not B – the article does not say how the family will be chosen. Not D – the article mentions the technology that will be used but not how technology has advanced over the past ten months.

TASK 2 1 D. Not A – the house is an *old* farmhouse. Not B – the gadgets were designed by *some of the world's best known manufacturers*. Not C – the article says nothing about who owns the house.

2 B. Not A – David, Clare, and their children are imaginary. Not C – the situation is real. Not D – scientists will monitor the experiment but not live in the house themselves.

3 B. *What makes the house different is that the phone* … Not A – some of the technology is established. Not C – this is not special. Not D – it uses *new* and *established* technology.

4 A. Not B – it will make a shopping list but not do it. Not C – it will not prepare or cook the food. Not D – it will plan a nutrition programme but not an exercise programme.

5 A. Not B – this answer does not include the technology. Not C – they don't know whether the technology will make things easier or not. Not D – this answer does not mention people's reaction to the technology.

Writing p.13

TASK 1 The college where you study is consulting students and staff about <u>the number of computers available for use in the college and the rules for their use</u>. The policy document is given below.

You have made some notes about points that you wish to bring to the attention of the Principal. <u>Write a letter to the Principal giving your opinion on the document</u>.

PETERSHAM COLLEGE
Information technology and computing Policy document

The college-wide information technology and computing policy committee has made a number of recommendations to the college administration regarding the provision and use of computers within the college.

1 The ten computers currently in use in the college IT room should be <u>replaced with twenty new and considerably more powerful PCs.</u>

2 Students should be <u>charged a standard termly fee for Internet use. A figure of £15 per term has been suggested.</u>

3 <u>The college reserves the right to check students' e-mail at any time to check for unsuitable or illegal content.</u>

4 <u>Students may not download any material from any source without the permission of a member of the college IT staff.</u>

We would appreciate hearing the opinions of students and members of staff on these proposed changes. All views will be taken into consideration before a decision is reached.

Amanda Williams

Amanda Williams
Principal

Notes on policy document:
- *keep old computers? what's wrong with them?*
- *or 12–15 new ones OK (max. class size 15)*
- *censor Internet (unsuitable material)*
- *check websites and programs (not just e-mail)*
- *no downloading: 1) cheating (using other people's work) 2) unsuitable material*

TASK 2 A 3b; B 4b; C 2a; D 1a.

Make a note of the different ways of saying the same thing:

FORMAL	INFORMAL
• I hope the college will not allow …	• You shouldn't let …
• I am not opposed to …	• I'm not against …
• These points should be given consideration …	• You should think about these points …
• I fail to see the need for …	• Why do we need … ?

🔍 Close up

There are obviously a number of ways of rewriting these sentences. Possible answers are:

1 I'd like to point out one or two things about …   the IT and computing
  I'd like to make one or two points about …   policy document.

2 I hope you'll think about these things   … when you make a decision.
                                            … when you decide what to do.

TASK 3
I 1 Many thanks for …
F 2 I was wondering if you could …
F 3 I would like to apologize for …
I 4 Could you send me …
I 5 Write soon.
F 6 I would like to complain about …
I 7 I'm dead against …
F 8 It will be totally inadequate.

F c Thank you very much indeed for …
I g Please could you …
I a I'm really sorry about …
F e I would be grateful if you could send me …
F b I look forward to hearing from you.
I h What were you thinking of?
F d I am completely opposed to …
I f It won't be nearly enough.

English In Use p.15

TASK 1 source, account, There, receive; preferred, Unfortunately, developing, weight, pieces.

TASK 2 1 … the answer,' said Kelly; 2 … a design classic, has helped …; 3 English; 4 It's; 5 … of global warming?'; 6 'Let's stop. It's …

TASK 3 1 to investigate people's reactions to technology; 2 to ensure more natural reactions; 3 they will use the information to add to the new technology debate and to benefit industry and commerce.

TASK 4 1 ✔; 2 ✔; 3 influence ; 4 usefulness ; 5 families ; 6 monitored ; 7 programme, which; 8 research; 9 project, said; 10 ✔; 11 developed; 12 'We; 13 won't; 14 ✔; 15 added, would; 16 contribute.

Listening p.16

TASK 1

writer	teacher	artist	doctor
rough draft	classes	sculpture	treatment
manuscript	subject	oils	symptoms
	problem kids	watercolours	
		collage	

social worker	politician	student	computer programmer
orphan	vote	classes	software
problem kids	govern	subject	disk
	election		

Obviously there are many other possibilities: if the teacher is an art teacher, anything in the artist column could apply to a teacher; anyone can use software and disks; doctors may well deal with problem kids, and so on. The point is, however, that predicting key words will help you to identify the matches you have to make.

TASK 2 TASK ONE: 1 C; 2 A; 3 D; 4 E; 5 B. TASK TWO: 6 D; 7 A; 8 F; 9 H; 10 B.

🎧 **2.1**

1 Exciting. So exciting. I mean, I've spent most of my creative life working in what I guess most people see as a very traditional way. I tend to use oils, but occasionally I work with watercolours and I've done one or two pieces of collage and sculpture that I think are quite successful. But then along came computers and they've opened up completely new areas for people to explore, completely new avenues and methods of expression. It's fantastic.

2 Quite frankly, in the fifteen years I've been doing this, they've revolutionized my working life. Time was I'd send in a rough draft, which usually had a lot of crossings out and bits added and arrows all over it. And it would come back with comments for revisions and whatnot. And in order to produce a final manuscript I'd have to start all over again from the very beginning. Whereas now, of course, I slap in a disk and I start from where I left off. Magic!

3 But, actually, I think what I appreciate most is the contact. Because, in my job, I can be sent off at a moment's notice to a disaster zone or a famine area. It's difficult, impossible even sometimes, to let my family know where I am, or how I am, or when I'm coming home. So yes, there's vital information on symptoms and treatment that I can access at any time and that's useful, but it can't beat being able to e-mail my kids on their birthday.

4 Well, yes, I can see the benefits. But unfortunately I can see the downside too. Working with problem kids, as I do, in their homes and with their families, I would much rather that these kids spent time interacting with other people, getting some of their problems out in the open rather than shutting themselves away in front of an endless succession of screen games. Sometimes I feel like unplugging the damn machines and throwing them out the window.

5 I'm on the Internet everyday. And not just playing, shopping, entertainment, and so on. It doesn't govern my life. It's useful stuff I'm doing. And as long as you're fairly selective about what you believe, it's incredible what you can find out. The web is probably the source that I use the most these days for keeping me up-to-date on my subject. And I encourage my classes to use it as much as possible too.

Language development p.16

1 creation; information; revision; revolution; donation; admission; examination; action; operation.

2 1 operations; 2 the creation of the universe; 3 donations; 4 'Action!'; 5 Admission free; 6 examinations; revision; 7 information.

Speaking p.17

TASK 2 1 ✔ … looks as if …   ✔ … maybe …
✔ … something like that …   ✔ I guess they might be …
It looks like …   ✔ Perhaps …
✔ … this might be some kind of …   I suspect it's …
✔ … it could be …

2 present continuous; 3 no, he uses words he does know to explain it: *some kind of machine for making clothes.*

Choose three or four of the phrases in question 1 and learn them.

🎧2.2

Well, the first picture looks as if it is the inside of a car factory or something like that. I don't know what exactly they are doing but there are some men here working on the car. Perhaps they're putting something inside the car, some controls or something like that, or I guess they might be putting in the seats or carpets. In the second picture, I can see a man operating some kind of machine for making clothes. I'm sure there's a special word for it in English but I don't know what it is. In my language we call it a *Nähmaschine*. I guess this might be some kind of clothing. I mean, I can only see this one person here but maybe there are others outside the picture. That would give you a connection between the two pictures, they're both in factories. Or maybe the connection is just that something is being made in both pictures. I don't know what is being made in the second picture because I can't see it very well. Perhaps it's a dress or it could be a shirt or something. Clothes, anyway, I think.

TASK 3 🎧2.3

W woman; M man

(Part 1)

W Well, my picture seems to be in a busy office type thing. There's five guys all on phones, landlines, on the telephones. One guy's got two phones to his ears so he's definitely, you know, very, very busy. There's stuff, computers in front of them or something and they're all, they're all on the phone actually, so … yeah.

M Very busy.

W Very busy.

M The picture I have is a very happy man. Outdoors. Sunny day and he's got he's got (W He's looking happy.) a smart suit on and he's got his mobile phone up to his ear. (W Right.) He's obviously had some happy news and there's … I don't know it seems to be sort of like an industrial area, kind of like offices and stuff in the background. (W Yeah, like he's just come out of the office, maybe.) Yeah, he's got his overcoat on and everything, so it seems midday.

W The guys in my picture are quite smart as well, so …

M Yeah. Yeah. There's … They're definitely at work. They're sort of like …

W Maybe telesales or something …

M Could be telesales or a switchboard or something. (W Definitely. Switchboard.) Could be sort of … sort of money exchange thing. They're very busy.

W Definitely. And it's a very crowded office as well so there's a lot going on there.

M I get the idea this guy's in a more superior position than these guys 'cos …

W Definitely. He's definitely higher up.

(Part 2)

W Right, so connections between the two.

M Well, they're all on phones. All the people are on phones, so …

W They're obviously doing some kind of business deal.

M It looks as if this one's business and it looks as if this one … or could be pleasure 'cos he's out of the office. He could be talking to a loved one.

W That looks more like he is talking to a loved one.

M And it's a personal call.

W Mind you, he could have, they could have just given him …

M He's got happy news.

W Exactly. He could have just got a job there in their office.

M He could have done.

W Mind you, I don't think he'd be too happy about that.

M He could be their boss and he's out to lunch and they're working hard.

W And they want to, they want to prove to the boss they're working hard by …

(M two phones) … by having two phone conversations at the same time. Maybe.

M Maybe it's some stockbroker. Money market or something.

W Maybe.

M And he's just made some money.

W Definitely.

TASK 4

1 Notice the <u>underlined</u> words and phrases used to show speculation.

a my picture <u>seems to be</u> in a busy office <u>type thing</u>

b there's <u>stuff</u> – computers in front of them <u>or something</u>

c he's obviously had some happy news

d it <u>seems to be like</u> an industrial area <u>kind of like</u> offices

e he's just come out of the office <u>maybe</u>

f <u>maybe</u> telesales or <u>something</u>

g <u>could be</u> telesales or a switchboard <u>or something</u>

h <u>I get the idea</u> this guy's in a more superior position

The speaker seems certain in c.

2 a looks as if; b could be; c could have; d could be; e or something.

---

3 Practicalities

Reading p.18

TASKS 1 & 2 2 – note the play on words in the title: the correct English word is *role play*. It has been changed here to *roll play* because different types of rolls are often served in sandwich bars.

TASK 3 (a); (f); g; h; b; c; d; i; e.

TASK 4 1E this adds to the preparations they made before opening their own shop

2A this carries on from the previous three paragraphs: it describes the site they eventually chose and explains further about their finances

3B this carries on from *We opened right from the start with four staff*, and talks about the opening day

4F this explains further about the staff (mentioned at the end of the previous paragraph)

5G *however* indicates the contrast between this paragraph (saying how conservative people are about sandwich fillings) and the previous one (which tells how many possible combinations there are)

6C the paragraph before is *the beginning of the day*, the paragraph after is *the end of the day*, so this one must be *the middle of the day*

Language development p.19

1 to start a business; to do a lot of research; to gain some practical experience; to get into a routine; to build an efficient team; to open a new shop.

There are some other possibilities: to start a new shop, to start an efficient team, to build a new shop, to open a business, etc.

2 1 gained some experience; 2 start a business; 3 did a lot of research; 4 got into a routine; 5 built an efficient team; 6 opening a new shop.

Writing p.20

TASK 1 1 to keep the reader's attention, and to make brief, and therefore memorable, points; 2 yes and no (!) – the fact they are shorter makes them more memorable and gives a more powerful effect; however, the reasons for some of the points have been left out and this may not be a good thing; 3 it draws the reader into the leaflet; 4 it is called a *bullet point*. They are often used in leaflets, brochures, and notices to identify important features or different sections of the text; 5 it breaks up the information / advice into different categories and makes it easier on the eye; 6 it separates different kinds of information / advice. You will not get extra marks for using columns but you do get marks for clear layout; 7 there is no right answer to this. In fact (see 2 above) both leaflets have their good points and their not-so-good points.

TASK 2 1 b – these are not laws – the leaflets are just saying what is good practice; 2 B – fewer reasons are given – it is more directive; 3 Whilst the purpose of the leaflets is to give advice, they intend to do so in a very strong way. They are, after all, concerned with people's safety. *Don't go on busy pavements and streets* is therefore going to be more appropriate than *It's probably not a good idea to skate on busy pavements and streets in case you knock into other people and hurt them*; 4 Young people, teenagers. Yes, it means that the writer of the leaflet can use slightly more informal language: for example, using the imperative rather than more polite and formal ways of giving advice; 5 a – the language used for this would be very informal, possibly even slang to catch teenagers' attention, and it would be encouraging and persuasive in trying to get them to come along and join up; sentences are more likely to be short; ideas presented in a short, sharp fashion with as few words as possible; b – the language used in this would not be formal but would not contain any slang (simple, neutral / informal); it would still aim to be persuasive but would probably be informative as well.

TASK 3 C; both A and B are too long. The sentences in A are far too long. B is better but still too wordy. C says exactly the same thing with fewer words and slightly less formal language (*hurt* not *injure*, for example).

TASK 4

Possible answers

In the DO'S column: Be careful if you jump off your board.
                     Make sure your board doesn't hit other people.

In the DON'TS column: Don't let your board hit other people.

English In Use p.21

TASK 1 1 It is going to be computerized; 2 50%; 3 a limit to the number of immigration officers (meaning long queues) and the increasing skill of forgers; 4 they think humans are better than machines.

TASK 2

✔ their   immigration ✔ will ✔ has   bypass
  occupy ✔ with ✔ to   long ✔ can
✔ by ✔ this   prevent   hi-tech   queue

You might also want to tick *prevent* as there will be a number of grammatical consequences for the rest of the sentence with this verb. For example: *Is it followed by **that** or the -ing form? What preposition can come after it?* and so on.

TASK 3 1 that / which; 2 their; 3 and; 4 to; 5 by; 6 are; 7 with; 8 that / who; 9 the; 10 of; 11 has; 12 too; 13 If; 14 would / do; 15 not.

Listening p.22

TASK 1 1 yes; 2 yes; 3 What do you think? – drive herself? pay for meals out? do her own washing / cleaning? There are lots of possibilities.

TASK 2 Probable answers

✔ tabloid newspapers ✔ to intrude into one's life
  a bookcase   a flower shop
✔ a huge star ✔ business affairs
✔ an agent   superstitious
✔ interviews   garage
✔ restaurant ✔ glamorous

TASK 3 1 more famous; 2 complain; 3 brother; 4 irritated / annoyed; 5 facts right; 6 look for work; 7 wonderful part; 8 book.

🎧 3.1

P presenter; K Katie Moon

P Now, turning to the question of fame, which has been a hot item in the press this week, our studio guest this morning is Katie Moon, the well-known actress and star of stage and screen.

K Hi.

P Good morning, Katie. Now I think it's true to say that you have become a household name over the past eighteen months. You've shot from relative obscurity to being the name and face that sells tabloid newspapers all over the country.

K (laughs) Well, it's nice of you to say so but I don't think that's really quite true. Lots of the people that I meet in the course of my work are more famous than me. I mean, I've just been doing some work on a film with Nathan Williams and he is like huge … a huge, huge star. So, yeah, I'm quite well known, much more so than this time two years ago. But let's be real, you know. I'm not in the top league.

P Well, that's very modest of you …

K (laughs)

P … but nonetheless, the amount of fame you have, be it large or small, does guarantee that the press are after you. They are going to intrude into your life in order to get a story.

K Sure. Of course, they are. But, you know, I have to be honest here. Any publicity I've got really hasn't harmed my career. I don't actually think I'm in a position to complain about the situation. And look at it from their point of view too, the journalists. I mean, they've got a job to do. For whatever reason, people are interested in actors. Perhaps they think we lead glamorous exciting lives …

P Don't you?

K I wish I did (both laugh). But the fact is, the press are going to be there.

P And how do you cope with it? Is it difficult for you?

K Well, I don't have an agent, if that's what you mean. But my brother, he's worked in public relations for five years, he's sort of taken over that role. We've always got on really well together. So, he kind of looks after all my business affairs and manages my life, and he also deals with the press, if people want interviews or background information. He deals with all that.

P I can see that that's a help but what about when you go out? You know, you step out of your house and there's half a dozen people there, poking cameras in your face.

K That is difficult. I'm quite a private person. And I do like to be able to go out and walk around the shops or go to a restaurant, so photographers … hmm … I get quite irritated, annoyed with them. But the media generally, I don't mind journalists, people doing stories on me, as long as they get the facts right. You know, if I've given an interview, as long as they quote me right, that's fine. I've got no problem with that. I mean it's their job. They need the work.

P But I guess there must be some advantages to the fame – money, meeting other famous people, going to fancy parties.

K Well, yes and no. I mean parties with famous people aren't much different from parties with your friends. And famous people aren't necessarily any more interesting. The one real advantage, and it's not the money, is that people know me. They know who I am and what I do. So if there's work available, they ring me up and say 'would you like to do this or that?' and I don't have to look for work myself. That's great. At the moment I just sit and wait for it to come to me. (laughs)

P I guess for an actor that's quite a luxury.

K It certainly is.

P So what are you up to at the moment?

K Well, I've got a couple of projects on the go at the moment. One's a film for a small independent film maker. It's obviously not going to be big at the box office but it's a wonderful part and even if the film doesn't make a lot of money I'm sure the people who do see it will really like it.

P That sounds interesting. And what else?

K Well, the other thing – I don't know whether I want to tell you this …

P Oh, go on!

K Well, the other thing is, I've started writing.

P Fantastic. A book or a film script or what?

K Well, I'm pretty sure it'll be a book.

P Great! What's it about? Can you tell me about it?

K To be honest I'd rather not. You see, I'm rather superstitious about these things. But if I finish it and someone decides to publish it … then I'll come and talk to you about it.

P OK. It's a deal. Katie Moon, thank you very much for coming on the programme, it's been very nice talking to you …

Speaking p.23

TASK 1 1 F; 2 T; 3 F.

TASK 2 1 & 2 The words and phrases are underlined in the transcript below.

🎧 3.2

W woman; M man

W OK. Looking at this list my feeling is that all these things are important. <u>What do you think?</u>

M Yeah, <u>I quite agree.</u> I don't think there are any factors here that we can easily say are less important – though perhaps the two things to do with the leader of the party should come at the bottom of our list.

W Appearance and personality.

M Mmm, yes.

W <u>I see what you mean but</u>, actually, I always thought that in, well, in the US presidential elections, I thought it was well-established that the most handsome candidate always got in.

M (laughs) I hadn't heard that one.

W Well, I don't know if it's true or not.

M In fact, looking at this list, I suspect that the least influential factors are probably education and health.

W Really!

M Yeah, I mean I'm not saying they're not important or anything, but I'm sure people don't think, 'Oh, this lot are going to put a lot of money into schools. I must vote for them.' <u>What d'you reckon?</u>

W Well, <u>I can't say I agree with you there.</u> <u>I'd agree that</u> they're probably not the most important thing, but I don't think they'd be right down at the bottom … Actually, I think international relations would probably be at the bottom.

M Yes. <u>Absolutely.</u> I mean, unless it was a time of crisis or something like that … but generally we don't think at all about foreign policy when we're electing a new government, do we? What about honesty? How important do you think that is?

W Not at all, really. <u>What about you?</u>

M Not at all? Really?

W Mm. I don't think people care much. I think they assume that politicians are probably not that honest anyway.

M <u>Well, I don't know.</u> <u>Wouldn't you say that</u> a party which was run by people who were generally regarded as being dishonest would have very little chance of being elected?

W I think that would depend to some extent on the degree of dishonesty, <u>don't you?</u>

M <u>True. True.</u> For me, though, I think the most important factor is going to have to be lowering taxes. Not general economic management because I don't think people really understand that …

W No, but taxes means the pound in your pocket …

M <u>Exactly.</u>

W … and people really relate to that. That's what really swings the vote one way or the other, <u>doesn't it?</u>

M <u>I couldn't agree with you more.</u> So taxes number one, then …

4 Danger

Reading p.24

TASK 1 1 F – they all still exist; 2 T – swan, cormorant; 3 F – the whale lives in the sea; 4 T – only the giant anteater and the trumpeter swan are not endangered (the swan has recently been taken off the endangered list).

TASK 2 1 – A (*eventually became flightless*)
2 – D (*the cormorant no longer flies*)
3/4 – C/B (C *they have adapted well to life in zoological gardens*; B … *zoos where they have been bred successfully*)
5/6 – A/G (A … *have no fear of man and can be easily approached and picked up*; G *is usually easily approached, even by humans*)
7 – B (*destroyed as a predator of domestic animals*)
8 – E (*it now survives only in zoos*)
9 – F (*they are mistakenly believed to kill dogs and cattle*)
10/11 – C/E (C *the smallest species*; E *only 1.2m high*)
12 – C (*when encountering people, it flees at once*)
13 – D (*have been removed from the list of endangered species*)
14/15 /16 – B/D/E (in any order) (B *is legally protected*; D *now legally protected*; E *strict legal protection since 1926*)

Choose five or six words and phrases which you think will be useful when talking and writing about endangered animals. Write them down and learn them.

Writing p.25

TASK 1 1a There are four parts to the question: (1) you have to tell guests what to do in case of fire (2) you have to tell them how to raise the alarm (3) you have to tell them where to go (4) you have to tell them how to get there
b Yes
c Yes
d Yes, it does need one in order to catch people's attention. Yes, it has a heading
e The imperative, because that is the verb form most often used for giving instructions
f Yes: the sentences are short and bullet points are used before each section

2a Your friend is going to read these directions so they do not need to be particularly formally presented
b Yes, the paragraph answers the task fully
c Yes
d No, they don't really need a heading; no, they don't have one
e The imperative – because it is often used for giving directions. It is also possible to use *you + present simple* (*You turn left out of the front gate … You go … You take the first turning right*, etc.)
f Probably not – directions are not usually given in short paragraphs with bullet points, but personal styles differ and it would not be 'wrong' to present them like that

3a Someone who picks up the extinguisher in order to put out a fire. They will be in a hurry, and will need short, simple, very clear instructions
b Yes … but see c and d
c No – the instructions contain a lot of unnecessary information and could be expressed in far fewer words
d No – they are not short, they are not simple, and they are not clear
e No – a heading would be a good idea so that people using the extinguisher would immediately know this was what they needed to read

TASK 2 1 and 2 are good; 3 is not.

TASK 3 Instructions and directions…

X	should always be in short paragraphs with bullet points.
I	should be appropriately presented.
I/D	often use the imperative (*Go …, tell …,* etc.).
I/D	should be in a logical order.
X	will never be in the form of a letter.
I/D	should be in clear and simple language.
X	must have a heading.
I/D	should contain all the necessary information.
D	can sometimes be written in ordinary paragraphs.

TASK 4 Possible answer

IN CASE OF FIRE
- Hold in upright position.
- Point away from you.
- Break seal.
- Stand one metre back from fire.
- Point at base of fire.
- Press trigger.
- Move from side to side over flames.
- Do not breathe fumes.

English In Use p.27

TASK 1 1 T; 2 F.

TASK 2 1 catastrophe – noun; catastrophic – adjective; catastrophically – adverb
2 extinct – adjective; extinction – noun
3 nature – noun; natural – adjective; naturally – adverb; unnatural – prefix + adjective; unnaturally – prefix + adverb; naturist – noun (person)
4 alarm – verb or noun; alarming – adjective; alarmingly – adverb
5 expect – verb; expected – adjective; unexpected – prefix + adjective; unexpectedly – prefix + adverb; expectedly – adverb; expectation – noun.

When you come across a new word, find out and learn as many different forms of the word as you can. When different parts of speech are formed from the same word it is easier to learn them all together.

TASK 3 1 catastrophically; 2 extinction; 3 natural; 4 alarming; 5 unexpected; 6 Uneaten; 7 shortage; 8 hatred.

TASK 4 1 threatening; 2 drivers; 3 possibility; 4 scientific; 5 approval; 6 information; 7 conventional; 8 motorists.

Language development p.28

1

NOUN	VERB	ADJECTIVE	ADVERB
threat	threaten	threatening	threateningly
possibility	–	possible	possibly
science	–	scientific	scientifically
approval	approve	approving	approvingly
information	inform	informative / informed	informatively
convention	–	conventional	conventionally

2 unthreatening(ly); impossible (impossibly); unscientific(ally); disapproving(ly); uninformative(ly), uninformed; unconventional(ly).

3 impossibility; disapproval, disapprove; misinformation, misinform; disinformation.

Note *Misinformation* is wrong information; to *misinform* is to give someone wrong information (usually accidentally); *disinformation* is wrong information that is given deliberately in order to deceive. There is no verb *to disinform* – we say *to spread disinformation*.

Listening p.28

TASK 1 1 bungee jumping; 2 climbing; 3 skiing; 4 motor racing / rally driving; 5 it is not clear what she is talking about.

TASK 2 1 C; 2 B; 3 A; 4 C; 5 A; 6 C; 7 B; 8 C; 9 A; 10 B.

🎧 4.1

1 It was fantastic. I mean, I've always wanted to go bungee jumping but it's just seemed a bit too scary. So I said to myself I'll just go along and pay my money and see how I feel and at any point I can say 'OK. Stop. Forget the money. I don't want to do this,' but that never happened. I must admit, as I jumped off the top I closed my eyes and thought, 'Oh my God! What happens if they haven't checked the bungee rope thingy properly and I go straight on down into the river?' But luckily that didn't happen.
2 I guess I like climbing so much because it's both a mental and a physical thing. Physically, you have to climb the rock or the mountain or whatever and not fall off. And that's not always that easy. I mean, I've escaped serious injury but I've tumbled a few times. But there's also the mental challenge too of finding the way up and helping the other members of your team to do the same. That's why I prefer getting a bunch of my friends together and finding something challenging.
3 Yes, I come every year, if I can. I missed last year because I broke my leg. But that was riding, not skiing. I just love it. The fresh air, the snow, the sunshine. I have to be careful, actually, about that. Put lots of suncream on. And, of course, the days of it being so expensive that it really was the rich man's playground have long since gone. I mean – true, it's more expensive than a weekend at a guest house in Brighton but it's well within the reach of a lot of people these days.
4 I've been driving for five or six years now. It's enjoyable but really I don't know that I'd want to do it full-time as a job. It's been more of a hobby to me but I can't see myself going on beyond next season really. One reason is the expense. I mean, I race for a good team, which is great, and it means that the car is looked after, the sponsorship is in place, and so on. I think that's really important. Some other teams are really badly organized. I can't imagine what racing for them would be like. But despite being in a good team it still costs me a lot personally.

5 Would you believe it! It was a birthday present. I had to book it two weeks in advance and then went down on the Friday night to be ready for the weekend's training. Then, at about two o'clock on Sunday afternoon, they took us up. I was quite surprised. I thought I might get in a terrible state about it or want to back out but, actually, I just couldn't wait. When they opened the door, I was the first one on my feet. I really wanted to do it. The parachute opened and I floated down. It was absolutely brilliant.

Speaking p.29

TASK 1 Discussion 1
    The man develops the discussion well.
    ✔ The man speaks too much.
    The woman is rude when she interrupts.
Discussion 2
    The man speaks too little.
    ✔ Both speakers share the conversation equally.
    ✔ The conversation develops fairly naturally.
Discussion 3
    The woman does not encourage the man to speak.
    ✔ The man does not really participate in the conversation.
    ✔ The man does not say enough to get a good mark in the exam.

🎧 4.2
A, D, F men; B, C, E women
1 A Well, the thing about mobile phones is they give you cancer, don't they?
  B Well, …
  A But, to be honest, I think that's ridiculous. I mean, you can't do anything these days without it giving you cancer. There was an article in the paper only yesterday about people who don't clean their teeth properly getting cancer.
  B Yes, I …
  A You saw it too, did you? I mean, what did you think? Stupid or what? The next thing is they'll say breathing gives you cancer. Well, I suppose it does if someone's smoking near you. (*laughs*)
  B (*laughs*) Wh …
  A Anyway, I don't think mobile phones are particularly dangerous. But the ozone layer, now that's a real problem. I mean, what's your view on that?
  B Well, excuse me –
  A Well, I'd just like to say that governments still aren't doing enough. I know things are much better than they were, but …
  B Sorry. Can we just go back to mobile phones a second …
2 C Well, let's think of things we can add to the list first. Erm … well, smoking for one.
  D Yes, and drinking.
  C Drinking?
  D Yes, the government's next health target is to try and stop people drinking so much.
  C Because it contributes to so much disease?
  D Yes. That's right. Now … can you think of anything else?
  C Well, one thing that I think is really dangerous, though probably most people wouldn't agree, is dieting, and encouraging young girls to be ridiculously thin. Did you know that …
  D Hang on a minute. I mean, I'm sorry to interrupt you but do you think it's the dieting to blame, the dieting industry, you know, keep fit, go to the gym and so on, or is it the fashion industry that's really at fault? It's the fashion industry that really causes people to diet. Don't you think so?
  C I see what you mean. That's a good point. But what do you think about …
3 E Of course, you also have to think about dangers that we choose, don't you?
  F Like smoking?
  E Well, yes, I wasn't thinking of smoking exactly but that could be one. No, I was thinking more of dangerous sports. Bungee jumping, white water rafting, base jumping, …
  F Base jumping?
  E Yes. It's sort of like parachuting only you jump off high buildings with a parachute that opens right at the last minute.
  F Wow!
  E It's illegal in Britain, in fact, but that doesn't stop some crazy people doing it. Can you think of any more things like that?
  F No. Not really. So … which items are most dangerous – what do you think?
  E Well, in the long term, I think it has to be the ozone layer. I mean, we can see what it's doing to the world's climate, can't we?
  F Mm.
  E And there's more people dying of skin cancer.
  F Right.
  E So, I think the hole in the ozone layer is the most dangerous thing on the list. What about you?
  F Hmm. Well, I don't know really.

5 Dilemmas

Reading p.30

TASK 1 1 four; 2 there was rain, strong wind, and heavy seas – the weather was stormy.

TASK 2 1C *Once on Vancouver Island* follows on from being at the ferry terminal.
2H *Eventually* indicates that the storm has been going on for some time – the *few exhausting hours* in the paragraph before. *As the wind rose again* indicates that it has risen and fallen already. The *two men* looks forward to *they* later in this paragraph and to more explanation as to who they are in the next paragraph.
3A *Later* and *they* reflect back to the last paragraph and the two men. *Us* and *to Tofino* refer back to earlier in the day. *That night* keeps the reader aware of the timing – also a useful concept for helping to organize the development of the writing.
4D *Our subsequent decision* prepares the reader for what is about to happen. *Rather than retracing our … journey* tells the reader what happened before they got into this situation; *an open stretch of water* looks forward to *halfway across*.
5F Think about who the *We* is here. It is not four people. You can see this because Brenda is obviously not part of the *We*. *We turned in towards Tofino* hints that the next part of the story may take place on land.
6B *Brenda … while David …* refers back to *two extra figures*.
7G *The airline* refers back to the *airport check-in desk*.
    E is the extra paragraph. It is about Vancouver Island but it is factual information rather than part of the story that is told here.

Writing p.31

TASK 1 to inform
TASK 2

	A	B	C
Does the notice catch the eye?	2	3	1
Are different sizes of writing, layout, etc. used to good effect?	2	3	1
Is the information clearly expressed?	2	3	1
Does the notice contain all the information?	2	3	1
Is the information arranged logically?	2	3	1
Is the style of language appropriate?	2	3	1
Is the notice easy to read?	1	3	1
Has the writer added some of their own ideas?	3	3	1

As you can see from the chart, C is a full, model answer. It contains all the information, clearly expressed in an appropriate style, and is well laid out. The writer has also added some intelligent ideas of their own: the questions across the top and the bullet-pointed list of why you should attend the day.
A is OK as far as it goes. However, it omits information (about tea and coffee, and the cushion). B does not catch the eye. The information is difficult to find, because it is poorly laid out, and some of the information is missing. In addition, it is far too chatty in tone.

English In Use p.33

TASK 1 The first text is informal / friendly; the second is very formal.

TASK 2 1 attend; 2 express; 3 agree; 4 achieve; 5 redecorate; 6 reduce; 7 aware.
1 I – F; 2 I – F; 3 about the same formality; 4 I – F; 5 I – F; 6 I – F; 7 I – F.

TASK 3 1 attend; 2 business; 3 short notice; 4 opportunity; 5 express;
6 question; 7 aware; 8 reduce; 9 plan of / course of; 10 redecorate;
11 suggestion; 12 favour of; 13 achieve / accomplish.

Listening p.34

TASK 1 1 an image consultant; 2 how business people should present themselves in restaurants ; 3 yes; 4 probably not. If it was a good idea it would probably be more apparent from the question; 5 no; 6 very important: you need to have some *interesting* ideas.

TASK 2 1 act with confidence; 2 you are driving; 3 bad mannered; 4 childish; 5 civilized; 6 conversation; 7 their holidays; 8 brush your teeth.

See p.118 for transcript 5.1.

🎧 5.1

P radio presenter; N Nicola Leonard

P We're talking with image consultant, Nicola Leonard, this afternoon and what we've been discussing so far is how you can present yourself when you go for an interview and how you can, well, make the most of your appearance and skills and so on. And so, Nicola, you've had the interview and you think it's gone well and the boss asks you out for lunch. Is this <u>a problem area</u>? Is it still part of the interview? What should I do?

N Well, you're right, it is still part of the interview and they'll be having a good look at you to make sure you know how to behave in a restaurant because this is a very important skill in modern professional life. So the first thing to do is act with confidence. Just behave as if it was a normal trip to a restaurant. Choose what you want to eat and don't change your mind. Showing confidence, even if you're feeling a little bit nervous, is really the most important thing you can do.

P What about drinks?

N That's a good point. If you don't want to drink alcohol, and you probably won't – actually, you probably shouldn't as it's an interview – you know, it's best to keep a clear head – so if you refuse, you should do so graciously. Make an excuse. Say you're driving or something like that. That's always perfectly reasonable. If it's clear that you're drinking and driving that may well count against you. And there are other 'rules' if you like. Don't ask for a pint of beer, for example. Apart from the fact that you'll probably have to start jumping up to go to the lavatory, a pint of beer can make you seem rather bad mannered. Wine may give an air of civilization and refinement but a pint of beer won't. And, if you're not having alcohol, don't ask for Coke. That may sound strange but it has a sort of … well, it just may make you seem a bit childish, that's all. I know it seems weird but these things work on a subconscious level and it's really not going to be helpful at all if people think you are a youngster. Then if we move on to the meal itself and eating – all the usual table manners apply. I mean, you want to try and appear civilized so, for example, don't put unwanted food on the table; put it on the side of your plate. Again this sounds so obvious but I know a number of people, extremely competent people, but they've lost out on new jobs or promotion because of uncivilized <u>table manners</u>. And then of course the other thing to think about is the conversation. After all you need to show them that you do possess reasonable social skills.

P Quite.

N So what you need to do is think of some interesting topics for conversation. Make sure you've thought about this before you go for the interview. Preferably think of subjects that are nothing to do with work, interesting subjects, mind you, and try and bring them up. But for heaven's sake keep away from boring topics like what everyone's doing for their holidays this year. I mean, you're not a hairdresser and people won't necessarily want to hear about your three weeks in Benidorm.

P (laughs)

N And one final tip – especially if you're going back to the office after lunch – and this applies not just to interviews but every day – is brush your teeth. There's nothing worse than trying to do business with someone who's got garlic breath and bits of food stuck in their teeth!

P&N Errr. Yuk!

Independent On Sunday

Language development p.34

1 see above

2 package holiday; income tax; credit card; burglar alarm; death penalty; windscreen wiper; junk food; blood pressure.

3 1 credit card; 2 burglar alarm; 3 blood pressure; 4 income tax; 5 death penalty; 6 package holiday; 7 junk food.

Speaking p.35

TASK 1 1 correct; 2 she's studying history at university (or she's studying Tai Chi at a place in Wales); 3 she went to Wales not China; 4 her course is four years.

TASK 2

TECHNIQUE	EXAMPLE (S)
repeating a key word / phrase	Going back?
asking a short question	And it was good? And then what?
making a comment	How interesting! Really?
asking for more information	What sort of things did you do? What are you studying?
asking for clarification	You mean the Chinese exercise thing? Two more?
changing the topic	But, anyway … So what about you?

The woman shows that she thinks she has spoken enough by saying: *But, anyway, I've talked enough. So what about you?*

🎧 5.2

A man; B woman

A So what are you planning to do when you go back to your own country?

B Well, I'll be going back to university in September.

A Going back?

B Yes, I'm halfway through a course at the moment. I just took a year out to travel a bit and also I'd become interested in Tai Chi …

A You mean the Chinese exercise thing?

B That's right. And I wanted to take a solid period of time – like a couple of months or so and do an intensive course and really get into it.

A How interesting!

B It was really interesting, actually. I came over here and went to this place in Wales where there's an old Chinese man who runs courses. And I stayed there for ten weeks.

A And it was good?

B Excellent. Really, really good.

A What sort of things did you do?

B Well, a lot of it was learning and practising the moves of Tai Chi. That's the really slow stuff that you see Chinese people doing out in parks in the morning sometimes. But we also did some self-defence.

A Really?

B Mm. It's not all sort of health and relaxation and slow movement. The self defence bit was really useful too. Though I must admit I hope I never have to use it.

A I'm sure. So, getting back to university then. What are you studying?

B History. I've done the first two years and I've got two more to go.

A Two more?

B Yes. Well, I'll get a master's degree after four years.

A And then what?

B After university?

A Mm.

B I don't know really. I haven't decided. I'll get a job obviously but I really haven't thought much about what I'd like to do. But, anyway, I've talked enough. So what about you? What are you planning to do when you get back to your country?

6 Natural assets

Reading p.36

TASK 1 3 … he's the only man here who looks exactly like Bill Gates
… he isn't the only professional Bill Gates lookalike in the world

TASK 2 1 C is correct (*it's not hard to spot Steve Sires*). Not A – he has never met Bill Gates and the article does not say that he has worked for him; not B – he is a civil engineering consultant with his own business; not D – twice a month he is paid to pretend he is Bill Gates, the rest of the time he runs his own business.

TASK 3 2B is correct (*I imagine a few furtive glances sent our way*). Not A – there is no hint that he is a regular customer; not C – the journalist booked the table in the name of Gates; not D – *our dinner proceeds without interruption.*

3D is correct (*Sires initially shrugged off the much-remarked-on resemblance*). Not A – people asked him for tips but he did not sell them; not B – his wife contacted the agent; not C – he shrugged it off until his wife called the agent.

4C is correct (people say of his real driving licence *That's just a fake you had made so you can trick people*). Not A – he is introduced to audiences; not B – he shows his driving licence if people don't believe that he is not Bill Gates; not D – he always puts the signature in quotes and tells people he isn't really Bill Gates.

5A is correct (*I've got a great deal. I get a little attention … but at the end of the day, I can always go home to my real life.*) Not B – *it's celebrity without any of the complications of actually being Bill Gates*; not C – he likes a *little* attention – but also to go home to his real life; not D – it doesn't say so in the article but it does say that he doesn't have the complications of being Bill Gates.

🔍 Close up

The colloquialisms are underlined and explained / given in British English.

• He isn't even <u>the real deal</u>.
the real Bill Gates / (colloquial British English) the real thing

• Then <u>I guess</u> I'd be in trouble.
I imagine / suppose / (colloquial British English) reckon

- *I didn't know who this Gates guy was.*
  this person called Gates / (colloquial British English) this Gates bloke
- *I did it for free.*
  without asking for any money / without charge / without payment / (colloquial British English) for nothing
- *What's with this quote-unquote?*
  Why have you written this … / I don't understand this … / (colloquial British English) What's this …
- *This is Bogus Bill were talking about.*
  fake / it's not really Bill
- *It's a kick.*
  It's exciting. / It's good fun. / (colloquial British English) It's a gas.

Writing p.38

TASK 1 B or C are the better openings. A has no introduction. It is not very original, and quite boring. It doesn't grab the reader's attention at all. It starts with a list of places and some not very original reasons for going to them. B is much more interesting because it is quite personal. It tells of the writer's excitement and the unusual way (s)he chooses the first place to go. C is interesting in that it offers a theme for the trip. The list of different words to describe a journey is interesting though possibly too long. Both B and C contain questions to catch the reader's attention. B is more personal (*I couldn't believe it. My hand was shaking …*); C grabs the reader's attention with the very first sentence. (*Every journey needs a purpose.*)

TASK 2 A or B are the better endings. C is a very ordinary and unexciting reason for wanting to do the trip. A is well expressed and gives a sound, practical reason why the writer should win the prize. B is also well expressed. It displays a good use of language (*to broaden my horizons, to witness vastly different cultures, a wide range of perspectives on life,* etc.) It also gives a good reason why the writer should win the prize. However, B's reason is far more personal than A's in that it expresses a desire for a 'life experience' rather than specifically demonstrating how the writer will translate the benefits of the trip into anything immediately practical.

TASK 3

Win A Round-The-World Trip
Traveller's Choice, the award-winning travel company, is offering <u>free round-the-world air tickets stopping off in five different places, one in each continent: Europe, Asia, Australasia, America, and Africa (sorry, not Antarctica!).</u> To win this once-in-a-lifetime journey, <u>make a list of the five places you would like to go to (one in each continent), explain why you would like to visit them,</u> and <u>tell us why you are the person we should choose to send on this journey.</u>

The three parts are:
1 list the five places you would like to go
2 explain why you would like to visit them
3 say why they should choose you to send on this journey

English In Use p.39

TASK 1 3 is false.

TASK 2 an extra word in each line that is grammatically incorrect or does not fit in with the sentence

TASK 3 1 it; 2 all; 3 being; 4 real; 5 ✔; 6 other; 7 than; 8 the; 9 was; 10 very; 11 quite; 12 to; 13 can; 14 so; 15 been; 16 ✔.

Language development p.39

1 For the purpose of; 2 on the basis of / as a consequence of; 3 as a consequence of; 4 in the absence of; 5 in relation to; 6 by way of; 7 in a variety of; 8 in contrast to.

Check that you understand the meaning of these phrases and learn them.

Listening p.40

TASK 1 The last sentence in the paragraph is false. The sentences in task 2 make it clear that there is doubt as to whether the process could be speeded up enough to raise the temperature sufficiently within 60 years (*People who think … / Other scientists say this will take …*).

TASK 2 1 climate; 2 dry, airless; 3 greenhouse effect; 4 –40 degrees Celsius; 5 liquid water, plants; 6 (space) mirror / mirror (in space); 7 optimists; 8 600 years / much longer.

🎧6.1

P presenter (Victoria); J Jeremy Hartshorne
P   And on now to what sounds like science fiction, but is it? We go over to California and the Ames Research Center where Jeremy Hartshorne reports on a conference that is out of this world.

J   Thanks, Victoria. Yes, this is a conference that certainly is 'out of this world'. Scientists here have been discussing the planet Mars and the possibility of developing it as a warm, Earth-like planet by transforming its climate. And how would they do that? Well, it all sounds surprisingly easy. At the moment Mars is a dry and airless planet. Of course, another problem is the temperature. The surface of Mars is about –60 degrees Celsius, so although there have been claims of life there, it's nothing really for you and me to get excited about. However, modern technology makes it sound simple. The plan would be to introduce some man-made gases into the Martian atmosphere. These would react with the planet's atmosphere and Mars would then experience its own 'greenhouse effect'. In other words temperatures would rise as a result of the sun's warmth being trapped by these man-made gases. In much the same way as we have been experiencing on Earth in recent years. This, in itself, wouldn't be enough though. What it would do, however, is raise the temperature from –60 to –40 degrees Celsius and then, at that temperature, there would be a release of frozen carbon dioxide which would warm the atmosphere up even more … I'm not losing you, am I?
P   No no.
J   Right, well, the solar energy would come from machines that could be dropped at various points on the surface of Mars. The release of man-made gases would create an atmosphere that was rich in carbon dioxide and, more importantly, would be warm enough to support liquid water and plants. And then it's easy – sort of. Once you've got plants you've got food so you could live there – although in an atmosphere of carbon dioxide you'd obviously need to wear a spacesuit. As for a time scale on all this. Well, the whole thing could be vastly speeded up by focusing light from the sun down onto the planet from a large space mirror. Believe it or not, optimists here have been saying that it would take only 60 years to raise the temperature to a pleasant 15 degrees Celsius. Realists, though, would disagree, and the sort of estimates that they are coming out with suggest that it might well be 600 years before Mars becomes in any way a green and watery planet like the Earth is now. And how likely is all this?
Well, at the moment, not likely at all. First and foremost, there is, of course, the huge ethical question of whether we have the right to interfere in something as dramatic and as important as the climate of another planet. After that they need to survey Mars. But who knows? One day we may well have colonised small areas of Mars, if not the whole planet.

The Independent

Speaking p.41

TASK 1 1 a diamond mine; 2 he thinks they're not well paid and they have a hard life; 3 they are a contrast: the beach is natural and the mine shows what man has done to nature; 4 there are people in the mine but the beach is empty; 5 they are both connected with beauty but the beauty of the beach is free and the beauty of the diamond isn't.

TASK 2   ✔ I see you mentioned …
  ✔ Another thing I noticed was …
    I was surprised at your comments about …
  ✔ I was interested that you …
    I notice that …
  ✔ Have you noticed that …
    It's interesting / surprising that …

Choose three or four of the expressions above and learn them. Try and use them when you discuss the photos in task 3.

🎧6.2

A a man; B a woman
A   This picture here looks like a mine. I've seen pictures like this before and it was a diamond mine. This is a sort of open mine where they dig straight into the ground and take out what they want. Not like a coal mine, you know, where they dig down into the ground and there are lots of tunnels going all round under the ground. And you can see some men here working in the mine. I guess they're not very well paid and they have quite a hard life probably too. And then this picture is a beach, an empty beach in fact. You can see the sky and the sea and the sand and that's all really. A bit of a sand hill here. And if I compare them, well, I guess they're a contrast, sort of. I mean, the beach is natural, completely untouched if you like. And the mine is very unnatural; it's like what man has done to nature.
B   I see you mentioned that contrast – because that's the first thing I thought of. Another thing I noticed was that, well, it's a really obvious thing really, there are people in this picture but the beach is empty – so that's like another contrast. And I was interested that you think it's a diamond mine – so perhaps in a strange way we could say both the pictures are connected with beauty. And if we stay with that idea, have you noticed that the beauty of the beach is free and the beauty of the diamond certainly isn't?

7 Senses

Reading p.42

▶ Exam technique
Read the headline of the text before you start reading. This will help you predict what it might be about.

TASK 1 There is not really a definitive answer for this question.
The following ideas are *almost certain* to be discussed: university life for the deaf, provision in schools for deaf people.
The following are *very likely* to be discussed: different kinds of deafness, numbers of deaf in the community, sign language, grants for deaf people. The others are much less likely to be discussed: housing for the deaf, dyslexia, job prospects for the deaf, blindness.

TASK 2

question	paragraph(s)		question	paragraph(s)
1	c		4	j
2	e f g h		5	k
3	h		6	a–k

TASK 3
1D *You have to work considerably harder than your peers.* Not A – *there are few role models*; not B – she says that she was lucky enough to get a lot of support from her family but she does not say that it's necessary; not C – she can lip-read but she doesn't say it's necessary.
2B *Universities run on talk.* Not A – Jude organized an earpiece for Catherine but the article doesn't say that they are difficult to get; not C – the article doesn't say this. In fact Queen's is a centre of excellence; not D – again the article doesn't say this. It does say that *for deaf students casual spontaneous discussions are out* but not that people won't talk to them.
3D *We're offering them deaf awareness training – how to adapt to the needs of deaf employees, and where to apply for grants.* Not A – they don't go to the schools to teach; not B – the article does not say they collect facts and figures; not C – it advises employers on grants and it is a self-financing organization but the article does not say that Jude finances deaf students.
4A *many people did not believe she had a problem.* Not B – she had a tailor-made service at Queen's that made it easy for her to be independent; not C – what caused her pain was the fact that people did not notice her difficulties; not D – she presented a challenge to the staff because it was difficult for them to appreciate she had a problem. It was easy to talk to her.
5C *You are accepted by a university on the basis of your ability to learn and carry out mental tasks. You have a right to be there.* Not A – she doesn't say this; not B – she thinks the support should be available to all disabled students but not that they should have to pay for any of it; not D – she thinks they should provide excellent support. The reason she thinks this is because they don't.
6B *Stephen Hoare looks at the problems and the successes.* Not A – it says something about her life but that is not the main purpose of the article; not C – it is encouraging in that it outlines how support for the deaf is improving but it does not try and persuade deaf people to go; not D – it does praise Queen's but that is only a small part of the whole article.

🔍 Close up
Check your answers in a good dictionary.

Writing p.44

TASK 1 Introduction; Guided tours; Museums; Shopping; Other attractions; Outside Oxford; Nightlife; Conclusion.
TASK 2 The paragraph about museums is in an inappropriate style. The language is too informal: *lots of, all over the place, aren't too bad*. It also expresses the writer's opinion in the wrong place: *we loved the Ashmolean*.
1 T; 2 F; 3 T; 4 F; 5 T; 6 F; 7 F; 8 T; 9 T.

Reports should be written in clear factual language and organized into well-defined paragraphs, which will probably have headings. Opinions in the main body of the text will tend to be expressed impersonally or objectively. Any personal opinion or recommendation will come at the end.

TASK 3 Possible answer
There are a number of good museums in Oxford. The Ashmolean is the most famous and contains exhibits from all over the world: coins, paintings, drawings, etc. The University Museum, the Museum of Oxford, and the Museum of Modern Art are also worth a visit.

English In Use p.45

▶ Exam technique
Read the article first without worrying about the gaps. This will help give you a good understanding of the text.

TASK 1 You should have ticked: what many people think of airline food
the problems of preparing airline food
some recent developments regarding airline food
what professional chefs recommend regarding airline food

TASKS 2 & 3 1 F; 2 H; 3 D; 4 A; 5 B; 6 C.

🔍 Close up
air travel   runway
airline food   turbulence
the airlines   altitude
transatlantic   cabin pressure
in-flight meals   35,000 feet
on board   airline caterers

Listening p.46

▶ Exam techniques
• Read the sentences for completion before you listen and predict the type of information that will be required.
• You should look at the questions while you listen.

TASK 1 1 a percentage – 6;   3 a number – 4;
2 a reference to time – 2;   4 an adjective – 3, 5.
TASK 2 1 Lasik eye; 2 (far) shorter time; 3 legally blind; 4 a / one million;
5 painless, quick; 6 95%; 7 support group; 8 nothing.

🎧 7.1
P presenter; A Ann Fairchild
P And now over to Ann Fairchild who has a report for us from the ophthalmology department of St Thomas' Hospital in London. Ann.
A Thank you, Peter. Well, what do businessman Richard Branson, actress Courteney Cox, and Spice Girl Mel G have in common? The answer? All three of them've had Lasik eye surgery – that's L-A-S-I-K – a form of corrective eye surgery that's being hailed as little short of miraculous.
The treatment, which as the name suggests, involves the use of lasers, has only been on offer here in Britain for the last six years, and a far shorter time in the United States, yet reports from stars like Courteney Cox, who is rumoured to have said, quote – I feel I've been given a new life – unquote, are helping to lengthen queues at clinics around the country. In Cox's case her comments hold more than a little truth – her eyesight before the operation was so bad that she qualified as 'legally blind'.
The popularity of this new procedure is not in any doubt. The figures are astonishing. Last year the Lasik procedure accounted for 90 per cent of all eye operations. In Britain 12,000 people signed up for it; in America there were close to a million.
Although the procedure is not cheap, coming in, as it does, at £3,000 a go, it is, I am told, extremely painless and quick – taking only ten minutes for each eye you have treated.
All this is amazing, you might think. Ah, for the wonders of modern science! But what about the success rate? At 95% it sounds excellent but … might there be more to all this than meets the eye? Indeed there might. A support group in the US called Surgical Eyes, set up to help people whose laser treatment has gone wrong, now lists over 1,000 people who've suffered long-term eye damage as a result of the Lasik procedure.
That's not many you might argue … and you'd be right. But the problem is, when the procedure does go wrong, it goes very wrong. Nothing can be done about it. As one of the country's experts on laser eye surgery told me earlier this morning, there is no 'plan B'. You could end up with worse eyesight than you had before.
Well, those are the facts about the Lasik procedure, and I have with me here a couple of people who have just arrived at the hospital …
The Guardian

Language development p.46

1 The presenter means that the eye operation might not be as simple and as successful as it first appears.
2 1 b; 2 d; 3 f; 4 a; 5 c; 6 e.

3 1 in the public eye; 2 keep an eye on; 3 pulling the wool over our eyes; 4 catch his eye; 5 have eyes in the back of my head; 6 more to him than meets the eye.

Speaking p.47

TASK 2
✔ to compare them
✔ there was no comparison
✔ they are completely different
more uncomfortable
✔ whereas
✔ much quieter

not so loud
busier than
not as easy as
✔ while
✔ but
✔ compared to

🎧 **7.2**

Well, this photograph here is of a blind person, a man, and he's out in the street somewhere, and he's got a dog, er, you know, the sort of dog that blind people often have. I don't know what they're called. And I guess it's a very well-trained dog. You know, it helps him to cross the road and it makes sure he knows where the doors to different shops are, and so on. It's quite a busy street. And I guess it might be quite noisy. And then this other picture, this is a woman who's going to tell you your future and that you're going to meet a tall, dark man and fall in love with him. (*laughs*) Now <u>to compare them</u> … well at first … before you mentioned the idea of sight … well, I thought <u>there was no comparison</u>, <u>they're completely different</u>. I mean, one picture is obviously noisy <u>whereas</u> the other one is <u>much quieter</u>. One has a lot of people in it <u>while</u> the other has only one person. <u>But</u>, actually, when you told me about the connection. Yes, I can see it. The blind person can't see anything at all but the old woman in this other picture … Well, <u>compared to</u> the blind person she can see everything in the physical world <u>but</u> I guess the picture is also saying that she can see the future as well. I don't know whether I'd call it a strong connection between the two pictures but it's certainly a clever one. Perhaps it makes us think about whether sight is an entirely physical kind of skill or ability or whatever … and perhaps it's saying that intuition is a kind of sight. You know … a second sight or a sixth sense. As I said, it's a clever choice of pictures to put together.

🎧 **7.3**

First I'll give you a set of pictures to look at (pictures A1, A2, and A3). They are all to do with communication. I'd like you to compare and contrast the pictures talking about the importance of each type of communication and what the future holds for it. Don't forget you have about one minute for this.

🎧 **7.4**

Now it's your turn. I'll give you another set of pictures to look at (pictures B1, B2, and B3). They are all to do with different types of discovery. I'd like you to compare and contrast the pictures talking about the importance of each method of discovery and what the future holds for each. Don't forget you have about one minute for this.

8 Control

Reading p.48

▶ **Exam techniques**
- The title will give you some idea as to what the text is about.
- You should read the text through carefully to get a general idea of the meaning and to see how it is organized, before you look at the missing paragraphs.
- Look for words which link the paragraphs, especially: pronouns (*he, she*, etc.), demonstratives (*this, that*, etc.), possessive adjectives (*his, her*, etc.), and link words (*however, although*, etc.).

TASK 1 It is quite possible that all the questions will be answered by the article.

TASK 2 1 shoppers have to leave a thumbprint if they pay by cheque or credit card; 2 to stop fraud; 3 human rights campaigners think that it will lead to an increase in state control and a loss of freedom; 4 Margaret Reid, a Scottish businesswoman; 5 Hull, large parts of Kent, some areas of London.

TASK 3 A *It* is probably the scheme. *She* is probably Margaret Reid because she is in favour of the scheme. Margaret Reid is first mentioned before gap 4. Where do you think paragraph A will come?
B It probably does introduce the police viewpoint because the police spokesman's name is given in full. Generally names are given in full the first time they are mentioned in an article. The quote between gaps 5 and 6 could be a quote from a police officer. If so, where will paragraph B come?
C *They* are people who object to the scheme, namely human rights campaigners. They are worried about state control and loss of individual freedom. An explanation of the system will probably come near the

beginning of the article. Where are the human rights campaigners first mentioned? So where will this paragraph come? Remember *they* will refer back.
D Liberty are against the scheme. *However* will contrast their view with a view in favour of the scheme. Where are views in favour of the scheme expressed? Yes, Deborah Clark has other things to say. There is a *she* in the paragraph between gaps 6 and 7. Could this be her? So where is D likely to go?
E Ms Clark is Deborah Clark of Liberty. She will first be referred to as Deborah Clark. So where will E go?
F *Fraudulent* reflects *fraudster*. *The print* refers back to a *thumbprint* in the previous paragraph.
G Cheques and credit cards are not contrasted anywhere. There is no mention of the comparative safety of credit cards nor of the opinion of the banking world. This paragraph would therefore seem to be the odd one out.
H *This security system* refers to the thumbprint scheme. *Bluewater* refers immediately back to its first mention.

TASK 4 1 H; 2 C; 3 F; 4 A; 5 B; 6 D; 7 E.

🔍 **Close up**
1 perturbs; 2 spotted its potential; 3 to evade detection; 4 virtually; 5 via.

Writing p.50

▶ **Exam techniques**
- As you read the question, you should underline the different parts that need to be included in your answer.
- Before you start to plan and write your answer make a list of ideas for possible inclusion.
- When you have listed all your ideas, check them against the different parts of the question. Cross out any that are irrelevant and organize the rest into a coherent plan for your answer.
- Catch the reader's attention with a strong opening paragraph.

TASK 1 The key points are:
– your experiences
– where you studied / learnt English
– what you liked
– what you didn't like
– some tips on how to become better learners

TASK 2 Compare your ideas with those in task 3.

TASK 3

Possible answer
learnt at school
– ~~teacher wore terrible clothes~~
– ~~school food was awful~~
– English lessons poor
– four lessons a week (Mon, Wed x2, Fri)
– teacher was very strict
– we never spoke English in class
– exercises were boring

likes
– speaking English
– ~~going out (in UK)~~
– ~~being in UK~~
– meeting people from other countries
– ~~comfortable desks & chairs in UK school!!~~
– good class in UK
– friendly teacher
– English jokes

tips
– ~~eat breakfast~~
– ~~exercise every day~~
– write new words on little pieces of paper and keep them in your pocket until you know them
– speak English sometime every day
– read a lot of English
– ~~don't do your homework if you can think of a better way of spending your time~~
– ~~eat chocolate (chocolate and breakfast both give you energy!)~~

learnt in UK
– stayed 10 weeks (Jan–Mar)
– great teacher (funny)
– ~~never been so cold in my life~~
– stayed with UK family
– ~~10 yr. old daughter; 8 yr old son~~
– son supported Liverpool football club (*might have been a shared interest!*)
– ~~wonderful food (surprise!)~~
– learnt a lot and had a good time

dislikes
– homework
– grammar
– short words in English (especially prepositions!)
– ~~classmates who ask the teacher boring questions~~

TASK 4 1 c; 2 a; 3 b. There isn't really a best answer. They all have their good points.

TASK 5 Model answer

I hated my Dad when he told me I was going to Britain for a year to learn English. 'It's THE international language,' he said. 'It's important that you speak it well.' 'What does he know?' I thought. I was 16 at the time and I knew everything. But, actually, he was right!

I'd had five years of English at school before I went to Britain. I didn't work hard and I guess I was a low intermediate level. Then I spent a year at a language school in Edinburgh. When I left I took the CAE exam and passed with a grade 'B'.

What was so great about learning English in Britain? Well, the classes for one thing. Our teachers were young, in their late twenties, and interested in the same things as us. Because of that, their classes were always interesting and lively. In addition, the classes comprised people from all over the world. It was fascinating to talk to people from many different countries and find out about their attitudes and opinions and their way of life.

All this was a long way from the boring classes we had back home in my country. There we learnt long lists of vocabulary, practised prepositions until I never wanted to see another one, and discussed boring subjects like holidays.

So if you want some tips on how to become better learners, my advice is this: learn English in an English-speaking country. Speak the language the whole time, make friends from other countries not just your own. Live with an English-speaking family and chat to them when you're not at school. And work hard! The harder you work, the better your English becomes and the more you enjoy your stay abroad.

English In Use p.51

▶ Exam technique
Looking at the title will give you an idea what the text is about.

TASK 1 2

TASK 3 6C This tests the meaning of an individual word in the context of the whole scenario. The other words do not fit.

7A This tests the choice of one word from several with very similar meanings. *Adapt* means to change something so that it can be used for a slightly different purpose or in a different situation, which fits this context.

8B This tests collocation: tubes, lines, and syringes are inserted. You introduce something *to* or *into* something else.

9D Collocation again: medical staff *monitor* vital functions.

10C This is a fixed collocation: hospitals have *intensive care units*.

11A Another collocation (though not fixed): you can *display* speed and efficiency. None of the other words fit in this context.

12D Collocation: *a close parallel*.

13B Fixed collocation: *to make an improvement*.

14A This tests knowledge of words which go together in groups: *teams* have *members*.

15C Phrasal verb: you *draw* up a plan.

Listening p.52

TASK 1 Possible answer
Remember that not all the words you think of will necessarily occur in the recording.

a presidential election	vote, candidates, results, poll, winner, loser, speech
a flight in an aeroplane	flight attendant, pilot, speed, height, duty-free, aisle
a weather forecast	rain, sun, umbrella, temperature, wet, dry, tomorrow
a football match	crowd, fans, match, goal, referee, team, supporters, game
a demonstration	peaceful, violent, march, placard, police, speech
a lesson in a school	teacher, class, blackboard, subject, classroom
a royal wedding	prince, princess, church, prime minister, guests, crowds
a trip up a mountain	climb, ropes, height, equipment, weather, hard work, summit

TASK 2 TASK ONE: 1 D; 2 A; 3 F; 4 C; 5 H.
TASK TWO: 6 E; 7 F; 8 A; 9 B; 10 H.

🎧 8.1

1 We managed to keep the fans apart. I think that was by far the most successful part of keeping everything under control. In fact everything was pretty good natured. Lots of singing and chanting from both sets of supporters – deafening but not threatening at all. What was less successful and it's perhaps a lesson we should learn before the next game is that it would be a good idea to make sure that pubs and bars are closed before the kick-off. That would keep people a bit more sober before the match and

our lives would be that much easier.

2 It all went off very peacefully really. I mean, people do have a right to march and express their feelings, tell us how they think we should all be voting, and as long as it's peaceful I don't see a problem. In fact, in some ways, I'm very much in favour of it as a way of letting politicians know what people are regarding as the really important issues of the moment. There were complaints, though, because they went through a residential area. A lot of people phoned in saying they weren't able to hear their televisions and what were we going to do about it.

3 I was just sitting there, marking papers. Everyone had their heads down, working away and there seemed to be a very studious atmosphere. Then I got the impression that something had flown across from one side of the class to another. And then suddenly all hell broke loose. Rolls, biscuits, cakes, flying all round the class. I knew I'd never discover who the ringleaders were or who started it all. But I was chiefly concerned with restoring order and once I'd threatened to keep everyone in after four, they were very keen to start behaving properly again.

4 It was a wonderful occasion and it was such a pity that they got let down by the weather. Of course, the heads of state and presidents and prime ministers and what have you, were all in the church keeping dry, and all of us, who just wanted to catch a glimpse of the princess, we were all outside getting absolutely soaked. They ran some loudspeakers out so we could hear the service but nobody seemed that interested in listening – we were just there for the excitement of being there.

5 By the time we reached eight thousand metres I could see that a number of the party were feeling like giving up. Although it had been a gorgeous day, it was really a bit too warm. People had had enough and it was still a couple of hours to the summit. In fact a couple of people asked if we could divide up the food, the ropes and the equipment so that they could go back down. But I knew that if we split up it would be a disaster, especially as night would fall quickly, so I worked hard at keeping everyone's spirits up.

Language development p.52

1 (I'll) keep my fingers crossed for you – P; 2 (I'm) at my wit's end – N; 3 It's not the end of the world – P; 4 (He) drives me round the bend – N; 5 (There seems) to be light at the end of the tunnel – P; 6 (That)'ll be the day – N; 7 (I suppose) things can only get better – P; 8 (I was) completely out of my depth – N.

Speaking p.53

TASK 1 The ideas mentioned are:
– raise the price of petrol and diesel
– increase tax on cars
– increase public transport
– subsidize public transport
– ban leaded petrol
– subsidize research into other forms of fuel or electric cars
– cars can only travel with two or more people
– ban cars and lorries from city centres

TASK 2 1 *That's a good one / That's a great idea / I hadn't thought of that.*
2 *The point is … / The main reason is …*
3 *Do you think so? / Don't you think … / You might be right, but I think …*
4 *I'd go for … / I'd much rather …*
5 *You mean …? / How do you mean? / What you're saying is …*

Choose two of these expressions for each negotiating skill and learn them.

🎧 8.2

A Well, I guess we can start with the obvious things like raising the price of petrol and diesel.

B Yes, and increasing tax on cars themselves so they're more expensive for people to buy.

A Yes, that's a good one. What else? Oh yes, increasing the amount of public transport so that people feel … well … I mean, the thing with cars is they're so convenient and public transport often isn't. I mean, if you have to wait ages for a bus or it doesn't come people are obviously going to use their car.

B Exactly. And, of course the government should subsidize public transport … or perhaps in towns and cities it should be free then people would have no excuse not to use it.

A That's a great idea. Though I can't see many governments thinking it's a good idea.

B No. Expensive.

A Mm. They could ban leaded petrol.

B You mean completely?

A Why not?

B I hadn't thought of that.

A The government should actually subsidize research into other forms of fuel or into developing electric cars, things like that.

B Sure. And then perhaps we can think of some really impractical ideas like you can only use your car if there are two or more people in it.

A Ban lorries and cars from all city centres. Tomorrow.

B (*laughs*)

A How many have we got?

B 4–5–6–7–8.

A OK. Now, the three most effective. Well, <u>I'd go for</u> raising the price of fuel. I think that's pretty effective.

B <u>Do you think so?</u> <u>Don't you think</u> people just make the journey anyway and pay more for it?

A <u>How do you mean?</u>

B Well, I think <u>the point is</u>, we use cars so much it's just a habit. I don't think people consciously think, 'Oh, petrol is so expensive I won't drive over the other side of town to buy some plants for my garden or whatever.' They just go anyway.

A So <u>what you're saying is</u>, the price of petrol doesn't affect how much people use their cars.

B Yes.

A Yes, I think for short journeys <u>you might be right, but I think</u> for longer journeys people would perhaps think about using a bus or a train.

B Mm. Maybe.

A <u>I'd much rather</u> choose subsidized or free public transport. And <u>the main reason is</u> that it's a positive action. I mean, increasing taxes is very negative, people feel bad about it, they have to pay more money, but providing free public transport is a very positive thing, people can feel happy about it. It's a plus sort of thing.

B I see what you mean. Yes, I can go along with that.

A OK. We need two more things now …

9 Music

Reading p.54

▶ **Exam technique**
You should read the text through quickly to get a general idea of the meaning before you look at the questions. One way of doing this is to read the first sentence (or two) of each paragraph.

TASK 1 1 listen to music; 2 it affects the heart rate; 3 no; 4 Nike.

TASK 3 1 – A; 2 / 3 – C / E; 4 – F; 5 – B; 6 / 7 – C / D; 8 – H; 9 – D; 10 – I; 11 – G; 12 – C; 13 – A.

Writing p.56

▶ **Exam technique**
It is a good idea to underline the important parts of the question so that they are highlighted while you are planning your answer. When you have written your answer, you should then check back to make sure that you have answered the question fully.

TASK 1 pair A: thanking; pair B: request; pair C: warning; pair D: giving information.

TASK 2 A1 / A2: 1 A1 is more polite. 2 It is a little longer; it makes a favourable comment about the borrowed CD; it talks about their next meeting. 3 It would make it slightly less polite.

B1 / B2: 1 B2 says a lot more than is necessary. In doing so it is very polite, though it is also a very personal expression by the writer. It gives an indication what sort of person she might be – an exuberant, rather extravagant person. 2 B1 is brief, to the point, and there is no extra information at all. B1 verges on rudeness. It needs something more to ensure it is read as a 'polite' request, for example: *Thanks a lot.* 3 probably about 11.00; *I'm going to the cinema with Evie; you know I love them!* is all unnecessary. 4 An acceptable note would be: *Dear Alan, I'm afraid I won't be back till late. I've just noticed there's an All Stars concert on Channel 5 tonight. Could you video it for me? Thanks. Fizz*

C1 / C2: 1 C1 is OK in length. The explanation may be a good idea in persuading people to keep off the piano. 2 C2 is just about acceptable. *Please keep off* would be better. 3 No.

D1 / D2: 1 You would write D1 if you were in a hurry. 2 D2 is a little more formal. You would probably write this if it was to be read by someone with whom you had a more formal relationship: someone you did not know very well or an elderly and slightly distant relative perhaps. 3 The name of the video is not essential.

English In Use p.57

▶ **Exam technique**
You should read the text through and get a general idea of the meaning before you start trying to complete the spaces.

TASK 1 2 is correct.

TASK 2 1 noun; 2 noun; 3 noun (person); 4 noun; 5 noun; 6 prefix + verb; 7 noun.

TASK 3 1 collection; 2 sales; 3 critics; 4 anticipation; 5 compilation; 6 reawakened; 7 success.

TASK 4 8 handful; 9 profitable; 10 exclusive; 11 badly; 12 unable; 13 advertisements / advertising; 14 users; 15 trial.

Listening p.58

▶ **Exam techniques**
• Before you listen to the recording you should read the questions carefully to find out as much information as you can.
• Continue to look at the questions as you listen to the recording; you only hear the recording once in this part of the Listening Paper and it is important not to miss anything.

TASK 1 1 Westbeach; 2 three; 3 four days; 4 £60; 5 yes.

TASK 2 1 fourth; 2 north end; 3 (Northern) Ireland; 4 June; 5 running order; 6 £80; 7 cooking facilities; 8 dairy ice-cream; 9 train; 10 coach.

🎧 **9.1**

Welcome to the information line for the Westbeach Summer Pop Extravaganza. All relevant phone numbers and website addresses will be given at the end of this announcement so please have a pen and paper ready. This is the fourth year it has run, and, as in previous years, the event will be held on Wilson's Fields. Come to the north end of the town of Westbeach and follow the signs. Camping is also available to the north of the town. Bands already booked for this year's event include Inspiring Tide, the well known up-and-coming American country band from South Carolina, Perfect Harmony led by Gwyn Morrison, arguably the best guitarist to come out of Wales, and Green Metal, the new and successful rock band from Northern Ireland – a 'must' for all fans of Irish music. There will, of course, be an opportunity to see many other bands over the four days of the extravaganza and a full running order of bands and tickets are already available over the Internet via the Westbeach Extravaganza website. Dates for this year's extravaganza are the 13th to the 16th of June. Tickets and a complete running order are also available by post from the Westbeach Community Theatre. Day tickets cost £20 for the Thursday and Friday, £30 for the Saturday and Sunday. Tickets for the whole four-day event cost £80. Camping facilities will be available at £10 per person per night. Full toilet and washing facilities will be provided. As one of the improvements implemented since last year, there will be limited cooking facilities available. However, bear in mind they will be limited and it is recommended that, as far as possible, you bring whatever you might need in the way of cooking equipment. As in previous years, there will be a large number of food stalls set up around the site providing everything from fish and chips and Mexican food to Thai food and, of course, Westbeach's own special dairy ice-cream, a 'must' to cool you down if the weather is as hot as it was last year. For people not coming by car, special train services will run between London Liverpool Street and Westbeach throughout the week of the festival. Eastern Rail Services will be able to provide more information about these services and their information line number will also be given at the end of this announcement. It is only a short walk from Westbeach station to Wilson's Fields. Alternatively, the Anglian Coach Company will be running extra direct services to the extravaganza from Victoria Coach station during the same period. For more information and ticket booking forms you can ring Westbeach Community Theatre on …

Language development p.58

1 You should have crossed out: definite, serious, strong.

2 You should have crossed out: 1 adequate; 2 state-of-the-art; 3 adequate; 4 splendid; 5 old-fashioned (possibly *adequate* – you would expect a *new* sports centre, however small, to have better than *adequate* facilities).

Speaking p.59

► Exam technique
See task 3 below.

TASK 1 1 M; 2 M W; 3 neither; 4 W M; 5 M; 6 M.

TASK 2 1 M; 2 W; 3 W; 4 M; 5 M; 6 W; 7 M.
As far as I'm concerned …; With all due respect …

TASK 3 *I think we'll just have to agree to differ.*

🎧 **9.2**

M man; W woman

M This man here, the busker, street musician, whatever you want to call him, as far as I'm concerned he serves no purpose at all except to irritate people who are trying to get on with their shopping or get from A to B.

W Oh, I think that's a bit hard, actually. I mean, to be perfectly honest I rarely give money to buskers, but it seems to me that they do brighten up the streets and underground stations.

M Well, possibly. It depends what they're playing really.

W (*laughs*) Yeah. Er, this picture here, the orchestra. Now that definitely has a social role. (**M** Yes. Yes.) People go along because they enjoy playing but they also want to meet their mates …

M … and have a few drinks afterwards.

W Exactly. And I suppose it's uplifting for people who listen to it too.

M Oh, very much so, very much so.

W And this is folk music I guess.

M Yes, traditional. Ethnic folk music. Chinese, in this case, by the look of it.

W Yeah.

M This has a sort of social role too – at weddings and parties and things like that.

W And a brass band.

M Well, the same sort of thing as the orchestra, really. Perhaps more so. More of a social role with people getting together to have a good time and enjoy themselves really.

W Mm. Yeah. And then pop … Well, some pop is certainly political. In the late 60s and early 70s quite a lot of it had a political flavour to it though it's probably less so now.

M Well, that's probably true but, as I see it, pop doesn't have much to recommend it. Now, classical music … to my mind this is the most spiritual form of music and because of that the best.

W Hmm. I think that's a view that quite a few people hold but in my opinion some pop music is spiritual. I mean pop in the sort of broadest sense of the word here, so you know pop, rock, country, whatever … but some of that can actually have a spiritual effect on people.

M You are joking!

W No. No. I'm serious. And not just at concerts either, you know, when there's a lot of mass feeling generated. But I do think some pop music can be spiritually uplifting even if you're just, you know, sitting at home listening to the CD player or driving in the car or whatever.

M Well, with all due respect, I really can't agree. I don't see how you can compare Beethoven and the Beatles.

W Oh well, in that case I think we're going to have a bit of a problem then. I mean, we seem to agree on some things but on the question of classical music or pop music, I think we'll just have to agree to differ.

M Yeah. I guess so.

10 Places

Reading p.60

► Exam techniques
• Before you look at the questions, you should skim the text to get a general idea of the meaning. This will prepare you before you read the questions and it will also give you an idea of how the text is organized.
• There is a lot of text to read in Parts 1 and 4 of Paper 1. However, it is not necessary to understand, or even to read, every word of the text. After reading a question, you should first identify the part of the text where you expect to find the answer. Then you should read that part of the text more closely in order to identify the correct answer.

TASK 1 Probable answers
A 2; B 3; C 3; D 2; E 1; F 3.

TASK 2 1 / 2 – B / F; 3 / 4 – E / F; 5 – E; 6 – A; 7 – F; 8 – E; 9 – E; 10 – A; 11 – D;
12 – F; 13 – A; 14 – B; 15 – D; 16 – A.

🔍 Close up

highly-illustrated, design-heavy, guide, presentation, content, graphics, writing, tone, photos, visuals, chapter, section, feature inserts, introduction, references, guidebook, intelligently-presented, well-illustrated, expressions, textual, stories, illustrating, quotations, authors, books, front cover shot, cover illustration, introductory section, descriptions, translation, series, pages.

Language development p.61

1 unreliable; impractical; uninteresting; incomprehensible; unconvincing; uninspired.

2

POSITIVE	NEGATIVE
thorough	dull
up to date	clumsy
knowledgeable	repetitive
concise	insulting
balanced	simplistic
lively	humourless
detailed	
cool	

Writing p.62

TASK 1 1 B; 2 A; 3 A; 4 A; 5 A.

TASK 2 1 bright blue seas, hurricane season, older generation; 2 you think *of* a cruise, cruises appeal *to*, to pay *for* the cruise; 3 it sounds a great job, didn't really *live* up to expectations, I think he *is* going to want to know.

English In Use p.63

► Exam techniques
• You should read through the text and get a general idea of the meaning. This will help you when you try and decide how to fill the gaps.
• This part of Paper 3 tests *grammar* words rather than *vocabulary*. You should look at the sentence around the gap and decide what is missing grammatically: prepositions, conjunctions, a missing *to* in front of an infinitive, etc. The meaning of the text will obviously help but what is missing will usually be an important grammatical element of the text, sentence, or phrase.

TASK 1 1 and 3 are true.

TASK 2 1 of; 2 You need a conjunction that indicates additional information: *and* is possible or *while*; 3 The airport could be in the middle of the countryside. The countryside would therefore be *around* the airport. The airport could also be *near* the countryside; 4 According; 5 *is*: the -*ing* form in *serving* indicates that there needs to be part of the verb *to be* in the gap to complete the verb. The article is talking about the situation now so the verb will be in the present.

TASK 3 6 since; 7 However; 8 to; 9 itself; 10 into; 11 can / will / may / might; 12 the; 13 be; 14 with; 15 as.

Listening p.64

► Exam technique
You should read through the questions and options. You will be able to make predictions about the text based on the questions. This will prepare you for what you are about to hear.

TASK 1 1 T; 2 T; 3 T; 4 F.

TASK 2 1 B; 2 A. You can work out the answer to question 1 from what the presenter says: *Was that wise do you think? Taking a four-year-old to India? What about the health risk? I mean, surely that must have worried you.* However, the presenter's intonation is also rather doubtful. The answer to question 2 can be found in Jane's words (*And you survived?*) *Oh more than that, much more than that – we had a fantastic time!* You should work this out much sooner, however, from Jane's enthusiastic intonation.

TASK 3 1 B; 2 D; 3 D; 4 A; 5 B; 6 A; 7 C; 8 C.

Parts to underline:

1 *Was that wise, do you think? Taking a four-year old to India?*
2 *Well, in many ways, yes, I think it was. A great experience for him.*
3 *I thought it would be foolish, irresponsible even, to take the risk.*
4 *He just wanted to help and always wanted to give them money. He was quite upset by children begging.*
5 *Everyone should do it once. What an eye-opener!*
6 *From my point of view that couldn't have been better.*
7 *Absolutely no problems. Not at all.*
8 *… we had a fantastic time.*

🎧 **10.1**

P presenter; J Jane Brewer

P And now, continuing the theme of 'journeys-that-not-everyone-would-want-to-do', my next guest is Jane Brewer, a single mother who has just returned from a five-week backpacking trip to India. Now I'm sure a lot of people would want to go backpacking in India for five weeks, it's certainly the dream of many people I know, but not everyone would want to take a four year-old boy with them. Jane, you took your son, Marlon, along with you, didn't you?

J Yes. That's right.

P Was that wise, do you think? Taking a four year old to India?

J Well, in many ways, yes, I think it was. A great experience for him. Marlon's still at nursery school so it didn't interfere too much with his schooling. If I'd wanted to go later when he was at primary school it would have been much more difficult.

P Yes, I can see that, but what about the health risk? I mean, surely that must have worried you.

J Well, yes, to some extent. And partly because I've never let Marlon have all the usual childhood inoculations. I've always thought they did more harm than good. But, well, …

P But for India you changed your mind?

J Yes, I felt I had to. It really was such an unknown quantity that I thought it would be foolish, irresponsible even, to take the risk. So we had just about everything we could. And of course we stocked up on malaria pills and so on before we went.

P So what were your first impressions? How did Marlon react to it all?

J Well, we arrived in the middle of the night … I don't know … have you ever been to Delhi or to India?

P No, never.

J It's unbelievable. Fantastic but unbelievable. It's total confusion, busy like you can't imagine, and complete and utter chaos. Fortunately, we arrived in the middle of the night so it wasn't too bad. Things were a lot quieter than during the day. But then the next day was really hot and that took a bit of getting used to. Also the poverty. It's really quite difficult, I think, for people living in the west to imagine the poverty. As well as a lot of adult beggars, there are desperately poor, half-clothed kids running around on the streets, begging, asking for money.

P And what did Marlon make of it all?

J It was sweet really. He just wanted to help and always wanted to give them money. He was quite upset by children begging.

P So what did you actually do?

J We stayed in Delhi for a few days and did the sights there. Then we travelled around a bit by bus and train. Agra, Jaipur, and Udaipur and then down to Kerala in the south for some time on the beach.

P I understand travelling by train is quite something in India.

J *(laughs)* It certainly is. Everyone should do it once. What an eye-opener! We usually travelled in reasonable style – not first class, I have to say, but not crammed in like sardines either. We always opted for an air-conditioned coach, and if it was an overnight journey, we had a sleeper.

P And what about the stations?

J They're extraordinary! Well, compared to stations here, anyway! There are people cooking, sleeping, begging, picnicking, and on every bit of space in the station. Like everywhere else, very chaotic.

P So I guess the time in Kerala must have been a bit more restful, then?

J Yes, it certainly was. We felt we deserved a bit of a rest after all the hard travelling. We stayed in a cottage on the beach. The weather was fantastic, of course. Marlon tried every sport and beach game that he could. And he even became great friends with a local teenager called Ram. From my point of view that couldn't have been better. They used to go off for breakfast every morning while I sunbathed. In fact, by the end of the trip Marlon had given up using a knife and fork and was eating just like the Indians do, using his right hand. I was really surprised by that.

P And so how about your health? You must have had some problems. Nobody comes back from India without having had something.

J Absolutely no problems. Not at all. We met a lot of travellers who had, in fact as you said, most people seemed to have had something wrong at some time. But we just took sensible precautions. And we never made the mistake

of thinking that we might have built up an immunity. We always peeled fruit, we ate only hot food, we always drank bottled water. We even brushed our teeth in bottled water just to be on the safe side.

P And you survived?

J Oh, more than that, much more than that – we had a fantastic time. In fact, when we got home Marlon decided he wanted to go to South America next year.

P Ha ha.

J Yes, he was really keen. But only until one of his friends brought in a home movie of her holiday to Disneyland!

P&J *(laugh)*

The Independent

Speaking p.65

▶ **Exam technique**
While your partner or the examiner is speaking you should listen carefully and show interest. You will need to react in some way to what they have said so a good understanding will be very important.

TASK 1 1 Oxford; 2 yes; 3 it is an unfortunate necessity; 4 they think the queues in them are crazy; 5 it limits the number of people.

TASK 2 ✔ Let me put it another way …
✔ What I meant was …
Look at it this way …
✔ No, my point is that …
✔ Put it this way …
What I'm trying to say is …

Choose a few of these expressions and learn them.

TASK 3 You should have underlined:
for instance
for example
take (these theme parks)
Let me give you an example
just to give you an idea

Choose a few of these expressions and learn them.

🎧 **10.2**

A a man; B a woman; C another man

A … No, wait a minute. Let me put it another way. Just think about Oxford, for instance. Where I live. It's dreadful in the summer. Absolutely dreadful. For example, I wanted to park in the centre of town the other day. It's not a usual … I mean, I wouldn't normally. But on this occasion I had to take a desk in to have some repairs done … and park? … in the centre of Oxford? You must be joking. There were tour buses … Seriously, I counted twelve tour buses … and people everywhere.

B Yes, I know. But what I meant was: we may not like it but we have to put up with it. The fact of the matter is … money. They come here. Lots of tourists. See the sights. Give us the money.

C But there should be a happy medium. Because after a while, if it gets really, you know, crowded, people just won't want to come. They'll think 'Oh I don't want to go there, it's going to be awful.'

A No, my point is that it's too late. When that happens it's already too late.

B Do you really think so? I mean, take these theme parks. On a busy weekend in the summer you've got kids standing for an hour and a half. Can you …? An hour and a half. Just to go on one of these rides, which is what? Two minutes. An hour and a half for two minutes.

C Mad.

B Crazy. But they do it. The queues don't make a difference.

A True. But you can stop this sort of madness. Let me give you an example – what's happening in some of these villages in north, on the north coast of Devon.

C Lynton, Lynmouth.

A Exactly. Car parks is the answer there.

B Car parks?

A Car parks. The only way to get into the town … well, put it this way, if you go by car, you have to park. If you can't park, you can't go by car. So, there's a set number of car parking spaces and basically that's it. The number of tourists is limited by the number of car parking spaces.

C That's right. Actually, just to give you an idea. I was in, not one of those places, not exactly, but somewhere like it last year and it was a lovely day, and up at the top the car park was packed but down at the bottom, like in the village by the sea, it was fine. I mean, busy, sure, but not over busy …

11 Remember

Reading p.66

► **Exam technique**
You should look for words which link the paragraphs, especially: pronouns (*he, she,* etc.), demonstratives (*this, that,* etc.), possessive adjectives (*his, her,* etc.), and link words (*however, although,* etc.).

TASK 1 The following sentences are true: 1, 2, 3, 5.

TASK 2 3 is correct.

TASK 3 1 C; 2 A; 3 F; 4 B; 5 G; 6 D.

Writing p.67

► **Exam technique**
You should organize your writing into paragraphs. Each paragraph should focus on an area / topic that is relevant to the answer.

TASK 1 2 reference; 3 complaint; 4 request for information; 5 letter of thanks; 6 request for advice; 7 explanation; 8 apology.

TASK 2 Suitable topics would be: your word-processing skills, your personality, the skills required in your present job, evidence of how you work independently.

TASK 3

PARA	TOPIC(S)
1	reason for writing
2	present job, evidence of working independently
3	personality, present job
4	word-processing skills
5	why I would like the job

TASK 4 Paragraph 4 is written in an inappropriate register.
Possible answer
I am competent at word processing and familiar with the latest versions of a number of popular software packages, among them Word, Excel, and Powerpoint. I am also proficient at shorthand and audio-typing.

TASK 5 The greeting is too informal and the closing is incorrect. A suitable beginning would be *Dear Mr Howard* and a suitable ending *Yours sincerely*. *Dear Sir* or *Madam* is only used when you do not know the name of the person you are writing to. *Yours faithfully* is only used with *Dear Sir* or *Madam*.

English In Use p.69

► **Exam techniques**
• You should read through both texts and get a general idea of the meaning. You need to be able to understand the texts in order to fill the gaps in the second one.
• There are many different ways of saying the same thing in English in a variety of different registers. It is important to be aware of this and to know a number of ways of saying the same thing in more formal and less formal English.

TASK 1 1 eight weeks before you leave; 2 when they are paid for; 3 you may have to pay a cancellation fee; 4 six months; 5 it is a good idea to.

TASK 2 1 to pass on information; 2 travellers – to find out what to do; 3 the same; 4 it is written to a friend; it is not a general notice to all travellers.

TASK 3 1 c; 2 e; 3 a; 4 b; 5 f; 6 d; 7 j; 8 i; 9 g; 10 h.

TASK 4 1 full amount / whole amount / whole lot; 2 before we; 3 changes / alterations; 4 new; 5 make sure; 6 at least; 7 after; 8 let us / allow us; 9 check; 10 back / home; 11 need; 12 should / ought to; 13 touch with.

Listening p.70

► **Exam technique**
While you are waiting for the recording to start you should read through the multiple choice questions and options to get an idea what the recording is about and what sort of information is required.

TASK 1

recording	no. of speakers	relationship between speakers
1	2	mother and son
2	2	boss and secretary
3	3	teacher and students
4	3	radio presenter and guests

🎧 **11.1**

1 M mother; S son
M You haven't left your football kit at school again, have you?
S   I'm sorry. I was in a hurry. I just forgot.
M But I told you on Wednesday I wanted it back so I could wash it for the match on Friday.
S   Sorreee.
M You're hopeless!

2 B boss and S secretary
B   Now about the meeting tomorrow …
S   Yes, I think everything's ready for that. The room is ready, lunch is ordered, and everyone can come.
B   Excellent. And did you remember to arrange for a video player in the room?
S   Yes, that's taken care of.
B   Good. Good.

3 T teacher; C1 and C2 students
T   Now for the exam on Friday don't forget you'll need a pen, a pencil, and a rubber.
C1 Can we take dictionaries?
T   No, I'm afraid not.
C2 Do we need our passports or ID cards or anything?
T   Yes, you'll need to take those along and also the piece of paper with your exam number on.

4 P presenter; R and S guests
P   Well, here in the studio with me this afternoon are Dr Sheila Matthews, who describes herself as a Memory Improvement Consultant, and Reginald Potter, the well-known author, who at the age of 86 has just published his twenty-seventh novel. Now first I must apologize for having kept you both waiting but …
R   No, no don't apologize, we've just been chatting outside the studio and I must say it's been a complete education to me …
S   (*laughs*)

TASK 2 The recording is about *The effect of age on memory and what you can do about it.*

TASK 3 1 C; 2 D; 3 A; 4 B; 5 C; 6 A.

🎧 **11.2**

P presenter; S Sheila Matthews; R Reginald Potter
P   Well, here in the studio with me this afternoon is Dr Sheila Matthews, who describes herself as a Memory Improvement Consultant. She runs courses around the country helping people to improve their memories, and she has a number of famous people among her clients. And also with us is Reginald Potter, the well-known author, who at the age of 86 has just published his twenty-seventh novel and we'll hear a bit later from him what that novel is all about, and undoubtedly when and where you can buy it. Now first I must apologize for having kept you both waiting but …
R   No, no don't apologize, we've just been chatting outside the studio and I must say it's been a complete education to me. I'm beginning to think there might be hope for me yet …
S   (*laughs*)
P   I'm sorry, but perhaps you could explain for the benefit of our listeners. Just give us a brief idea of what you were talking about.
R   Yes, well, I have the most appalling memory. Absolutely terrible. I've always put it down to old age myself. That's quite a good excuse for anything, actually.
S&P (*laugh*)
R   Anyway, I'm not joking when I say that I often turn up at restaurants to meet people and I forget who it is I'm meeting. I usually just hope that they recognize me and that I can remember their names when they do. But even that's not always the case, unfortunately. I mean, it really can be most embarrassing. But, well, out there in the discussion, in the twenty minutes we were chatting out there, Sheila has persuaded me that this isn't a permanent state of affairs and that I *can* improve my memory. So, as I say, there is some hope.
P   (*laughs*) Sheila Matthews? Perhaps you could tell us a bit about how you managed to lift Reginald Potter's spirits so much and convince him that all is not lost.
S   Yes, certainly. I think a lot of people … or I should say I *know*, because I've done a lot of research into this, I know a lot of people associate old age with

loss of memory. And to a certain extent it's true, memory does fade. As the years go by we do become a bit less sharp than we were. But, and it's a simple 'but' really, if we keep exercising our brains, if we pay attention carefully – and paying attention is probably the most important part of remembering something – there really is absolutely no reason why our memory should become that much worse.

R The other thing you said that I found most interesting was about strengths and weaknesses.

S Yes.

R I mean, despite my saying I have a bad memory, much to my wife's astonishment sometimes, I can always remember passages from books, or poems or quotes … the written word … things like that. You know I can recite a poem that I read in the newspaper that morning.

P Whereas names and places and more routine things just disappear.

R Exactly. Along with where I put my glasses and the name of the person who's coming for dinner.

S But this is very common. Very common. People have a sort of selective approach to memory. I mean, I knew a songwriter once who found it impossible to remember the lyrics of songs – a bit of a handicap for a songwriter – but she could remember long passages of music with no problem at all.

P Extraordinary.

R But the other thing I must tell you. The other thing that gave me hope was the different techniques that Sheila suggested for improving one's memory.

S Well, it has to be said that some of these things are related to good health more than anything. It's really common sense in a way. You know, things like diet; have a healthy diet, get enough sleep, take exercise. A fit, healthy person is more likely to have a better memory than someone who is not in great condition.

P Yes, I can see that would be true but are there other things as well?

S Oh, yes. There are endless little things you can do. One thing that a lot of people find difficult is remembering people's names when they are introduced. A very simple idea for this is just repeat the person's name as you are introduced. So if I say to you, 'I'd like to introduce you to Reginald Potter', you don't just say 'Hi!', you say 'Reginald, hi! Nice to meet you'. And if you can manage to say the name a couple of times in the first few minutes, you know, just drop it into the conversation, you are much more likely to remember it.

P I'll remember that. That's a great idea.

R But that wasn't the only good idea. One big problem I have is …

The Daily Telegraph and The Independent

Language development p.70

1 retrospect; 2 memory; 3 remember; 4 remind; 5 memorable; 6 Memorize; 7 memo; 8 memoirs.

Speaking p.71

TASK 1 Possible ideas for extending your answers

1 Say why you think your memory is good / bad. Give an example to show how good / bad it is. Mention friends or family who have exceptionally good or bad memories.

2 Give examples of remembering things easily or forgetting things. Give examples of when this has been useful or caused you great problems.

3 Talk about your own habits but you can also mention people you know who have unusual ways of remembering things, and even possibly people you have seen on TV performing memory tricks.

4 Again, don't just talk about yourself, mention other people you know who use different and possibly unusual methods to help them remember English words.

5 Tell the story. If you can't think of one, make one up or tell a story about someone you know.

Note It is worth remembering that it is not absolutely necessary to tell the truth in the interview. If you can't think of an example, you can always make one up. As long as you use good English you will impress the examiners and they will not know that you are not telling the truth. In any case you only lose marks for bad English.

🎧 **11.3**

M man; W woman

M OK, how good do you think your memory is?

W Well, it's OK, I suppose. Good. OK to good. Good. I think.

M I would say mine is awful.

W Really. Why?

M Terrible. I have a terrible, terrible, terrible memory. I'm permanently forgetting stuff.

W OK. Number two. What things do you remember easily and which do you find difficult to remember?

M OK. Names terrible.

W I'm bad at names.

M Really bad.

W What's your name? I'm really bad.

M No. Very, very bad at names.

W But I do always remember a face.

M Same here. I can see somebody once and if I see them again two years later I will recognize them, but it doesn't matter how many times they've told me their name, I will not remember it.

W Yeah, but I'll kind of, you know, be able to place them.

M Yeah. Things you have to do.

W Very good.

M Yeah. I'm good at that, I suppose.

W I'm quite annoying, actually, 'cos I hate everyone who doesn't remember what they have to do.

M Yeah. That's true.

W Numbers?

M Well, I'm bad at remembering phone numbers.

W Really?

M Because with the advent of mobile phones I just put them all in there and just use that to pull things out, so I never remember other people's phone numbers.

W No, that's true. I know my mum's number. That's about it. And directions. I'm afraid to say I'm appalling.

M Are you?

W Yeah.

M I'm pretty good … (W Really?) … I have to say. You know, once I've been to a place a few times, it goes in my head. Mental map.

W So if we're driving, you can direct.

M Yeah. I'll do that. OK, how do you try and remember to do something? Write it down?

W No. I'll remember. You know.

M You just remember?

W I just remember.

M It goes in your head.

W If someone tells me once (M Yeah.) then I'll stew it over and I won't forget it. No.

M I suppose it depends what it is. If it's, I don't know, if it's an appointment I will always write it down but I'll often (W If it's a job …) lose the piece of paper.

W Really?

M I don't write stuff on my hand 'cos it just makes you look a bit messy.

W And like you're at school.

M And like you're at school. Yeah. And I don't have a handkerchief, so I'd never tie a knot in it.

W No.

TASK 3 The woman seems to have the better memory for everything except directions.

1 He says I'm permanently forgetting stuff.

2 He says he can meet someone and remember their face two years later.

3 She gets annoyed with people who don't remember things they have to do.

4 Because he puts them in his mobile phone.

5 Once he's been somewhere a few times.

6 He thinks it's messy. They both think it's like being at school.

12 All the rage

Reading p.72

▶ **Exam techniques**
• First you should read quickly through the text (three or four minutes maximum) to get a general idea what it is about.
• Yes, the questions will follow the order of the text. When you have read a question, you should identify the part of the text where you think you will find the answer and read it very carefully.

TASK 1 You should have ticked *Why is Shigeru Miyamoto so important in the video game scene?*

TASK 3 1 l.5–7; 2 l.12–21; 3 l.22–28; 4 l.29–42; 5 l.43–50; 6 l.55–59.

TASK 4 1 B; 2 C; 3 C; 4 A; 5 C; 6 D.

Language development p.73

1 1 d; 2 f; 3 a; 4 e; 5 c; 6 b; 7 h; 8 g.

2 1 recent creation; 2 technical accomplishment; 3 gaming experts; 4 enchanted forest; 5 exalted figure; 6 industrial design; 7 artistic background; 8 intimate experience.

Writing p.74

TASK 1 C is the best introduction. It gives the aim of the report. It tells you how the research was done and it tells you what different criteria were examined in the report. A is in an inappropriate style. It is quite vague and there is an opinion in the introduction. B is not very detailed. It is also rather personal (as is A) using *we*. Reports tend to be impersonal, often written in the passive: *The clothes shops were all visited* …

TASK 2 B is the best conclusion. It is objective, pointing out the good and bad points of each shop. A is very subjective and the language is inappropriately informal (*nasty, the coolest place in town*). C is better than A but has fewer reasons than B. The language of C is also rather informal (*really rather expensive; stuff*)

TASK 3 A for (twenty), do (appeal), the (men's), so (reasonable). B range, handkerchiefs, designer, traditional, priced, knowledgeable.

English In Use p.75

TASK 1 1 holding on to the outside of moving trams; 2 parts of the tram are being removed to stop tram-surfing; 3 the same thing but on trains; 4 in Brazil; 5 holding on to the back of trams; 6 because people may injure or kill themselves.

TASK 2 1 to stop children holding on to them; no they don't; 2 *to* + infinitive; 3 the outside of the train; a noun or a preposition; 4 train-surfed or done something similar; 5 the rebirth of streetcar systems in towns in Britain; thanks to; 6 they have tried to stop them; to end.

TASK 3 1 B; 2 A; 3 F; 4 H; 5 D; 6 I.

Listening p.76

TASK 1 1 There might be some connection with the previous week's programme since he obviously mentions it. 2 You can see that Charlie will be using onion and garlic, tomatoes, water, olives, parsley, and black pepper. There will probably be other items too. 3 From the ingredients you can tell that he's cooking a main course. 4 You can see from the sentences that he fries the onion and garlic. There is no mention of an oven or temperatures so it seems unlikely that he will be using an oven.

TASK 2 Cooking words are: slice, crush, skin, recipe, gently, freshly, shrimp, leaf.

TASK 3 1 pasta; 2 (tasty) fish sauce; 3 invented; 4 (good) olive oil; 5 peel / skin; 6 wine; 7 sliced; 8 flat leaf; 9 freshly ground.

🎧 **12.1**

SP studio presenter (Victoria); FP food presenter (Charlie)
SP And now over to the most popular part of our morning programme, Charlie's Cook-in. Charlie, what have you got for us today?
FP Thanks, Victoria. OK. Last week I told you how to cook pasta. This week we're going to cook something to put on the pasta. A tasty fish sauce. If you were Italian you would call this *marinara*, and it's absolutely delicious. But before I start I must confess that this isn't authentic Italian cooking. It's just a little something I invented. But we'll call it *marinara* anyway. So first of all, you need a small onion and a couple of cloves of garlic. Dead simple. Get a knife. Chop the onion. Crush the garlic and fry them both in some oil. Good olive oil is best, of course. Just leave them frying on the cooker. In the meantime, you need to peel and chop three large tomatoes. So get some boiling water, pour it on the tomatoes, and leave them for a minute or two. You'll find then that the skins should peel off very easily. To chop them …

no, I don't need to tell you, do I? When the onion and garlic mixture is golden, add the chopped tomatoes. Slosh in a little water or wine, if you like. It depends how dry it looks and whether you'd rather drink the wine. Then cook the mixture, simmer it gently that is, for 10 to 15 minutes. You should stir it occasionally too to break up the tomatoes. While that's cooking, get everything else ready. Drain any liquid off the tuna – a 200 gram tin is what you need; get the prawns out of the fridge – about 300 grams will do. Slice some olives – or you can cheat and buy them sliced in the first place – and chop a handful of parsley. Go for the flat leaf variety. There are times when flat leaf is so much nicer than the boring old springy sort – and this is one of those times. Then, when the tomato mixture looks ready, throw all the other ingredients into the pan. Stir it round and heat it all through. Don't let it cook too long as it'll get very mushy. Just spoon it onto some delicious fresh pasta. And then, if you like, add a bit of black pepper – freshly ground, of course – and that's it. It may not be authentic Italian … but it's a tasty meal for a weekday evening. OK? Back to you, Victoria.
SP Thanks Charlie, that sounds delicious and for listeners who would like details of the recipe you can find it …

Speaking p.77

TASK 1 ✔ models   ✔ ordinary people
✔ designers   film stars
tailors   ✔ photographers
✔ buyers   ✔ journalists

TASK 2 models – to model the new clothes; designers – to see what other designers are doing; buyers – to see the new fashions and decide what to buy; ordinary people – to see the collections and decide what to buy / to be seen; photographers – to take photos; journalists – to get a story or article.

TASK 3 You should have underlined:
I guess they're doing that because …
they've perhaps gone along in order to …
perhaps to …
… so that …
the main reason they're there is to …
another reason is so that …
(they are) there to …
(they) want to …

🎧 **12.2**

E examiner; C candidate
E Now I'm going to give you some pictures to do with fashion. I'd like you to talk about your pictures and say what the different people in the pictures are doing and why.
C Well, this one's a fashion show. There's like a stage here where the models walk along wearing the new clothes, and here you can see the audience or whatever watching them. The models, well, they're just modelling the new clothes and I guess they're doing that because it's their job. But the people in the audience might have a lot of different reasons for being there. Some of them might be clothes designers themselves and they've perhaps gone along in order to see what other designers are doing; or perhaps to get some new ideas for themselves. There might be buyers from clothes shops who are there so that they can see the new fashions and decide what they're going to buy for their shops. There might be some ordinary people, well, very rich ordinary people, and the main reason they're there is to have a look at the collection and decide what they want to buy. Or perhaps another reason is so that they are seen there and everyone knows they were there. You know, just promoting themselves as the sort of people who can afford expensive designer clothes but without actually buying any. A much cheaper alternative! And then I guess there's other people around who are just doing their jobs too … like photographers, you know, there to get pictures for fashion magazines or newspapers and maybe fashion journalists who want to get a story or an article for their newspaper or magazine or whatever.

13 Conflict

Reading p.78

TASK 1 This question practises *skim reading*. It is useful to skim the text quickly to get a general idea what it is about before looking at the questions.

✔ Which country does it come from?   ✔ How old is it?
✔ Does it train the mind and the body?   ✔ Do you need a weapon?
✔ What techniques are involved?   What time are classes?
Where can I learn it?   How popular is it?

TASK 2 This question practises identifying the parts of the text which contain the answer. It is important in the Reading Paper to find the answers quickly and efficiently.

Possible answers

For statement 1 – *There is no attack in Aikido; Shotokan Karate is a weaponless martial art…; Wushu athletes spend considerable time training with weapons such as … ; Today Kendo … is practiced with* **shinai** *(bamboo swords) … ;*

For statement 2 – *Aikido originated in the centuries-old tradition of the Japanese martial arts … ; Shotokan Karate … developed in Okinawa, Japan; Capoeira is a breathtaking Afro-Brazilian art … ; Kenpo includes movements from both Chinese and Japanese martial arts styles; Wing Chun Kung Fu's roots can be traced from the Southern Shaolin Temple in China … ; Modern Wushu … combines a foundation in the traditional Chinese fighting arts … ; Taekwondo … originated in Korea … ; Kendo is a Japanese style of fencing … .*

TASK 3 1 / 2 – F / H; 3 / 4 – C / G; 5 – D; 6 – B; 7 – C; 8 – A; 9 – H; 10 – G; 11 / 12 – C / F; 13 – E; 14 / 15 – B / G.

Note Where there is more than one answer, answers can be in any order.

🔍 Close up

physical training; spiritual discipline; profound effects; physical self; mental self; acrobatic movements; personal growth; unarmed combat; pure strength; protective equipment.

Language development p.79

1

NOUN	ADJECTIVE	NOUN	ADJECTIVE
protection	*protective*	*popularity*	popular
harmony	*harmonious*	*confidence*	confident
injury	injured	tradition	*traditional*
efficiency	efficient	*sensitivity*	sensitive
competition	*competitive*	effect	*effective*
spirit	*spiritual*	*flexibility*	flexible

2 1 injury; 2 effective; 3 efficient; 4 protection; 5 popularity; 6 traditional; 7 confident; 8 harmonious; 9 sensitive; 10 flexible.

Writing p.80

TASK 1
✔ the plot / story
✔ the writer's style
✔ the main characters
✔ strengths of the book
✔ other books by the same author
✔ the organization of the book
  the picture on the cover
✔ the development of the characters
✔ weaknesses of the book
✔ the theme / idea behind the book
✔ the opinion of the reviewer
  the number of copies printed

TASK 2

B The main themes of the book The victim	C The investigation The story
A A general description of the book The sort of books this author writes	D How the book is structured Opinion

TASK 3 Possible answers
remarkable, an ambitiously-structured detective thriller, it succeeds magnificently, psychological thrillers, compassion, a strong social conscience, to create unease / suspense / horror, angrily concerned with …, reveals, the frightening reasons for …, reconstructs, not-quite-convincing, a superb exploration of guilt and revenge.

TASK 4

positive adjectives	negative adjectives
remarkable	unimaginative
brilliant	dull
witty	humourless
superb	hopeless
magnificent	boring
amazing	predictable
fascinating	awful
original	dreadful

English In Use p.81

The English In Use sections for the following three units (13, 14 and 15) each focus on two parts of Paper 3 rather than just one. Unit 13 looks at multiple choice cloze and word formation; unit 14 at error correction and register transfer; unit 15 at open cloze and gapped text.

Multiple choice cloze

TASK 1 1A A fixed collocation. A *submarine base* is where you find submarines. No other word is possible.
2C Magistrates *order* the public to do things. *Calling* and *threatening* do not fit grammatically; *forcing* is possible grammatically but an odd word to use of magistrates.
3B This is the correct word to use describing what happens in court.
4D She thought she would have to spend some time in jail. Therefore she was *expecting* it. *Intending* sounds as though she wanted to be in jail.
5C A fixed collocation meaning a demonstration designed to achieve peace.
6B Meaning a *short time*. The others are wrong: *season* refers to spring, summer, etc; *turn* implies that she was taking turns in some way; *cycle* suggests that this was a regular event in some way.
7A Meaning *part* of the law. The other words do not fit the context.
8A Used of colours which go together. *Fit* is to do with being the right size; *suit* means the clothes look good on the person wearing them; *join* does not have any meaning here at all.
9D Meaning the things that happened. The other words are not general enough for this context.
10B This is the correct term for the punishment given to someone found guilty of a crime.
11C *primarily* and *principally* imply that this was the main part of her sentence, *newly* suggests that this was a new development. None of these are the case.
12D You *organize* a blockade.
13A The correct term for delaying the imposition of the jail sentence.
14C What she did. The other words are wrong in this context: *performances* sounds theatrical; *operations* is medical or military; *measures* sounds legal.
15B A fixed collocation: *to make a difference.*

Word formation

TASK 2 **Workers denied right …** 1 they are not being given paid holidays 2 four weeks' paid holiday a year 3 because employers are evading the law
Mobile phones to carry … 1 a Government health warning 2 children 3 because there are worries about potential health risks, particularly among children

TASK 3 1 allowance; 2 employees; 3 variety; 4 organizations; 5 incorrectly; 6 dismissal; 7 employers.
8 government; 9 harmful; 10 finalising / finalizing; 11 uncertainty / uncertainties; 12 specifically; 13 continuing; 14 discouraged; 15 radiation.

Listening p.82

TASK 1
boat: condition, price, sleep, engine, river, old, wheel
car: condition, price, engine, road, old, wheel
caravan: condition, price, sleep, road, old, wheel

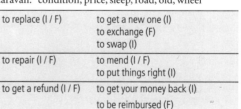

to replace (I / F)	to get a new one (I) to exchange (F) to swap (I)
to repair (I / F)	to mend (I / F) to put things right (I)
to get a refund (I / F)	to get your money back (I) to be reimbursed (F)

TASKS 2 & 3 1 A; 2 C; 3 C; 4 B; 5 A; 6 B; 7 C; 8 B; 9 C; 10 C.

🎧 **13.1**

E examiner
E You will hear five short extracts in which people are complaining about current or recent situations. For questions 1 to 10, choose the correct option A, B, or C.
1 It was OK to begin with. I mean, I know it was quite old but it seemed in good condition and the price was fine. It was large but, of course, we had to get something that sleeps five. And then as soon as we got out on the river I realized that it was a big mistake. The engine was in a terrible state. Well, I took it back to the yard and the boss there, he was very apologetic. Deservedly so. I told him I wasn't happy at all and I wanted my money back. He offered to put things right and even to find a new engine but I said I wasn't having that. So now I'm still looking for one.

2   I don't know how much longer I'm going to go on working for her. It's not the money, you know, it's just not much fun. I mean, I do my best, I do the things she asks and I'm always in on time. But I'm supposed to keep her diary and I never find out about half of her meetings … because, well, she just doesn't talk to me that much. It's kind of lonely because there's just the two of us. I've sent off a few applications so I'll just wait and see if I get any interviews.

3   We had a great time except for the trip home. It should have taken about 12 hours but it ended up taking 48 because there was something wrong with the plane. A lot of people were quite cross but there was nothing we could do really. Anyway, they put us up in a hotel overnight – not luxurious it has to be said, but quite reasonable. And we got our luggage back. And then the next day we flew home via New York and Paris. And after 48 hours I walked through the front door and thought, 'Thank goodness I'm home!'

4   I was stopped at the traffic lights on Church Street at about nine o'clock. The lights were red. And there were a few cars about. And Cathy Green, you know, from number 23, crossed the road in front of me and just raised a hand in acknowledgement. And I guess I smiled at her and must have missed the lights because all of a sudden there's all this hooting behind me and the man in the car behind has got out and is coming towards me shaking his fist. I tell you I didn't hang around to see what he wanted. I just put my foot down and drove.

5   No, I don't think you can leave things as they are. I know you're not happy. I mean, you've been complaining about him for the last six months and the fact that he doesn't do his job properly. But you know that going over his head won't do any good. So come on! Stop all this grumbling. Calm down, and have a chat with him and find out what the matter is. I don't necessarily think you're being unreasonable but I do think that a more moderate approach might be beneficial.

Speaking p.83

► **Exam technique**
If you cannot reach an agreement with your partner you should agree to differ.

TASK 1

Saying what is good about something	Saying what is bad about something	Expressing a preference
What I like about … is …	The problem with … is …	I'd go for …
The good thing about … is …	The disadvantage of … is …	My choice would be …
The advantage of … is …	The drawback with … is …	That would be my preference.
		If it was up to me, I'd choose …

TASK 2

Write down some phrases that you think might be useful.

🎧 **13.2**

A young man; B young woman

A   What do you think?
B   Hmm. Well, I think the problem with the ballet … I mean, I love ballet but I just don't think it would be a good idea … the problem is it doesn't have universal appeal.
A   Selective.
B   Exactly. Rather elitist.
A   Yes. The same's true of classical music too, I guess.
B   Hmm. I think of the cultural … sort of music-based ideas … the rock concert is going to have the widest appeal. And I'd probably go for that.
A   What about the sporting ideas, though?
B   Well, the drawback with sport is that not everyone likes it.
A   But you can say that about music too – any sort of music.
B   Yes. I suppose so.
A   The good thing about sport – for a charity event that is – is that you can do something different. I mean a rock concert is a rock concert. But if we chose football, say, we could have something unusual like a five-a-side tournament. And the advantage of that would be that we could invite all sorts of stars, you know, just for this special competition.
B   You prefer football to tennis or basketball?
A   Oh yes. It would get a much bigger crowd and make more money for charity. That would be my preference.
B   Mind you, you could do the thing for a rock concert – you know, have lots of different acts throughout the day. Like Live Aid or whatever. It needn't just be one group, one band.
A   Mm. I'm not against rock music, you know, but it has been done before. I just think the idea of a football tournament would be sort of new and

exciting.
B   Oh well, perhaps we'll just have to agree to disagree on this one then.
A   OK – pity it's not for real though. It'd be fun to organize. Either of them. Football or a rock concert.
B   Yeah. Who'd you get? – For a concert that is?

TASK 3

Saying what is good about something	Saying what is bad about something	Expressing a preference
What I like about … is …	✔ The problem with … … is …	✔ I'd go for …
✔ The good thing about … is …	The disadvantage of … is …	My choice would be …
✔ The advantage of … is …	✔ The drawback with … … is …	✔ That would be my preference.
		If it was up to me, I'd choose …

Make a note of a few useful phrases and expressions in the chart above and learn them.

TASK 4   They decide that they cannot reach agreement and 'agree to differ'.

TASK 6   🎧 **13.3**

W woman; M man

(Part 1)

W   OK. So these are the options. Well, …
M   Bottle of wine. I don't think Mrs Ashton really is a wine drinker.
W   She doesn't look like a drinker, does she?
M   I've never seen her come in with a hangover or …
W   No.
M   No.
W   But that's quite a neutral present, I suppose.
M   Yeah, it is. And a good bottle of wine is something perhaps she can …
W   Would you like a bottle of wine?
M   Yeah, I like, I like wine.
W   OK, so that's a possible.
M   That's a possibility. A pen. A nice pen. With an engraving perhaps on it or something like that.
W   It's a bit boring and you always lose pens.
M   Yeah. Yeah. Yeah. But she would use it a lot, wouldn't she?
W   That's true.
M   CD I think is out.
W   I could, I could never pick any music for her.
M   No way.
W   It would be impossible, wouldn't it?
M   No way.
W   OK, that's out.
M   A book. Well, …
W   What kind of book?
M   Yeah. I mean, I think we've seen enough books.
W   I know.
M   I'm sorry, but you know.
W   I know. Yeah, but she's a teacher. She likes books.
M   I suppose something, some fiction, some nice fiction.
W   She likes fiction.
M   I don't know.
W   But what if we chose the wrong book?
M   Oh yeah. Or she'd probably have it, you know …
W   Yeah. That's too difficult.
M   … being an English teacher. I mean, you know.
(Part 2)
W   So, what's the options? We've got the short list. We've got a potential bottle of wine.
M   Yeah.
W   You quite liked the pen, didn't you?
M   Pen with an engraving on it.
W   OK. Possible. Photograph of the class… too much hassle.
M   But it's a still good idea.
W   And an umbrella.
M   Or a bunch of flowers. I think we should ask the others, just see if we can get some votes.
W   I think we should just order the flowers.
M   OK.
W   I think, I think we collect the money from the class and get them delivered
M   That's a good idea.
W   …on our last lesson. I think that would be a nice thought. We could all be there.
M   OK.

W And you can't go wrong.
M So I can leave it with you then.
W Yeah.
M OK.
W Great.
1

PRESENT	FOR	AGAINST
wine	neutral present	she's not a wine drinker
pen	she would use it	boring / people lose pens
CD	–	impossible to choose
book	she likes books	difficult to choose; she'll probably have it

2 a 1 So what's the options? 2 We've got the short list.
  b He thinks they should ask the others.
  c She thinks they should just order the flowers.
  d They decide that the woman will order the flowers.

14 Work

Reading p.84

TASK 1 This question asks you to predict the content of the article from the title. It is useful to have an idea what the article is about before you start reading it. All the summaries are possible. The third is probably the least likely and the second the most likely.

TASK 2 It is important to get a good idea of the meaning and the organization of the text before you start trying to put the paragraphs into the numbered gaps.
a 4; b 7; c 2 ; d 5 ; e 3; f 8; g 1; h 9; i 6.

TASK 3 1 E; 2 G; 3 B; 4 F; 5 A; 6 C.

Language development p.85

1 to patronize – to behave in a superior way towards someone
to ignore – to pay no attention to something or someone
to put down – to make someone appear stupid or silly
to trivialize – to make something appear unimportant
to be impatient – to be intolerant of delay and eager for something to happen
to fidget – to make continual (often annoying) small movements
to slump – to sit in a tired manner

2 1 ignore, trivialize; 2 slumped, fidgeting; 3 patronizes; 4 be, impatient; 5 put, down.

Writing p.86

TASK 1
I've applied for a job as a youth organizer at a summer camp in the States this year. They'd like a letter of reference from someone who knows me well. They want to know how long you've known me, what my personality is like, what experience I have with young people (teenagers), and how well I am likely to adapt to living in an English-speaking environment. I'd be really grateful if you could write to them for me. The address is Vermont Summer Camps, Stowe, Vermont, USA. Thanks.
Carlos

There is nothing in the answer about Carlos' personality.

TASK 2 B is best. A is far too informal and colloquial. C is OK but a little short. B gives a full picture with extra information.

TASK 3 It is important to organize your writing into paragraphs.
a how I know Carlos and how long I've known him
b what experience Carlos has with young people
c what experience Carlos has of organizing groups
d how I feel Carlos would adapt to an English-speaking environment
e my recommendation

English In Use p.87

Error correction

TASK 1 1 the; 2 ✔; 3 and; 4 over; 5 up; 6 been.

TASK 2 1 ✔; 2 the; 3 such; 4 ✔; 5 that; 6 away; 7 off; 8 (other)of; 9 how; 10 ✔; 11 ✔; 12 were; 13 far; 14 round; 15 (must) to; 16 ✔.

Register transfer

TASK 3 Text 1 is formal. Text 2 is very informal. Text 1 is an advertisement. Text 2 is a suggestion.

TASK 4 1 T; 2 F (Sir Jeremy is going to Australia); 3 T; 4 F; 5 T.

TASK 5 1 offered; 2 charge; 3 make; 4 been in; 5 don't need; 6 well; 7 working for / under; 8 (foreign) trips / trips abroad; 9 good; 10 a chat; 11 in touch; 12 in; 13 be / get / come.

Listening p.88

TASK 2 1 full-time; 2 communicators; 3 shift work; 4 night work; 5 mail bags; 6 high standard; 7 your vehicle; 8 Staff Manager.

🎧14.1

Thank you for phoning the Mail UK employment hotline. For the latest information on employment opportunities with Mail UK, the nation's fastest-growing delivery system, please hold the line. We have currently filled all available positions at our Romford and Brentwood centres. However, we are still looking for and recruiting drivers, able to put in a 38-hour full-time working week, at a number of locations around the country. Please note that we have no part-time positions at the moment though some may become available later in the year. Mail UK is a growing, nationwide, mail delivery business which serves the whole community – both the world of business and the nation's homes. As such, we are looking for employees who are good communicators, who can work with other people, serving the needs of our customers and being effective and courteous with other people, whether in their jobs or going about their daily lives. We put the highest priority on communication skills and their effective use within the context of working for Mail UK. Candidates will require a certain degree of flexibility as regards their working hours and must be available for shift work, which may on occasions involve night work. Also, when delivery deadlines need to be met, an early start may be required. Some degree of physical fitness is necessary. Vans will need loading and unloading. Our mail bags may weigh as much as 16 kilograms and you will have to lift and carry these. In order to serve the needs of the community as well as we possibly can, we are, in particular, looking for enthusiastic people who are committed to working to a continually high standard. Many of the tasks you will have to perform are repetitive but they are nonetheless essential in providing a quality customer service. As a driver, you will also need to be conscientious in the upkeep of your vehicle. Some mechanical knowledge will be necessary as you will be required to maintain your vehicle in good condition. We offer good rates of pay and excellent holiday entitlement. Good health provision is made for all our employees through a reputable health insurance company and each centre has its own social and sports club. If you feel you have the necessary qualities and are interested in applying for one of these posts, please write, giving details of your previous work experience and the names, addresses, and contact telephone numbers of two referees, to the Staff Manager at Mail UK, Romford, Essex. Thank you for calling the Mail UK employment hotline.

Speaking p.89

TASK 1

ASKING FOR AN OPINION	✔ What do you think? What about you?
GIVING AN OPINION	✔ It seems to me that … ✔ I also think …
CLARIFYING	✔ You mean … ✔ How do you mean?
AGREEING	Absolutely. ✔ I'd agree with that.
EXPRESSING AN OPPOSITE IDEA	Wouldn't you say that … ✔ Don't you think …?
COMPLIMENTING	I hadn't thought of that. ✔ That's a good point.
EXPRESSING PREFERENCE	✔ I'd go for … My choice would be …
DISAGREEING	✔ Do you really think so? ✔ I see what you mean but …
GIVING AN EXAMPLE	✔ Take … for example. For instance …
SUPPORTING AN ARGUMENT	✔ The point is … The main reason is …

For further similar expressions look back at the Speaking sections in Units 3, 6, 8, 9, 12, and 13.

🎧 14.2

E examiner; C candidate 1; D candidate 2

E OK, so now I'd like you to have a look at this list of qualities and circumstances and discuss what it is that makes people succeed at their jobs.

C Well, what do you think?

D (laughs) Oh, thanks for letting me go first! Erm … I guess … well, it seems to me that hard work is pretty important. I think most people who are very successful really put in the hours.

C You mean they live to work rather than work to live.

D In some cases, yes – but not all.

C Yes, I'd agree with that. But I also think that ability is important, or talent, or whatever you want to call it.

D Hmm. D'you really think so? I can think of quite a few people who made a name for themselves with very little ability. Just pure determination.

C Yeah, that's a good point. You mean, like pop stars?

D Yeah.

C But, to be honest, if I had to choose the single most important factor, I'd go for luck.

D Luck? How do you mean?

C Well, you can produce something really special like a great song or film or something and it can come out at just the wrong time. Or you can have the potential to be fantastic at your job but there aren't any vacancies. Or you can have a brilliant idea but it's too early or too late.

D So, timing as well. Yes, it's not on this list, but yes, timing.

C I see what you mean, but don't you think that if you're that good or your idea is that brilliant then you will succeed anyway?

D Well, take the great impressionist painters, for example. I mean, were they successes in their lifetimes? No, they weren't. The point is, they were years ahead of their time and it took the public ages to realize that …

TASK 2 🎧 14.3

E examiner

E Now I'd like you to discuss something between yourselves but please speak so that we can hear you. Here are some pictures of different types of jobs. I'd like you to talk about the pictures, saying what sort of job is shown, what sort of person would choose to do each type of job, and which of these jobs you would choose to do if you had the opportunity.

TASK 3 🎧 14.4

M man; W woman

(Part 1)

M She looks like a secretary.

W A secretary, I'd say.

M Yeah.

W Definitely.

M All sorts of people are secretaries, aren't they?

W Yeah, loads of different people. My mum used to be a secretary.

M Yeah.

W It depends what type of place you're working for, I suppose.

M Yeah. I suppose there's specialist secretaries, aren't there?

W You've got to be organized.

M Yeah. Organized. You've got to be …

W You've got to have a good head on you really, on your shoulders. You don't really have to have any qualifications, I suppose.

M Not really. To be punctual.

W Definitely.

M You have to be helpful.

W A good timekeeper. Definitely.

M You have to care about the place you work …

W Polite. Yeah.

M … or the person you're working for.

W Yeah, you've got to be …

M Otherwise, it'd be very dull.

W Yeah.

M And I certainly have never wanted to be a secretary.

W No. No. I can't say I have either.

M No.

W No. Not something I aspire to.

M Too much running around. Bit of a dogsbody.

W I'm not very punctual really either, so …

M No.

(Part 2)

W Artist. Now that's something I would like to be if I could draw.

M Yeah. Step one. Learn how to draw.

W You've got to be talented, I think.

M I think you have. Although these days it would appear that maybe you don't. You just have to have a good idea and then sometimes that's enough.

W Yes. Maybe.

M But what kind of artist would you like to be? Like Sculptor? Painter? Sketcher?

W I think a cartoon … a cartoonist or something.

M Cartoonist, yeah.

W Or graphic design I've always been interested in. What other qualifications? I suppose you need a degree or you don't really, actually, do you?

M No. I don't suppose you have to have anything really other than a creative mind.

W Mind. Yeah.

M Or body. Either of those things really.

W Yeah. That's the only creative thing, actually, we've come across so far.

M Yeah. There's no professional qualifications …

W No.

M … anyone can be an artist.

W Definitely.

M And finally, well, he looks like a …

W Some kind of site … construction site worker.

M Or something.

W Yeah. Definitely. My uncle's a construction worker.

M OK.

W And I think you've got to be strong.

M Yeah. You've got to be strong.

W You've got to be …

M I don't want to be …

M It's manual labour, isn't it, really? You have to be unafraid of lugging stuff around all day.

W Yeah. Definitely.

M Working very hard.

W Yeah. Also early mornings. Long days.

M Yeah.

W Hard. Good hard graft.

M Good hard graft. Manual labour in the old style.

W I don't think you need any qualifications.

M No. I wouldn't have thought so. Again, it's construction work – open to anyone, I'd have thought …

W Open to anyone. Yeah. But you can make good money.

M Yeah. You've got to be big.

W You can make good money out of it, so … how about you? Is it for you?

M No. No. I think. No.

W No. It's not for me.

M No. I think I'm too artistic. I'd probably get beaten up or … crushed under a girder or something like that. I don't think I could carry a hod of bricks anyway.

W No. Scaffolding and all that.

M No.

W Too much like … hard work.

M I'm a bit scared of heights too.

W Oh well, you definitely couldn't then.

M No. Forget it.

1

secretary	artist	construction worker
– organized	– talented (perhaps not these days)	– strong
– good head on your shoulders	– creative mind or body	– unafraid of working very hard
– punctual		– unafraid of early mornings, long days
– helpful		– no qualifications
– you must care about the place / person		– big

2 Secretary

Definitely!	agreeing
My mum used to be a secretary.	giving an example
I certainly have never wanted to be a secretary.	expressing preference
I can't say I have either.	agreeing
Too much running around.	giving a reason

Artist

That's something I would like to be.	expressing preference
What kind of artist would you like to be?	asking about preference
Sculptor? Painter? Sketcher?	giving an example
Cartoonist or something … or graphic design.	expressing preference

Construction worker

My uncle's a construction worker.	giving an example
Is it for you?	asking about preference
It's not for me.	expressing preference
I'm too artistic.	giving a reason
I'm a bit scared of heights.	giving a reason

15 Behaviour

Reading p.90

TASK 1 It is important to skim read the text to get an idea what it is about before you read it more carefully. 1 T; 2 F; 3 T.

TASK 2 1C A and B are true but not the reason he became powerful; D is true but happened after he had become powerful.
2B (*the newspapers had blown up his reputation from murk to myth.*)
3D (*his chief business, he felt, was legitimate in human terms, even if it was against the strict letter of the law.*)
4D (*In a curious way, however, it was legitimate business as well as corrupt State governments and the prohibition law, which had given American gangsters their chance … Their opportunity was prohibition.*)
5B (*His name still reaches to every household, as do the fingers of his greedy followers.*)

Language development p.91

1 Cross out: 1 prohibit; 2 reach; 3 apply for; 4 confirm.

2 1 She joined an organization. 2 They condemned violence. 3 He looked for business. 4 She went into business. 5 He enforced the law. 6 They prevented violence. 7 They founded an organization. 8 They did business. 9 He provoked violence. 10 They changed the law.

English In Use p.92

Open cloze

TASK 1 You should read the text through carefully and get a good idea of its meaning before you try to fill the spaces. 1 on Mondays; 2 more often; 3 they cry; 4 they swear; 5 money; 6 their current partner.

TASKS 2 & **3** 1 contrary; 2 not ; 3 more; 4 are; 5 of; 6 other; 7 and; 8 with; 9 when / if; 10 to; 11 by; 12 in; 13 those; 14 were; 15 their.

Gapped text

TASK 4 You need a good understanding of the text before you start filling the gaps. 1 it is the world's first sculpture; 2 by using powerful microscopes; 3 probably a woman; 4 arms, breasts, and possibly feet; 5 it was a natural shape.

TASK 5 1 F; 2 C; 3 G; 4 A; 5 I; 6 D.

Listening p.94

Sentence completion

TASK 1 While you are waiting for the recording to start think about the type of vocabulary you are likely to hear.

✔ the lowest possible price ✔ simple rules   ✔ respect
✔ a fair price   football   ✔ reasonable
✔ cultural background   ✔ friendly   ✔ tourists
✔ Third World countries   ✔ experience   introduce
✔ western countries   ✔ negotiation   magazine

TASK 2 1 (the) locals; 2 lose money; 3 fair price; 4 (paid) more; 5 help; 6 friendly way; 7 (almost) two days; 8 shopkeeper's wife; 9 in favour of.

🎧 15.1

P presenter; T Tricia Broadbent; G Geoff Haynes
P In today's programme we're going to look at the practice of haggling, or bargaining, or to put it another way, negotiating the price of something – it's common in many countries but less common here in Britain and many Western European countries. Now Geoff Haynes, you work for Aidrelief, a charity that has a presence in many Third World countries and you're not really in favour of bargaining, are you?
G Not at all. I mean, I think it's OK for the locals. After all, it's the way they've always done business and they know the rules. It's part of their cultural background. What I object to most strongly, however, is what I would call irresponsible tourism. That is, people from western countries who bargain way beyond what is acceptable and in doing so force local shopkeepers to lose money. Money they need to support their families. They can suffer real distress.
P Tricia Broadbent. You're editor of the magazine *Worldwide Travel* and you're very widely travelled yourself. How do you feel about what Geoff is saying?
T Well, I can see his point but I think he is rather overstating the case. Yes, sometimes I think westerners do drive too hard a bargain. They don't realize that the object of the exercise is to arrive at a fair price. And they don't realize there are some simple rules for doing that. However, for every westerner who manages to buy something really cheap at a lower price, say,

than the shopkeeper would normally sell it, for every one of those I'm sure there are three or four other customers, westerners, who've come up against a wily and experienced shopkeeper and paid more than they should have done.
G I don't think that's the case at all. Certainly not in some of the countries I visit. In places where there are a lot of tourists I can believe it. Shopkeepers will be more experienced at dealing with tourists and it will be difficult to get a bargain at all. But in the much poorer countries where there are fewer tourists we really should be paying a fair price, not only to help the economy of the country but also to help the individual that we are buying from.
P Tricia, you said there are some simple rules for bargaining. Could you explain a bit more about those perhaps for people who are unused to the practice?
T Yes. Certainly. I think the most important thing of all, and it's something that a lot of westerners really don't understand, the most important thing is that the negotiation is done in a friendly way. Don't think of the other person as your opponent or your enemy. Bargaining is more about spending time with someone from another culture and getting to know them. You also have to be prepared to spend time doing it. Quite serious time.
P (*laughing*) What do you mean by 'serious time'?
T Well, my partner and I once bought a carpet in Pakistan and it took almost two days.
P You're joking!
T No, seriously. Not all the time, of course. I mean, we spent a couple of hours on both mornings in the shop and then all of one afternoon and most of the following evening. And we drank tea and discussed the carpet and how well it was made and we talked about our families. I was introduced to the shopkeeper's wife and got an amazing insight into the life of women in Pakistan. It was an experience that I treasure.
G If I could just say, and assuming that you paid a reasonable price for the carpet from the shopkeeper's point of view, which from what you've just said I'm sure you would have done, that sounds like bargaining at its best. Respect shown for another culture, genuine interest in the people, no desire to exploit a poorer people. I'm thoroughly in favour of that. What is unacceptable, however, what we have to stop, is the people who think this is a great opportunity to …

Multiple matching

TASK 3 1 B; 2 C; 3 A; 4 F; 5 E; 6 D.

TASK 4 TASK ONE: 1 D; 2 B; 3 C; 4 A; 5 E;
TASK TWO: 6 A; 7 B; 8 G; 9 H; 10 C.

🎧 15.2

1 Of course, *The Sands of Time* came very close. It was shortlisted in 1998 – but then so many other people produced their best work that year that I wasn't really surprised when it didn't win. What is disappointing, I feel, is that I've always felt my best work was *The Attic Woman's Dream* – the characters just seemed far more real to me, probably because I was so young, and the plot is certainly the cleverest I've come up with – but the problem is that because it was the first thing I ever did its merits didn't really get recognized until later when I became well-known.
2 To be honest I think this is by far the best thing I've done. I very much like the way that I've managed to create an air of mystery about the house, a feeling that perhaps all is not as it should be. You can imagine going in through the front door and perhaps hearing strange, rather frightening, piano music, which sends a shiver down your spine. And I think the way that I've done that – without creating a dark and gloomy picture full of heavy, threatening brushstrokes – well, I think this is probably the most memorable and creative artistic work of the year, if not the last ten years.
3 Of course, there is some difference between what you find on the east coast and what you find on the west and I try to take from both when I'm doing my own compositions. On the east coast, where the climate is more changeable, the rhythms are usually faster but more regular. Give a kind of upbeat flavour to everything. Whereas on the west coast, where the weather is generally warm and the people are more friendly and relaxed, you'll find that the drums and bass frequently go off into slow and irregular improvisations. And everything is cool and relaxed.
4 I find the human body an absolutely endless and fascinating source of inspiration for my work. When I started, however many years ago it was, 50 or so, there were just a few of us around the country but we knew each other well and we used to exchange ideas. There was a real sense of community amongst us even though we were scattered around the country and none of us ever made the headlines; we all learned and developed together. I used to work with all sorts of materials in those days – wood, stone, anything I could get my hands on – but for ideas I always turned to the human body.

5 It sounds glamorous but I'm afraid it's not. Imagine a five a.m. start to see some arrogant film star. Dragging a reluctant cameraman along with you. Hours of work on the word processor trying to make it readable – not literary, just readable. Then there's nothing more depressing than having it rejected. You've spent hours working it up until you're satisfied and the editor takes one look and throws it in the bin. And even when you do get a piece accepted, the only way you can earn enough is to rewrite the same piece and sell it on to a different newspaper or magazine. Frankly I don't know why I do it.

Speaking p.95

TASK 1 They have been deciding what present to get their teacher.

TASK 2 1 thought; 2 pointed out; 3 wondered; 4 mentioned; 5 explained; 6 persuaded; 7 agreed; 8 admitted; 9 decided.

🎧 **15.3**

E examiner; C Carlos; M Maria

E So what did you decide then?

C Well, we found it quite difficult to agree. I thought we should get him a bottle of wine because … well, I know from things he's said in class that he likes wine, but …

M … I pointed out that once he'd drunk it, it was gone. It's nothing to remember us by.

E OK.

M I wondered about a CD. I mean, I know he likes music but we didn't know what sort …

C Then Maria had a great idea.

M Yes. He mentioned that he'd had a really nice pen but he'd lost it. Carlos didn't like the idea much but I explained we could have his name engraved on it.

E And so she persuaded you it was a good idea, did she?

C No. No. She didn't persuade me. (laughing) I agreed it was a good idea.

M (laughing) No, Carlos. You didn't agree. You reluctantly admitted it was a good idea.

E Well, let's just say you decided to give him a pen, shall we?

C & M (laughing) OK. OK.

How well have you done?

Congratulations! You have finished the book. You have done all the preparation and should feel confident about tackling the exam. Before you sit the exam you should do at least one practice paper in exam conditions. You can find one complete paper on pp.96–110. If you feel you require more practice, you can find further papers in CAE Practice Tests (OUP) by Mark Harrison and Rosalie Kerr.

Good luck in the exam!

Practice Test Key

Paper 1 p.96

Part 1 1B; 2A; 3A; 4E; 5D; 6C; 7D; 8E; 9B; 10C; 11F; 12D; 13A; 14F; 15E; 16C; 17B; 18E.

Part 2 19C; 20B; 21D; 22A; 23G; 24E.

Part 3 25B; 26D; 27A; 28C; 29C; 30A; 31B.

Part 4 32D; 33B; 34C; 35F; 36D; 37/38 – B/E; 39A; 40/41/42–C/D/E; 43F; 44/45/46–A/B/D; 47B; 48F; 49F.

Paper 3 p.104

Part 1 1C; 2A; 3D; 4A; 5B; 6D; 7C; 8D; 9A; 10B; 11D; 12C; 13A; 14D; 15A.

Part 2 16 as; 17 for; 18 since; 19 the; 20 their; 21 with; 22 a; 23 more; 24 to; 25 have; 26 up; 27 or; 28 on; 29 in; 30 towards / to.

Part 3 31 floating; 32 ✔; 33 lose; 34 ✔; 35 people; 36 magnificent; 37 independent; 38 spokeswoman, Kate; 39 However, it; 40 ✔; 41 their; 42 ship's; 43 Caribbean; 44 ✔; 45 its; 46 travel.

Part 4 47 successful; 48 choice; 49 promotional; 50 bribery; 51 unhealthy; 52 Trial; 53 consumption; 54 enthusiastic; 55 arbitrators; 56 complaints; 57 variety; 58 satirical; 59 consultation(s); 60 informed; 61 reassurance.

Part 5 62 introduced; 63 elect; 64 proposed / nominated; 65 appointed; 66 a talk / lecture / presentation; 67 circulate; 68 (some / much) discussion; 69 collection; 70 donation; 71 was reached / was made / was taken;

72 custom; 73 fund-raising; 74 organize / be organizing.

Part 6 75 B; 76 G; 77 D; 78 I; 79 A; 80 F.

Paper 4 p.108

Part 1 1 salary; 2 (lovely) (Victorian) sofa; 3 (lots of) money; 4 your bank manager; 5 an antiques centre; 6 specialization; 7 annoying / irritating; 8 better quality.

Part 2 9 problems / (long) delays; 10 an accident; 11 burst water main; 12 South Street; 13 (running) on time; 14 cancelled; 15 ground staff; 16 airport information hotline.

Part 3 17 food and cookery; 18 constructive; 19 two (different) covers; 20 an unusual photo; 21 thin people; 22 positive; 23 marketing; 24 dieting.

Part 4 25 B; 26 D; 27 F; 28 C; 29 E; 30 B; 31 D; 32 F; 33 H; 34 G.

🎧 **PT1**

E examiner; A antiques dealer

E You are going to hear an antiques dealer talking about his work. For questions 1–8, fill in the missing information. You will hear the recording twice.

A I haven't always been an antiques dealer. I started out as a teacher and antiques were really just a hobby. I loved old furniture, old pictures, bits of glass and china, and I used to buy and sell them at antique fairs at the weekends. I was just making a bit of money to supplement my salary. A lot of people get into antiques like that. Eventually, though, my wife got fed up because she could never guarantee that some household item wouldn't disappear. I mean, we had a lovely Victorian sofa but I happened to bump into someone who was interested in buying it and the next day we didn't have a sofa any more. She was a bit cross about that and suggested that if I was going to do this I should do it full-time and not with things from our house!

Actually, that's one of the biggest problems with being an antiques dealer – stock. In order to sell antiques you have to buy them and in order to buy them you need money. So the most important thing when you start up is to get hold of lots of money. It also helps to be on good terms with your bank manager because there are always going to be times in the future when you'll need to borrow money to build up your stock. I've been doing this for ten years now and our bank account is almost always in the red.

The other important thing when starting up is deciding whether to open up your own shop or to rent space in an antiques centre. My feeling is that opening your own shop can be quite risky. There are always unexpected bills coming in and you've always got security worries. However, the advantage is that it is your own place. The advantage of the antiques centre is that you pay a flat fee each month, which includes everything – heating, lighting and so on – and you also get a lot of customers who come to look at the other shops in the centre and drop in to yours because you are there. The disadvantage, of course, is that it's not yours and often space is limited.

The one thing we did by accident, but which turned out to be the best thing we could possibly have done, was to specialize. We happened to buy a couple of nineteenth-century French gilded mirrors and when we sold them the buyer said that if we came across any more he'd be interested in them too. So we found some more and that's how we started to specialize. Of course, we sell all sorts of things but having our own little area of specialization has been very good financially.

You have to get used to selling to the public and the fact that people can be quite irritating. For example, buyers always want to bargain. I find that quite annoying. I mean, they wouldn't bargain over a new wardrobe but because it's antique and they're buying from an antiques dealer they always want a discount. Also people aren't always logical. I had a wooden umbrella stand which I was selling for £100 and a woman looked at mine and then bought a similar one from a shop down the road for £500. I think she thought it was better quality because it was more expensive. In fact, it was almost exactly the same.

🎧 **PT2**

E examiner; S studio announcer; T traffic and travel announcer

E You are going to hear the traffic and travel news on Bartlebury Local Radio. As you listen, complete the sentences for questions 9–16. Listen very carefully as you will hear the recording ONCE only.

S Well, that's it for this week and now it's time for the news, but before that let's go over to Jo Haydon for the latest on traffic and travel in the Bartlebury area.

T Thanks, Gary. Well, things have quietened down a bit now since the morning rush hour when things were really very busy today. However, there are still problems on the ring road out to the north of the town where there are long delays. The police have been there for quite a while now sorting things out after an accident which happened at about seven o'clock this morning. It seems that a furniture removal lorry ran into a car towing a boat trailer and spilled the boat on to the road causing serious disruption.

The road should be clear again very shortly but, if you can, the police strongly recommend that you avoid the area for at least another hour. After that it should be OK. If you weren't tuned in earlier, don't forget to avoid the High Street. There is a burst water main there, just outside the Central Library, which has completely flooded the road. Pity the boat wasn't on the road there, I suppose! Anyway, the water is still pretty deep in places and the road will be closed for the whole day at least. If you need to drive through the centre of town the police are advising you to use Walton Street and South Street but they would really prefer you to stay away if at all possible. Rail news is very good – all the trains are running on time and there seem to be no problems there at all. News from the airport, however, is not so good especially for those of you off to Italy on your holidays. British Airways and Alitalia have cancelled all today's flights and you are advised to contact your travel agent for further details. Italian ground staff are on strike and only a handful of planes are being allowed to land. News has just come through that the strike is only for 24 hours so we are hoping that things will be back to normal tomorrow. If you want further information on flights later in the week, or on how today's flights are planning to be rescheduled, you should call the airport information hotline. This is usually only available during office hours but the service has been stepped up round the clock during the present difficulties. That's all for the moment but I'll be back in half an hour with more. This is Jo Haydon with the latest in traffic and travel news for Bartlebury Local Radio.

🎧PT3

E examiner; P presenter; N Nancy Allbright; V Nero Varley

E   You will now hear a discussion between a publisher and a nutritionist. For questions 17–24 complete the sentences. You will hear the recording twice.

P   And now in the studio with me today to discuss body size – an issue which has had a lot of coverage in the newspapers this week – are two people who are both very well known in the food industry: the nutritionist and researcher Nancy Allbright …

N   Hello.

P   … and a man who is not only the publisher of an award-winning food and cookery magazine but is also an acclaimed chef himself, Nero Varley.

V   Hello.

P   Nero Varley, perhaps I could start with you and you could just explain why it is that body size has in fact become such a 'hot' issue this week and what your part in it has been.

V   Well, certainly, yes, we have played a part. We conducted a sort of experiment if you like. And I hope that it has been constructive in that our readers will think about what we've done and what it means. What we did was this. We published this month's issue of *Food for Thought* with two different covers. One had a thin supermodel type woman on the front and the other had a photo of an equally attractive woman on the front but it was a woman with a fuller figure.

P   This wasn't an original idea, was it?

V   No. No. Not at all. It had been done before but with a woman's fashion magazine.

N   If my memory serves me well, on that occasion only about 35% of the magazines sold were ones with the supermodel cover.

V   Yes, that's right. Well, I was just curious to see what would happen if we did the same thing. I mean, we always try and have an unusual cover photo …

N   I was going to say … don't you usually have food on the cover of a cookery magazine?

V   Actually, no! (*laughs*) We try and go for an unusual photo. Not necessarily to do with food. But something that will grab the attention. I mean there's often a link to food or maybe some food in it but that's not necessarily the main thing.

P   So, what was the result of your experiment? Do you know yet?

V   Yes, I think we do. We've sold almost all the copies we expected to sell this month, what we usually sell anyway, and it seems that an amazing 80% of our readership preferred the cover of the woman with the fuller figure.

P   Rather than the one with the supermodel figure.

V   Yes.

P   Nancy Allbright, your comments.

N   Well, two things really. First of all, the negative thing, I'm not sure how many thin people would actually buy a cookery magazine. Thin people are generally interested in not eating rather than eating! But the positive thing is that it shows that many people would rather look at a woman with a fuller figure. I know it's hardly reliable, scientific research – but it could show that the idea that to be beautiful and attractive you have to be thin, is not actually true.

V   I must say I agree with Nancy's reservation, if you like. I suspect we have few thin readers. But I've thought for a long time that women's magazines – and don't forget that as a publisher I look at all types of magazines for ideas on how to improve my own – I've thought for ages that the cult of the supermodel was more to do with marketing than with what people actually perceive is beautiful or attractive.

P   As a nutritionist, Nancy Allbright, I imagine you have similar views.

N   If anything my views are much stronger than Nero's. I feel certain, as he does, that marketing is responsible for women being so concerned about their body shape but, as a nutritionist, I come across … everyday I deal with people whose lives have been … er … 'ruined' is perhaps too strong a word but 'damaged', perhaps, by the desire to have a particular body shape.

P   You mean, people suffering from anorexia.

N   Well, yes partly, but not just them. On the whole, dieting is not something I would recommend to anyone. There are, there can be medical reasons for dieting. And that's fine. But there are people who lose weight quickly because there's a wedding coming up or a party or some other event that they want to look special for and this sort of up and down of one's weight isn't a good thing either.

V   Actually, we ran an article recently, last month I think, about how that sort of thing, the sort of up and down, up and down, that you were talking about, how that really isn't a particularly healthy thing to do.

N   Good for you.

P   So, what do you think the publishing industry as a whole can actually do about …

🎧PT4

E examiner

E   You will hear five short extracts in which people talk about influences on their lives and work. Remember that you must complete both tasks as you listen. You will hear the recording twice.

1   I used to live with my grandfather in a little village by the sea. We often used to go for long walks along the beach on a Sunday afternoon. Miles and miles. And I remember being fascinated by the clouds and the sea, the whites and the blues, the drama of nature, of how the land and the sea came together. Sometimes peacefully and calmly, and sometimes stormily. And I think you can see that fascination in my work. It perhaps explains why I concentrate on sea and the countryside. I find it much more exciting than people or anything urban.

2   I think I've always been interested in form. As a youngster, I was always making things and building things. I think I wanted to be an architect at one point but then I realized that there were always going to be structural limitations and I wanted an opportunity to be more artistic, to express myself more. I also realized it was living forms that excited and inspired me, particularly us, our form. I would sit in cafés for hours watching people and how they sat and stood. Then I would go back and create a whole new person of my own.

3   I've always felt that I was doing everything because of him. From the first time I ever stood for election right up to now – even though he died five years ago. Of all the people who've backed me through the years, his support was always unconditional. I still feel his influence over my actions even today. I think my mother does too. I can almost hear him talking to me as I have to make decisions about policy. Sometimes I feel him helping me make important decisions that will maybe change the lives of many people. It's strange how a parent can have that effect on one's life.

4   We didn't have television in those days so this was the big excitement every week. The whole family used to go. My grandad, he was a teacher at the local school, he always used to pay. And we used to sit right at the front and eat ice-cream and get transported into a completely different world. That's when I started thinking about storylines. It was always the plot, the different twists and turns that interested me. So when I decided to try my luck with a few publishers, a detective story was the natural choice really – so much plot.

5   I've never been worried about standing up in front of people. I suppose I've always been a bit of a show off. Anyway, I've found it certainly helps in this game. It was Mr Hayes who got me started really. He was just fantastic – never a dull moment in his classes. He was incredibly tall and his arms and legs seemed to be everywhere. What's more, he didn't just teach us the skills, the sort of stagecraft that we would later need. He also showed us how to enjoy the boring bits, like learning your lines.

OXFORD
UNIVERSITY PRESS

Great Clarendon Street, Oxford OX2 6DP

Oxford University Press is a department of the University of Oxford.
It furthers the University's objective of excellence in research, scholarship, and
education by publishing worldwide in

Oxford New York

Auckland Bangkok Buenos Aires Cape Town Chennai
Dar es Salaam Delhi Hong Kong Istanbul Karachi Kolkata
Kuala Lumpur Madrid Melbourne Mexico City Mumbai Nairobi
São Paulo Shanghai Taipei Tokyo Toronto

Oxford and Oxford English are registered trade marks of
Oxford University Press in the UK and in certain other countries

© Oxford University Press 2002

ISBN 0 19 433064 8 (book)
ISBN 0 19 437967 1 (pack)

Printed and bound in Spain by Unigraf Artes Gráficas, S.L.

Acknowledgements

The author and publisher would like to thank Joanna Cooke and Mike
Gutteridge for their invaluable comments on the manuscript.

The author and publisher are grateful to those who have given permission to
reproduce the following extracts and adaptations of copyright material:

Reproduced by permission of Guardian Newspapers Ltd.: p.8 'My inspiration'
© John Simpson, *The Guardian* 24 October 2000. p.28 'Long Welsh words
could be road hazard' by Martin Wainwright © *The Guardian* 5 December
2000. p.43 'Are you reading me?' © Stephen Hoare, *The Guardian* 14 November
2000. p.120 'Is laser eye surgery safe?' by Esther Addley © *The Guardian* 6 June
2000. p.80 'Has Ray Scarpetta solved her last case?' © Pater Guttridge, *The
Observer* 29 October 2000. p.81 'Grandmother has her day in court' by Kirsty
Scott © *The Guardian* 8 July 2000.

Reproduced by permission of Independent Newspapers (UK) Ltd.: p.9
'Stevenson's wife burnt Jekyll and Hyde "nonsense"' by Kate Watson-Smyth,
The Independent 25 October 2000. p.15 'On the internet at home? Big Teddy is
watching you' by Ester Leach, *Independent on Sunday* 29 March 1998. p.22
'Palm print i.d. to replace passports' by Keith Nuthall, *Independent on Sunday* 3
May 1998. p.27 'Vultures of India in danger of sudden extinction' by Geoffrey
Lean, *Independent on Sunday* 28 May 2000. p.30 'One length forward, two
lengths back' by Christine Campbell, *The Independent* 19 August 2000. p.36
'Just call me Bill' by Adam Sternbergh, *Independent on Sunday* 8 October 2000.
p.39 'Shorter, tougher life for lefthanders' by Laura Elston, *Independent on
Sunday* 13 August 2000. p.45 'Nothing we want to eat at 30,000 ft' by Amy
Anderson, *Independent on Sunday* 14 October 2000. p.49 'Shoppers made to
put thumbprints on credit card slips in war on fraud' by Robert Mendick,
Independent on Sunday 19 November 2000. p.51 'Motor racing experts to give
advice on speedy transfers of sick children' by Jeremy Laurance, *The
Independent* 9 November 2000. p.55 'Music – the drug of choice for Britain's
Olympians' by Jonathan Thompson, *Independent on Sunday* 29 October 2000.
p.61 'If you're going to San Francisco, be sure to avoid Fisherman's Wharf' by
Andrew Gumbel, *Independent on Sunday* 22 October 2000. p.63 'Heading for
Frankfurt? Here's Hahn' by Simon Calder, *The Independent* 19 August 2000.
p.125 Adapted from 'Delhi without the belly' by Jane Brewer, *The Independent*
9 September 2000. p.66 'Why it is crucial that elephants have good memories'
by Steve Connor, *The Independent* 20 April 2000. p.72 'Super Miyamoto' by
Hester Lacey, *Independent on Sunday* 17 September 2000. p.75 'Tram-surfing
craze sweeping cities puts children in danger' by Nicholas Pyke, *Independent on
Sunday* 13 August 2000. p.81 'Thousands denied their right to four weeks paid
holiday' by Barrie Clement, *The Independent* 4 September 2000. p.82 'Mobile
phones will carry government warning of potential danger to health' by Sarah
Schaefer, *The Independent* 27 November 2000. p.84 'More than just jaw jaw' by
Philip Schofield, *Independent on Sunday* 1 November 1998. p.93 'You'll lose a
year of your life looking for missing possessions' by Cherry Norton, *The
Independent* 26 June 2000. p.98 'Warning: exercise can damage your health' by
Roger Dobson, *The Independent* 24 November 1998. p.99 'These animals are
dying out. And all because the lady loves shahtoosh' by Peter Popham, *The
Independent* 20 June 1998. p.100 'My week: Sophie Ellis-Bextor' by Susannah
Prain, *The Independent* 19 August 2000. p.104 'Oxford Street shoppers may be
fined for dawdling' by David Brown, *Independent on Sunday* 3 December 2000.
p.105 'The ship that has everything – even its carpets are changed every day' by
Terri Judd, *The Independent* 7 October 2000. p.105 'Blair: We will give DNA
tests to every criminal in Britain' by Paul Waugh and Ian Burrell, *The
Independent* 1 September 2000. p.106 'Children used in television shows "lack
protection"' by Louise Jury, *The Independent* 5 June 2001. p.106 'New children's
food craze: veg' by Ben Russell, *Independent on Sunday* 10 September 2000.
p.107 'Hebridean island gets first roundabout to give children a taste of outside
world' by Andrew Mullins, *The Independent* 9 August 2000.

Reproduced by permission of Telegraph Group Limited: p.12 '£2m 'remote
control' house run by mobile' by Mary Fagan, *Sunday Telegraph* 28 January
2001. p.57 'Thoroughly modem Madonna stars on stage and screen' by Hugh
Davies, *Electronic Telegraph* Issue 2014. p.57 'CD of all Beatles' number one hits
sets sales record' by Rajeev Syal and Susan Bisset, *Electronic Telegraph* Issue
1983.

p.18 'Our fulfilling rolls' by Andrew Moody, *The Express* 24 August 1998.
Reproduced by permission of Express Newspapers. p.25 Text about Pygmy
Hippopotamus, Trumpeter Swan, Galapagos Flightless Cormorant, Snow
Leopard, Przewalski's Horse, Giant Anteater, and Humpback Whale adapted
from *Natural History Notebooks*, www.nature.ca. Reproduced by permission of
the Canadian Museum of Nature, Ottawa, Canada. p.91 Extract from Al
Capone by Fred. D. Pasley. Reproduced by permission of Faber and Faber Ltd.
p.93 'Lump of rock' turns out to be world's first sculpture' © David Keys,
Archaeology Correspondent, *Independent on Sunday* 24 September 2000.
Reproduced by permission of David Keys.

Although every effort has been made to trace and contact copyright holders
before publication, this has not been possible in some cases. We apologize for
any apparent infringement of copyright and if notified, the publisher will be
pleased to rectify any errors or omissions at the earliest opportunity.

The author and publisher are grateful to the following for their kind
permission to reproduce photographs:
Eye Ubiquitous p.10 (mobile phone shop / D Foreman), p.41 (weightlifter /
Sportshoot), p.56 (musician / B Battersby), p.59 (orchestra / J Mowbray), p.59
(rock musician / B Battersby), p.64 (Indian city / D Cumming), p.110
(mountains / P Field); Hulton Getty Archive p.47 (morse code); Image Bank
p.19 (young man in shop / G&M D de Lossy), p.27 (vulture / J Van Os); Impact
Photos p.17 (garment factory / C Cormack), p.41 (seashore / T Page), p.47
(fortune teller / C Penn), p.59 (Chinese musicians / M Henley), p.77 (fashion
model / D Reed), p.110 (volcano / Y.A.Bertrand / Earth, p.110 (aerial view of
housing / J Pimlott), p.110 (Eiffel Tower / C Bluntzer); James Davis p.17 (car
factory), p.110 (Japan); Manchester Evening News p.75 (tram surfing); OUP
Database p.17 (man on phone); P.A. p.17 (stockbrokers in India); Photonica
p.47 (e-mail / C Trochu); Popperfoto p.41 (model / Reuters / Popperfoto), p.47
(divining rod), p.77 (skateboarder); Robert Harding p.35 (Tai Chi / Corrigan)
p.41 (castle / R Rainford) p.41 (cottage by the sea / R Rainford), p.53 (traffic / J
Miller), p.77 (rafting / Int.Stock), p.110 (desert / Int. Stock); Sally & Richard
Greenhill p.47 (blind man), p.47 (postal worker), p.59 (busker), p.59 (brass
band); Science Photo Library p.10 (mobile phone / Tek Image), p.40 (Mars /
US Geological Survey), p.47 (scientist / C Cuthbert), p.47 (space probe / D
Ducros); Still Pictures p.41 (open mine / C Martin).

Illustrations by:
Adrian Barclay p.83, p.89
Ian Jackson p.23, p.28, p.51, p.71

The answer sheets on pp.96, 103, and 107 are reproduced with kind permission
of the University of Cambridge Local Examinations Syndicate.